D1436422

HISTORY AND THE SELF

HISTORY AND THE SELF

A STUDY IN THE ROOTS OF HISTORY
AND THE RELATIONS OF HISTORY
AND ETHICS

by

HILDA D. OAKELEY
M.A., D.LIT.

"Awake, arise, or be for ever fall'n"
JOHN MILTON, *Paradise Lost*

LONDON
WILLIAMS & NORGATE LTD
28–30 LITTLE RUSSELL STREET W.C.1
1934

PRINTED IN GREAT BRITAIN BY
UNWIN BROTHERS LIMITED, LONDON AND WOKING

TO THE

MEMORY OF

SIR ALFRED COMYN LYALL

CONTENTS

HISTORY AND THE SELF

CHAPTER I

INTRODUCTORY

"History is only in part a matter of 'fact'. Consider the 'facts' of the French Revolution! You must go down to hell and up to heaven to fetch them."

G. M. TREVELYAN, *Clio, a Muse*

WITH the first idea of history a serious ambiguity arises. For we are immediately conscious ourselves of an experience which is history before, or in a stronger sense than it is anything else. Or if we do not admit that merely as our individual experience it merits the name of history, we must allow that such is in an important sense the primal stock out of which all history grows. Unless this were going on in innumerable individual centres, or unless *we* were going on in this way of consciousness, there would be no history. This is the stuff, raw material perhaps, out of which it is made. For history in every other sense—this I must ask to be allowed to state here dogmatically —is secondary and derivative from the original experience. It is in this that we have its reality, and all its forms in solution. The present work will nevertheless be largely concerned with history widely understood in the more specific sense, history as recorded, or still more generally as a universal possession of the human race objectively viewed in its past activities. In this sense history is essentially or in the nature of the object common property or knowable to all men, though actually the immeasurably greater part may be unknown and beyond the reach of our instruments of knowledge. History as thus conceived, objective history, is, in its original form, connected in the closest way with primary history as above interpreted, as it is almost the first intelligent activity of a self possessing memory, aware of other similar selves to formulate however

vaguely and inadequately together with them some notion of a common past. At the very least there is implied the assumption of this past. And this is preceded by the barely intelligent operation continually and subconsciously taking place, in which the inner individual historic process is translated into something objective and as such shareable with others.

Throughout this work there will be references to history in both these meanings, though in the basic original form it is unique in the experience of each self, having a not fully knowable character. History in whichever of the lights cast upon it by the intellectual, emotional, and moral nature of man must have its *fons et origo* in the experience of selves, the arcana of individual consciousness. It may be staged as the theatre for the achievements of personalities, or the cultural progress of communities, as the drama of the manifestation of great values or the expression of mind in finite individuals. It may be presented as revealing the evolution of a logical or spiritual principle, or as exhibiting no general law, no uniform tendency. To some it may seem analysable only into cumulations of series of "events" inherently disconnected, a brief episode or succession of episodes in the measureless ages of the unmeaning, which seems to our narrowly limited view to have some significance, though in fact occurring in accordance with necessity or with chance in the course of endless occurrences of the meaningless in ages inconceivable to us. But for all interpretations whatsoever the idea of history must have its source in individual conscious experience. With this begins the history of all historic concepts. But it does not necessarily end here. In recognizing at the outset that in our search for a true interpretation of the historic form of all experience we must never forget or ignore its origin in the dual aspects of actuality and of the past as organized remembrance—subjective and objective forms—we are not thereby committed to any exclusion of theories of the real significance of history as lying in something quite other than the experience of independent and interdependent selves. Whether views of this type deserve serious consideration can from the standpoint of the present work only be examined after consideration of those leading factors of our historic experience and record which are found to be essential to its structure and content, and the most urgent questions which arise out of the relation of history to other aspects of life and knowledge. History is here referred to both as underlying all systematic experience and as itself a special type of system. Such principal factors are the problem of time in history necessitating at least consideration of the significance of past, present, future; the nature of the self and of our knowledge of other selves; the question of the historic object and historic categories. Fundamental issues have to be faced in regard to the character of historic knowledge and its relation to scientific knowledge, involving examination of the tendencies which I describe as animistic in our attitude to history, also of the relation of history to the values, in particular those of ethics, leading to the question whether there is a special historic value. Here will be encountered one of the most difficult problems in the interpretation of history in so far as we conceive it as primarily constituted by the activities of selves. For it is when we consider its meaning and value as pointing to and to a considerable degree derived from an interpretation by means of ethical principles, that a difficulty arises threatening the validity of our idea of history as constituted by the experience and deeds of selves. This is the central difficulty of the ethical interpretation of history. By this I do not mean its moral justification, but even the possibility of finding in the historic record as we should expect if its subject-matter is the activities of persons, the scene or field for the clear conflict of good and evil. Some aspects of the problem thus envisaged will be treated in connection with the concept of the "Other" in history, the non-moral or a-moral material and forces. As regards ethical theory in its own distinct domain, we are led by the existence of this problem to realize the generally un-historic character of the majority of ethical systems, the fact namely that their principles are elaborated for the most part in abstraction from and irrelevance to "the historic situation". The question here presents itself, whether a more historic method would increase the value of moral philosophy.

The truth of the dual aspect of history, which has been indicated here partly in the distinction of its more subjective and more objective sources, partly by means of the conception of history as consisting first in the activities of persons, secondly in the succession of events (in which factors have to be included impersonal, indifferent to value, unconcerned with the intrinsic effort of the personal principle to find meaning in experience), impresses itself with greatest effect in any attempt to study history as at once the scene of personal achievement and the record of the movements of races, the advance and decline of communities and nationalities. Of special importance in the interpretation I have attempted of this dualism is the fact that the impersonal may frequently be seen to emerge from the personal, or that factors alien to free personal activity and the direct pursuit of ends often enter in through co-operation of persons, and the instruments devised for joint or united action. These problems will confront us especially in the historic illustrations which are introduced and in the references to personality in biography and autobiography. Their investigation throws light on the difficulty which has so often made vain both the systems of philosophies of history and the hopes of practical reformers. This is the yet unsolved problem of transforming moral freedom into historic liberty, and so discovering the secret of continuous progress. In certain aspects this inveterate problem has haunted historical and dramatic treatments of human experience from the beginnings of civilization. In the chapter on the substance of history the admission of elements or agencies over which man appears to have no control receives some consideration in the various forms it takes in ancient and modern reflection generally on human life or specifically on history. Here we meet with the necessity or destiny of the Greeks, ἀνάγκη, the contingent or casual of the modern historian, *le hasard*, *zufall* (Aristotle's τύχη) of some philosophers.

"Sed mihi haec ac talia audienti in incerto judicium est, fatone res mortalium et necessitate immutabili an forte volvantur", in Tacitus' terse phraseology.[1]

From the standpoint of this book a philosophy of history as this has usually been understood is impossible, both because of the total inadequacy of our knowledge of the past as basis for such a system and because of the invincible relativity of all our historic valuations and judgments in regard to the permanent elements in civilization. It will be argued, however (in the chapter on "History and the Future"), that there are certain truths of the nature of personality, the inner core of all history, which go beyond relativity, and that in virtue of these a metaphysic of freedom may be held not as established but as speculatively possible or even probable. The grounds on which is based the hope of reaching an absolute principle here in the very seat of relativity, the centre or the innumerable centres of unique views of experience, of the world of meaning and personal relations, unique inspirations and struggles, the apparent cause of inescapable divergences, can only be exposed in the course of the argument. But here, it will be suggested, if anywhere, is a principle in regard to which we may think with Bosanquet—(in a different logical dilemma),[2] "Either this, or nothing." An examination of the Concept of the "Whole as Personal" appears to be demanded, mainly on account of the strong appeal which this conception has made to thinkers who have agreed in the position that a personal principle is central in reality. But that the very idea of personality is destroyed when we attempt to equate it with the totality of things or the All, is the conclusion to which our discussion of this notion will lead, whether it is investigated

[1] Tacitus: *Ab Excessu Divi Augusti*, Liber VI, 22.

[2] Cf. "On the Ontological Argument" and "Essence and Existence", "The Meeting of Extremes", in *Contemporary Philosophy*. Bosanquet does not actually express the dilemma in these terms here, but I think they occur in his *Logic*.

from the standpoint of the nature of the self, the process of history, or the ideas and laws of value. The ideal of a supreme Person loses its significance if it must absorb all the actuality of the innumerable grades of personality and of the non-valuable worlds of the impersonal. Or if these are conceived to be transfigured, neither do we escape dualism, nor do we find an atonement and a justification for the agonies of all separate souls. We have on our hands a metaphysical monstrosity, and for the folly of all our intellectual tortures and moral martyrdoms, in the struggle with the problem of evil we receive a final quietus in the news that it does not exist.

In rejecting the idea of a philosophy of history, are we in danger of rejecting philosophy itself as metaphysic? From the standpoint of the present book our whole experience begins in the historic process, and cannot escape it. The term "historic" is here used rather than temporal to emphasize the view that, although the temporal form may, and indeed must be abstracted from all content for the purposes of the most general reasoning and knowledge, it has no reality in this abstraction, and is only real in the original concrete passage as distinguishable aspect of a unitary successive experience. Time may be likened to an essential nerve of experience from which it cannot be torn and remain the same, contributing half the significance of our being in conscious living. Nor can this significance be bared of its temporal quality, and fully understood and known as a timeless object. To the degree in which the historical is contemplated in a static form, at least *now* unchanging in its eternal pastness it loses and cannot reflect something of its original actuality. But in this position is not an adequate metaphysic of experience ruled out? The whole content of knowledge, it may be held to imply, is abstract with an abstraction fatal to the truth. Philosophy aims at fixing and expressing the complete and final significance of that with which it deals. If all experience is historical and therefore temporal, if, as will be further argued in what follows, successiveness is creative, this aim must be unfulfilled. It does indeed result from the position indicated that philosophy as science is not possible. There cannot be a scientific metaphysic of the whole. Scientific knowledge is concerned with the general and abstract. Neither this nor any conjunction of the results of the separate sciences can ever exhaust the whole. This is due primarily to the historic nature of the real. A philosophy of history, in so far as it is not identified with all philosophy, would be an interpretation or rationalization of the totality of human experience and activity, *qua* taking place in the temporal succession. It ought not to be less than this, though in the great example of Hegel it takes as its field what will be characterized in this work as secondary, not primary history, the history of races and nations objectively or categorially presented. This it interprets as manifestation of an idea, or of the process of the one spirit. If the temporal succession is conceived as not ultimately real, its relation to the timeless has to be determined. But attempts to determine this relation appear to point to the following dilemma: Either the timeless real loses its essential form, since it must be conditioned by categories which involve time, such as the concept of the achievement of freedom by the spirit. Or the temporal process is illusory. The non-temporal and the temporal cannot be combined in the concept of a monistic universe. A philosophy of history is then from the standpoint of the present work not possible if by this is signified what Dilthey (who rejects it) speaks of as "a final simple word", corresponding to the true meaning of history.[1] Since the reality of history involves a process in which meaning is creatively given to events, there can never be a final interpretation of the process in its manifestations. Final interpretations belong to a static not a dynamic world. This admission does not however remove the possibility of philosophy as investigation of the real in experience, and the source of that significance without which there would be no sense of reality, no human experience. Such an investigation is fundamental and may claim to be

[1] Wilhelm Dilthey: *Gesämmetle Schriften*, Band I, p. 86.

prior to all other philosophical studies. It is to history, as theory of knowledge to the natural sciences. For it seeks to show how history and all other spiritual forms are possible, the ethical principles of life, science, art, and any other less well-defined higher experiences there may be. In such an investigation as is obvious, experience must be examined primarily in its historic basis. A reference to some words of Ernst Troeltsch may help to indicate the kind of study involved. Writing (in 1922) of a crisis in historic study, he proceeds that it lies, if not in the province of historic investigation, "in the general foundations and elements of historic thought and the conception of historic values out of which we have to think and to construct the system of history".[1]

"Historismus" cannot, in my view, be entirely overcome. Professor N. Hartmann in the Introduction to his recent work,[2] speaks of "Historismus" and its overcoming (*ueberwindung*) as one of the great groups of problems which enter everywhere into the thought of our day. In so far as "Historismus" (the word does not seem to be used always in exactly the same significance) means the fact that "our own life and knowledge are deeply set within history" (Hartmann), I agree with the view which seems to be on the whole (though he wavers at times) uppermost in Troeltsch's work. According to this the fact of "Historismus" must be taken as inevitably conditioning our outlook, and the significance we give to historic categories. As I should add, this need not mean that through historic sympathy these limitations may not in some degree be transcended, so as to enable insight into a life set in a different age. That this has taken place the historic genius at rare moments convinces us.

The idea of personality presented in this book is, in essentials, the same as that of my *Study in the Philosophy of Personality*, but it has been considerably developed, and in respect to the relation of this principle to history, modified.

[1] *Der Historismus und seiner Probleme*, Buch I, Kap I.
[2] *Das Problem des geistigen Seins*. It has not been possible to refer further to this important book as my work was completed before I had an opportunity of reading it.

As will be evident from the references to Troeltsch's *Historismus*, I am greatly indebted to this fine thinker for the inspiration given in his method of approach to the problem of historic knowledge and his treatment of the difficulty of relativity which so often threatens our undoing, as well as for various other fruits of his insight. In the works of Wilhelm Dilthey and of Heinrich Rickert I have also found most valuable statements of the historic problem, the relation between the cultural sciences and the natural (Rickert) consideration of the contribution of psychology, and of biography to history (Dilthey). In all these thinkers, whether expressly or not, we have the recognition of "Historismus" as an interpretation of the real human experience in the temporal process from age to age in its concreteness and its ideality, which marks I think the introduction of a new mode of thought. For this is not the historical method of the nineteenth century, with its search for origins and for the clue to all later developments in the beginnings. This has had its useful day, but its use in essential human history is limited. For according to the argument of this book the doctrine itself of development of the more complex out of the simple, the philosophical application of evolution in its various forms, and all formulations of the sub-historic stages of living experience, are methods of interpretation which must themselves be explained as derivative by abstraction from the fundamental need of the personal mind for value as order.

Without making any claim, which would indeed be unjustified, that such thinkers as Troeltsch or Dilthey take this view of method, I may at least attribute to them that pregnant treatment of historic reality which finds in it the primary field of human experience, on which the mind so to speak enters in full use of its categories of value, or at the minimum, already endowed with these though not perfected, employing them as instruments not derivable or fabricated from any activities in which value was yet unexperienced.

The references to historians may appear arbitrary, on

account of their narrow limitations. For the purposes of this work, which does not aim at the consideration of historical methods in general (a task for which I am not equipped), it is only necessary to refer to certain writers who, so far as my knowledge extends, furnish the best illustrations of the standpoint taken in this book in regard to history of the historian. Amongst recent works I am especially indebted to those of the late Professor Bury and of Dr. G. P. Gooch for their philosophical outlook, also, though rather by disagreement, to positions of the late Lord Acton. In the provinces of anthropology and archaeology, in works of Sir James Frazer, Professor J. Myres, and Dr. R. R. Marett, I have found much that is of great value for my purpose.

The choice of references to biography and autobiography may appear to be still more fortuitous. Here the selection depends entirely on the opportunity afforded by the personality of the subject for illustration of the argument. Those selected appeared to me particularly illuminating in this respect, but not exceptional, since the theory of personality is one that I have found without exception exemplified both generally in life and as might be expected in the literature of life.

Amongst philosophers there is no one thinker whom I can be bold enough to claim as the true source of the chief views or arguments adduced in these pages. No doubt I owe most to Plato and much to the English neo-Hegelians, in spite of a dissent in certain essentials both from the Ideal philosophy, and from such thinkers as Bradley and Bosanquet. We may owe the deepest gratitude to those to whose philosophies we are unable closely to adhere. In the ethical sections I have found Professor Nicholai Hartmann's work in the distinguished translation by Dr. Stanton Coit highly stimulating, even where I feel myself unable to accept his main position.

McTaggart's philosophy of selves, in his *Nature of Existence*, has been of great value to my work, on account of the genius of its presentation of the concept of a system of real selves timelessly enjoying an experience of the highest value. That such experience is conceivable in a timeless universe is a doctrine opposed by the general argument of this book, but McTaggart's fine statement of it makes easier the task of those who find it even in his advocacy untenable. Whilst I have referred in the course of the argument to conceptions belonging to Professor Whitehead's philosophy, I had not the advantage of seeing its latest brilliant development in his *Adventures of Ideas* before this work had been substantially completed for revision. References to this volume have been introduced in Chapter V and elsewhere, and will show that in spite of a very different method of approach to the problem of the relation of the self to history, there are certain principles in Professor Whitehead's argument with which those I maintain have a decided affinity. Especially is this the case with his conception of the "dichotomy" which dominates the history of ideas in such wise that the force of "consciously formulated ideals" is at odds with "senseless agencies driving 'civilizations' away from inherited modes of order".[1] The view of the factors in history which I have summed up as expressing the "Other", causing the dualism between free personal agency and the burden of alien material with which it has to work, appears very near to this though by no means identical. There is much also to which I could subscribe in his doctrine of the universally dynamic nature of the process of things. But that the essential in creativity, the increase in value is manifested except in that which is personal, I cannot agree. His treatment of the problem of evil, in spite of highly original features, is—on account of his doctrine of predominant harmony—irresistibly drawn into the class of solutions which fail to recognize that element in evil which admits of no transformation, or reconciliation.

The greatest debt I owe to the late Sir Alfred Comyn Lyall, who in his capacity as statesman and man of action, historian, philosopher, poet, and in his genius for friendship, showed what is the creative power of personality, working in many spheres. His memory is imperishable for those still here who

[1] *Adventures of Ideas*, Part I, Chapter I, Introduction.

knew him, and in another revulsion of literary and historical judgments, his works may be more widely consulted than they appear to be at present, both for their intrinsic value and charm, and for the light they throw on problems of thought and action vital to our civilization.

CHAPTER II

THE TEMPORAL PROCESS

"But thought's the slave of life, and life time's fool
And time that takes survey of all the world,
Must have a stop."

SHAKESPEARE's *Hotspur* [1]

"It is impossible to meditate on time and the mystery of
the creative passage of nature without an overwhelming
emotion at the limitations of human intelligence."

A. N. WHITEHEAD

THE form in which the problem of time appears to us when
we are enquiring concerning the reality of the historic process
is best appreciated if we start from the contrast between future
and past, and having attended to this proceed to examine
what it is that we are conscious of and attempt to discriminate
when we assert the existence of the past in a sense in which
the future does not exist. It does not belong to the purpose of
this study to investigate the general nature of the "form" of
time as something to be considered in itself and in abstraction
from its content. It is rather our task to concentrate on the
quality of the content in its concrete fulness, and penetrate to
that all-pervading and all-characterizing strain or central
nerve of it in virtue of which it becomes from future past.
Or should it rather be said future, *present*, past? At this point
I prefer to omit that central and in a primary sense all dominating stage we call present, because of its enigmatic character.
Is it not in one light everything, the only real, past and future
resting upon it whilst the past craves a little span of life, grant
of shadowy being out of present riches, and the future asks
some promise, some allowance of potential being wholly unde-

---

[1] I would draw attention to the fact that Shakespeare puts some of
his most philosophical reflections into the mouths of men of action
at supreme crises of life.

termined as yet? But in another light is it anything at all but a limit between future and past, or is it nothing for knowledge since in the act of knowledge we find it past? And if it is every-thing for action since it alone is life, yet this being of the present for action cannot be temporally defined, for the inex-orable law of the passage or process is to traverse the course from future to past leaving no central foothold for the present. The present then is experienced but not known. It may shake the temporal universe and yet have no place in time, for as it explodes it becomes past, henceforth to be cherished and protected for ever by knowledge, having entered the safe treasure-house of record from a foreign source. For knowledge has to ask for a "specious present", a little span which includes a fragment of the past when it claims to contemplate the present otherwise beyond its grasp. And for action there is no specious present, the pure moment of action is free from past as well as future; we may call its present all-powerful if we like, for without it there is no history. But we cannot know it as present and label it for knowledge. Hence our predicament as to what precisely it is. But knowledge (it may be said) in all forms of history, including "natural" as well as human history, is largely concerned with events in which the stage of the present is essential, and in a certain sense the whole of the interest. The knower is knowing in the present. What he knows is as it were spread out as a line, a series of successive occurrences which for him is, as a totality, past, but only intelligible on the assumption that each occurrence has in turn presented to its agents or patients the qualities of future, present, past. The point to be here noticed, however, is that we cannot in our act of knowledge apprehend a present in this past stretch. We cannot bring with that act the peculiar distinction which separates the present of lived experience from its preceding and later states. The exception to this lies in the possibility of an identification of the subject of knowledge with the point of view of a self in the past which he feels he can share, in virtue of a peculiar experience of union. Historic knowledge appears then to have the form of an outspread series of facts we term events, related to each other by the tie of temporal order. This tie not being in itself of rational rank, the scientific historian has constantly sought to trace relations of a strictly causal type between the terms of the series, under the postulate— to make which there is a strong tendency—that the search would be ideally completed by the demonstration of necessity in the causal relations. It is this presentation of the historic order of past events in a series, in the contemplation of which it is difficult to avoid spatial imagery, which is one easy approach to the concept of the really non-temporal form and relation of the series. For the scientific or philosophic student the form of his subject-matter for knowledge is all-important. The peculiarity of the historic fact, that as historic it at some stage has a form which (as universal experience, in a certain sense *de facto* admits) is everything for reality, but in this form and apart from transformation nothing with which knowledge can deal, must be in his systematic view ignored. There is no present then *as such* for his object of knowledge. As regards the future must he not conceive it as though spread out in a form similar to that of the past? I am here referring not to the average student of history, but to one who from interest in the foundation of history as knowledge proceeds to examine the concept of the continuation or completion of the series which his method seems to imply. He inclines perhaps to the idea which has been described as that of a *totum simul*. That this is by no means identical with the timeless for the meta-physician, Bernard Bosanquet once insisted in an interesting letter, in reply to some criticisms of the view expressed in his Gifford Lectures which I had ventured to make. "I don't admit the timeless real", he wrote, "to involve simultaneity or a *totum simul*. This I understand to be a temporal character-istic involving two or more temporal successions (as indeed Bergson points out). . . . I am strongly inclined to formulate a view that people confuse a 'timeless' below time—that of abstractions, e.g. mathematical truth—and above time, e.g.

that of a concrete whole."[1] Whether the timelessness of a concrete whole is thinkable it is not here my task to consider, nor to join direct issue with that neo-Hegelian position which Bosanquet so brilliantly maintained. An endeavour to obtain a systematic view of the historic series of events in abstraction from the dynamic movement whereby one passes into another, and exhibiting instead the form of distinct facts placed or set, as it were, every one next to another as objects on a spatial extent leads, it is here suggested, to the conception of an "all at onceness". This comes about through the transmutation of the temporal which naturally occurs for minds like ours, in the endeavour to construct into an ordered system the stream of the past upon which our attention is fixed. Our thought ranges over it backwards and forwards as though it were a geographical system, or a series of geological strata. We conceive a mind of greater capacity perceiving it in detail, in a single glance. The difficulties that beset such a reconstitution of the historic process, with the suppression to a minimum of the dynamic movement, and the approach to a static type of series, need not be considered here. They are most acute in regard to the content of history as events and deeds of selves, namely beings who have a continuity for certain portions of the series. The natural tendency to this scheme is only referred to here with a view to bringing out the result in the extended universe of history in which it culminates. All history past and future rises before us as one immense object of potential knowledge for some mind or minds, subject to similar laws connecting all its different parts. But again, ought I not to have said past, present and future? The stage of the present is omitted because it has no place in this system. There can be no dynamic creative point in this series, because a single such point would be enough to set the whole on fire as it were, and destroy the scheme for science. The idea of the future is assimilated to that of the past, for there can be nothing wholly novel in the world as

[1] Quoted by the writer in "Time and Eternal Life", *Church Quarterly Review*, July 1913. Note.

historic knowledge. Here we have one source of the power exercised over our understanding by the concept of a universally determined order in human as in all other affairs. We see also a preparation so to speak of the field of experience as history for the part it must play as exemplification in a metaphysic of the timeless, even though, as Bosanquet pointed out, the idea of a *totum simul* or of all succession of events as transferred to the plane of simultaneity is quite other than the concept of the timeless real. The only possibility of intrusion of the experience of present event or occasion into the plan of history outstretched for our examination is provided by that impulse which at times drives the student in his struggle for deeper understanding to the overleaping of the line between subject and object. Whether under the spell of illusion or not he seems then to identify himself with the agent in the events, and to know the deed as if it were his own. Perhaps even the possibility of this experience though it may delude us as to its truth-value, reveals the fact that history cannot be sufficiently presented in the general form of science, because it deals with the processes of selves, and the self is subject as well as object. The hope of finding thus a key which opens the door to a source of knowledge deeper than any which the sciences generally can achieve may be excited by a "will o' the wisp". But though missing this we may stumble upon a different and more revolutionary discovery, namely that of the creative activity of selves as the factor in history in comparison with which all other factors are minor. A gain in insight into the true character of history does not necessarily carry with it a perfecting of our knowledge. We may be thrown back to the admission that the problem of knowledge here presents itself in its most formidable shape. The point we have reached, however, brings recognition that in some form the present as standing between past and future has to be reinstated in our knowledge of history, though it does not occupy any span of time in the actuality of making history. We feel that it is there in the work of the greatest historians, as a gateway through which every event has gone in the passage from future to past. This is not because, as in F. H. Bradley's conception,[1] our ideas of past and future are always constructions on the basis of the present. He is contemplating the problem from the standpoint only of the subject of knowledge. The genius of the historian, however, of which I speak is that of the mind which knows its historic object, whether deed or event, or cultural creation, as something which has issued from the real source of history, the self, though we can only describe it as object related to other objects. He has insight into its uniqueness, though he can only speak of this in terms appropriate to more than one individual. The sense of the present then must illuminate history if we are to understand this form of knowledge as something which rightly aims at being a science but is less than science, though it possesses also a virtue which makes it something more. Further reference to this point will be made in the chapter on historic knowledge. It is not that the present, however conceived, is basis and source of all our ideas whether of past in memory, or of future in inference or imagination, or any modification of this view of knowledge with its obvious truth, such as Croce's principle "All history is contemporary". The position ultimately implied in the idea of the present here indicated, is that it stands for the creative push, so to speak, or intrusion of the personal principle into the process of change from which is derived all the significance of the temporal form, all its meaning for man and therefore we may truly say its reality as history. For here we are not concerned with any problem of physics, such as "the welding of space and time together with the mechanical laws of motion", by the relativity theory, because "the dimensions of time and space cannot be taken independently of one another, but must be welded together when there is question of the velocity of light *in vacuo*".[2] I merely quote this phrase, illustrative of the stand-

[1] *Essays in Truth and Reality*, XII. Some remarks on Memory and Inference.

[2] Max Planck: *Where is Science Going?* Chapter I. Translated by James Murphy.

point of modern works on physics, as a reminder, perhaps
not necessary, that my problem is that of the temporal process
of concrete experience, which with Bergson (though I do not
closely follow him) I conceive to be the reality of time. I may
here also quote Professor Whitehead. "Nature is a process. . . .
The process of nature can also be called the passage of nature.
I definitely refrain at this stage from using the word 'time',
since the measurable time of science and of civilized life
generally merely exhibits some aspects of the more fundamental
fact of nature."[1] But from my standpoint this process is to be
thought of as it is gradually unveiled in long ages of history.
In the dawn of culture man starts from the temporal, striking
him with its once for all and irreversible character, which is
first clearly realized in the passage of those things which are
of most significance and value to him. He proceeds to find
history everywhere—in the endless cycles of seasons and
years and the monotonous sameness of plant and insect life,
from which in time to come as poet he will remove the monotony
substituting infinite variety. It should be noticed that conceiving the present as representing the experience of originating
activity, there must (from my standpoint) be contemporaneity,
because of the principle of direct intercourse between selves.
This will be further treated in the following chapter. Even if
two subjects can experience the same two events in a different
order, they nevertheless experience simultaneously that quality
in the process which is presentness. Though in A's present
there occurs an event which is past in B's, A cannot have his
present in B's past. In principle my *now* is universal, I can
meet another self in it although his time-span may be wholly
different from mine, and what is ten years for him, a day for
me. The Psalmist rightly thought that he could meet his God

[1] *The Concept of Nature,* Chapter III. With Professor Whitehead's
view of fundamental time, as explained in this chapter, if I rightly
understand it, I am in close agreement, especially that time cannot
be dissociated from events. "There is time because there are happenings,
and apart from happenings there is nothing." But my interpretation
of "happenings" is more idealistic than his.

—though "a thousand years in Thy sight are but as yesterday". The truth I wish to make clear is that where in the order of succession of any individual experience there occurs the passage through that vital illumination we call the present, the subject knows this illumination to fall upon all other experiences of the universe. This does not make time absolute. Such a conception would be irrelevant, because time is the form of a series having an irreversible order since the series exists for a consciousness in which the past is real for knowledge, but inaccessible to action. It may be said truly that time is relative to each individual self together with all his experience. Yet if A could transfer himself to the inner side of B's experience without losing hold on his own, he would find that in respect to the quality of presentness the two are identical. There cannot be a present which is only present for one mind, since selves are directly related. Contemporaneity then means that there is or may be interaction. We may find that every test of original existence except activity vanishes on analysis. Is it conceivable that there should be an activity possible only at one point of the universe? If we examine this question carefully we see that this is only conceivable from the standpoint of the solipsist, or strictly on the condition that there is only one existent being, one activity. For granted that there is activity the universe must be in principle open to its operation. Apart from physical limitations the activity must be capable of operating at any point of the cosmos. The time quality required by the activity must then be found throughout. There can be no element which is dead to it, or has to it the relation of past or future. But that the moments of present illumination must be synchronous follows, as already observed from the interrelation of selves. There could not be direct knowledge of a *Thou*, over against the *I*, unless the quality of presentness were the same for both.

The problem whether reality can be attributed to the past and in what sense must now be further considered. The contrast from the metaphysical standpoint between the future and the past has been stated in a highly distinctive form by Professor

C. D. Broad, "Such a theory as this accepts the reality of the present, and the past but holds that the future is nothing at all."[1] Elsewhere he observes when discussing the objections to a naïvely realistic view of memory: "There is no general metaphysical objection. . . . It appears to me that once an event has happened it exists eternally."[2] In a paper on "The Status of the Past",[3] I followed Professor Broad on the whole in this position, though resting my view on arguments which he probably would not accept. More recent reflection on the problem has inclined me to question whether from my own standpoint the doctrine of the eternal existence of the past can be so well defended as from his. His view, if I rightly understand it, rationalizes the implication which may be found in ordinary thought. It assumes a type of modified realism. It is undoubted that ordinarily we ascribe in some sense a being to events of the past which we cannot attach to that which is thought of as future, whatever the degree of assurance with which we may anticipate it. The question of degree of certainty in our expectation is in fact irrelevant. The non-existence of the future event cannot be affected, whether by a psychical sense of reality of a coming event "casting its shadow before" or by necessity of scientific inference. The real import of this attribution of existence to the past is a more difficult problem on an idealistic than on a realistic theory of the nature of events. The strength of the idealistic view, as I tried to present it in the paper mentioned, if I may be permitted to refer to this, lies in the inseparability of self-consciousness from memory. This inseparability is a sign that the self has partly its being in the past, and its past is yet living and actual for it. Professor Alexander's view of memory appears to involve this position. "Remembering is the speculative desire of reinstating the past, or rather of reinstating ourselves in compresence with it. . . . The past is real as past. It is not

---

[1] *Scientific Thought*, Part I, Chapter II.
[2] *The Mind and its Place in Nature*, Chapter V.
[3] *Proceedings of the Aristotelian Society*, 1931–32.

real as being present, it is *now* no longer." In particular he
ascribes pastness to the "enjoyment". The experience of
enjoyment remembered is experienced as past. Thus it is not
only the object which is past but the subject which has a past
experience.[1] In my paper I went on to speak of the self as
continuous in past and present. Professor Johannes Volkelt,
however, whilst asserting that the self certainty of consciousness
"divides itself into certainty of present and of past", yet treats
the past as non-being. "I overcome 'the backward-lying
time' ", he writes, "and grasp immediately what no more is",
and "My past experience has irretrievably fallen into that which
is not."[2] It is this mystical notion of overcoming the backward-
lying time and grasping immediately that which is not, in
which the enigma lies. Is it not necessary to show that what is
thus grasped preserves a kind of being? In an article on "The
Nature of Memory-Knowledge" Professor Baillie observes that
"The past is an element of our reality, just as much as the
present",[3] and does not depend on the present for its being,
more than the present on the past. According to my argument,
then, with which the views of memory here referred to seem in the
main consistent, the existence of the past is necessary on account
of the nature of our experience as self-conscious beings in a process. But this existence is quite other than that we call present.
In a sense each event does vanish on the appearance of its
successor. It vanishes for sense and action. We are aware of
its existence in so far as we can put on the mortality of its
pastness. For it is mortal in respect to existence as activity.
To this it has died. In the same paper I argued that it was "the
necessity of a real past to our mental nature working through
categories which function more or less subconsciously, and
consciously expressed in memory", which "determines the
almost universally human interest in past events". It appears
to me that there is some force in the argument that "as beings
whose experience is of the nature of process, we are determined

---

[1] *Space, Time and Deity*, Book I, Chapter IV.
[2] *Gewissheit und Wahrheit*, III, 5.   [3] *Mind*, July 1917.

to seek to traverse this process in memory, or as if it were accessible to memory; to live through it to the utmost possible extent." "A real past is necessary to the form of our experience, and memory provides it with some content." The problem of the reality of the past for history, beyond the history of individual selves, is not, however, thereby solved. For on this line of thought it would appear that the idea of history as knowledge, the position that in principle there is potential knowledge of all past events, though the incalculably greater proportion is actually beyond all our instrumentation of search, involves the postulate of a universal self-consciousness with which we are unconsciously in communion. Without this assumption it might seem inconceivable that we could have a common knowledge of historic objects, since for each self his memory is unique, and incommunicable in its individuality. The philosophical standpoint of this book does not admit of the conception of a universal consciousness, as will appear in the work as a whole, and in particular the chapters on the self, and on "The Idea of the Whole as Personal". The concept might possibly be treated as a "regulative idea" required for the purposes of history in the ideal sense, namely as knowledge of the concrete actuality of the past in all its individuality. The realization of this ideal is, however, inconceivable for reasons which will appear in the examination of the nature of the subject itself, the real origin of history; the form which history has assumed as a great field of knowledge is different.

An argument for the existence of the past independent of any question of its accessibility to knowledge—the ontological rather than the epistemological problem might, I think, be grounded initially on the idea of continuity in the temporal process. It appears to be the nature of a continuous series that all its terms are in some sense "subsistent". The continuity it is presumed depends upon some principle which determines the order, in which there must from the nature of continuity be no gaps. Now the great reproach of history as knowledge is that to all the labours of philosophic historians it has remained irresponsive, and has not yielded up the secret of a law of order, upon which its events can be seen to follow in obedient succession. It remains a wild province of knowledge untameable by any of our categories unless reducible to the deterministic sequence in which it ceases to be history. Yet for such a law we must continue to seek. It must then have its interpretation in the fundamental form of the temporal, though we cannot distinguish in this any sure place for the types of value we find in many limited extracts from the total process. It is because this conviction returns again and again to the human mind, that there remains after all failure to find in history any continuous illustration of some principle that would give a coherent significance to the endless succession, the belief that this can only appear when the whole story is told. No petty incident in the backward and abysm of time can then have passed into nothingness. For its meaning is implicit in its relation to the whole, and the meaning of the whole cannot yet appear. This argument in fact rests on the postulate which history cannot abandon, that there is importance in its subject-matter. The subject-matter being—from any human standpoint—infinite, no atom of it can be conceived as wholly lost. Again, however, in the attempt to find ontological being, we seem to be driven back to the nature of the human mind. We are perhaps forced to conclude that the existence of the past in a metaphysical sense, apart from memory, is an undemonstrable proposition, though a necessary postulate. With regard to the problem of the future some further considerations will be adduced in the chapter on "History and the Future." The necessity of the idea of a real future will there be based especially on considerations in relation to the creative principle of personality. Here it may be observed that the reality of the temporal process involves the reality of the future as well as of the present and the past, in some sense. There must be a source of becoming. But the difficulty presents itself that we can only thus signify the form of the future, since we have no knowledge of its content, and the position has been taken that form is not validly abstracted from the concrete process. The content is indeed more or less vaguely or vividly imagined. It does not exist, but its imagination is essential to the temporality of the self. Also thought is not possible without assumption of the future. My thought at this moment is slain if it is not allowed an ideal successor. In emphasis of this point I may quote a passage from Professor Whitehead's new book, with which I am almost in entire agreement, allowing for the difference introduced by his philosophical standpoint which does not here affect the essential agreement.

"It belongs to the essence of this subject that it pass into objective immortality. Thus its own constitution involves that its own activity in *self* formation passes into its activity of *other* formation." (Professor Whitehead's italics.) "It is by reason of the constitution of the present subject that the future will embody the present subject and will re-enact its pattern of activity. But the future individual occasions are non-existent. Because the creative urge of the universe functions in each single individual occasion, the future is immanent in each present occasion. But no future individual occasion is in existence."[1]

In what respect I differ from Professor Whitehead in regard to the "creative urge of the universe" will appear in the sequel.

[1] *Adventures of Ideas*, "Past, Present, Future."

CHAPTER III

THE SELF AND HISTORY

"He builds the soaring spires
That sing his soul in stone; of her he draws,
Though blind to her, by spelling at her laws,
Her present fires.

Through him hath she exchanged
For the gold harvest robes, the mural crown,
Her haggard quarry features, and thick frown
Where monsters ranged."
GEORGE MEREDITH, *Earth and Man*

THE beginning of history, broadly speaking, coincides with the emergence[1] of selves. Perhaps it would be more exact to say that at this stage the conditions for the possibility of history exist, for where there is neither record nor the definiteness of self-consciousness which is expressed in rudimentary art or externalization by man of something in his experience, it is doubtful whether we can rightly speak of history. History will be found by the later self-conscious man, looking back from his own fully characterized experience at this sub-historic stage, because this is in accordance with the principle of our knowledge in all the data we approach. Our interpretation proceeds by applying, as far as possible, the categories which make intelligible our own more direct experience. This is the case not less with the historic and dynamic than with the static categories of the understanding. In the application, for instance, of the principle of evolution or development to throw light upon those fragments or phases of primitive human life we meet with, we are inclined to regard the process as stages in a growth of which the growth from seed or egg to mature being is a miniature epitome. If there are amongst the data some recalci-

[1] This word is not used in the sense of the philosophers of "Emergence" (C. Lloyd Morgan and S. Alexander).

trant to such inclusion showing those irregular unclassifiable events in which the peculiar individuality of man can be seen though not completely understood, these will frequently escape the net of the category, and uncomprehended tend to be forgotten. The main truth of our form of knowledge here to be emphasized is that it is and must be applied from the height of our present-day culture. We arrive indeed at the early culture (savage or barbaric) by reducing our principle of interpretation to the simplest form. We may be compelled to recognize that there is much that is complex, with a complexity not wholly intelligible in the behaviour of the primitive peoples. But we treat it, generally speaking, by seeing in it the shape appropriate as first pattern of the elaborately developed myth or the scientific system which arose after long ages. Our explanation in fact must be from the standpoint of the later, higher, less imperfect. If we attempt to explain the later by conceiving its gradual building up out of elements supplied by the earlier, we may be deluding ourselves by setting forth as members of a temporal series elements which have been analysed out of the whole at a more final stage. Not necessarily so, because there are series in which this procedure will be illuminating. It is not impossible that the temporal order should correspond with that discovered by analysing out simpler and more complex elements from our experience as representing earlier and later. But it does not necessarily do this, least of all where the problem under consideration is the history of value experience.

In the present work it is assumed that the principle which has been indicated is not only unconsciously followed, when a different principle is ostensibly applied, but is the only fruitful and valid one. We must conceive history primarily in its fully conscious form, experienced first in the intimate events of our own personal life in its past and present, secondly in the relatively direct knowledge of the doings of our fellows on their inner as well as external side. From the feeling and idea of history thus gained we turn to the record of the past.

As history began when mind in personal activity first made
events out of the processes otherwise indifferent to value, so
we can hope to comprehend its beginnings and developments
by interpretations from the point of view of the fully historical
with its historic value. This value as I conceive it is the fundamental contrast and union of the eternal and the changing.
It is the self which brings into the process, in the monotonous
cyclical nature of which there is as yet no delineation, no
distinction of the permanent and the changing, the definite
opposition of these principles. That history is not wholly
constituted by the experience of selves is revealed primarily
in the fact that so far as we can judge, without that reading
into the data which is almost inevitable, there is an amorphous
age, which is and is not history. In this the self (which is
however not as yet completely a self) takes the first steps on
the path or pathless way which is its own trail, not merely a
break of nature in the unpierced forest. The historic process
has then begun, with the vague hardly conscious attempt to
make, to humanize, in accordance with some image which
only man can see. Henceforth the labour to infuse value into
the process will never end, since the images of something
better will in time point to a notion of good, carrying with it
the law of its actualization. Nevertheless history is throughout
seamed with dualism. By this I mean not the dualism of good
and bad, but that of the activity of selves, and the agency of
another factor, which we may here (without strict accuracy)
call force, wholly indifferent to good and evil, or to the manifestation of value and disvalue in the events of the world.
On account of this it has seemed to some students of history
that the central factors are the historic forces and the events,
rather than selves and their deeds. This question and that of
the true significance of the notion "historic force" will meet
us later. We shall meet also with that question to which it
gives rise, whether there appears as appropriate to history
objectified for contemplation as knowledge, a standard different
from the moral standard—that of historic importance and

significance. If so, this would be due to the presence of factors which cannot be banned from history incompatible if not irreconcilable with the idea of history presented by some historians and by ethical and religious teachers, namely that it is a record of the doings of persons individually and collectively, the expression of their activity in realizing the good as it appeared to them, with results both good and evil. In respect to history as the course of events, these factors, summed up as the principle for which I suggest the name "Other" ($\tau\grave{o}$ $\H{\epsilon}\tau\epsilon\rho o\nu$), with a reflection of Plato's use, must be admitted to enter indissolubly and intimately into the web or fabric. They are not alien to history so understood, but essential. In this view, persons also and their deeds would be included as historic events. Persons are groups or series of actions of a special type. Into their very deeds there enters the element foreign to that free creativity which seems the essence of personality.

This subject will be further discussed and illustrated later. Reference has been made to it at this point in order to set in clear relief the method of the first approach we are making to the problem of history. This is the consideration of history as originally constituted by the experience of selves, without which indeed there would not be history, although as we find we cannot identify it with history. Some considerations in regard to the nature of the self seem required, and the problem of our knowledge of other selves. We cannot ask what experience would be without selves, because we cannot clearly conceive the possibility of such experience. We can, however, ask what it is that the kind of life which is that of a self gives to its world, because we discover this in direct inner experience. It is the self which endows experience with meaning, bringing to the things and events with which it meets, those meanings of which the outer shell of fact then becomes sign or symbol, and which are the sources of the life of emotion, thought, practice. It may be asked, Why conceive the self as bringing rather than finding meaning? One of the main problems of philosophy is here encountered, the interpretation of meaning.

What justification is there of attaching it to the self as source?
Why should it not have independent being, Platonic ideality?
Or phenomenological essence "Wesen" with the self as carrier
(Träger)? Some answer to this will be given in the general
position of the book, and especially the chapter dealing with
Platonic and other theories of moral value. The standpoint
adopted involves that without creativity of selves the world
of our experience would not be what it is, as through and
through made real by meaning. This work upon the data of
experience begins in the simple activity of perception, and is
found at its height in the creation of genius in thought, art,
and the Utopian scheme of the great visionary in practice—
Utopian here signifying the character of a world in which
some great value is realized completely, so that there is nothing
outside its influence. The arguments that follow will point to
the conclusion that the universe of meanings thus related to
the mind which is their source is inconceivable except as the
work of a multiplicity of selves. If this multiplicity were
illusory and the mind from which meaning proceeds were in
truth a unity the limitless variety of the world both in kind
and degree of meaning would be unintelligible. This is because
in important features the variety is such that it cannot be
interpreted except as outcome of distinct minds in co-operation,
or opposition. An idealistic interpretation, far from implying,
is incompatible with monism. This will be more evident when
the relation of selves to history has been further examined,
and also the bases of knowledge and of Ethics in the recognition
of the *Thou*, over against the *I*. This supreme human experience
would be excluded from the experience of a universal mind.
No self-objectification, no thought thinking upon itself can
offer anything but a weakened impoverished reflection of the
simplest human insight into that other self which is wholly
other. This is the fundamental fact which cannot be transcended or negated or absorbed into a wider unity of experience.[1]

The view that the self can best be understood in its historic

[1] Cf. "The Idea of the Whole as Personal," Chapter IX.

experience receives at least a negative confirmation when we
survey the attempts of philosophy to deal with this subject
by burdening it with the metaphysical weight of the notion
of substance. There appears to be little doubt that in its genesis
this notion (Aristotle's οὐσία) was inseparable from the
physically resistent spatial object. In Kant's treatment of the
category of substance there seems to be recognition of this,
though he does not consistently admit the implications involved.
As metaphysical thinking develops with the distinction of
"reality" and "appearance", and the discovery that mental
(or immaterial) objects may have more resistance and inde-
structibility than physical, as incapable of dismissal from our
total world, the reality of the immaterial begins to be more
clearly perceived. The test is no longer the impression of the
object on the senses and its spatial occupation. But substance
as the real retains for man's imagination properties which make
it an inadequate category for the subjective principle of all
experience. To attain the distinction between subject and
object in respect to this category marked perhaps the difficult
birth of the metaphysical faculty. A more concrete description
of this event would be that the distinction which had long
dimly haunted the thought of men agonizing in fear and labouring in action to avoid or propitiate beings not physical, not
sensibly visible or tangible, yet possessed of unknown power,
became a definite one. Yet substance is chiefly imaged and
thought of as object. As such it possesses characteristics common
to all objects. It endures amid change, it is there for A as well
as for B. Man's chief tendencies and interests in theoretic and
practical pursuits determine him to seek for its universal
properties. For the solution of the twin problems, the significance of history, as deriving its essential character from the
activities of selves, and the significance of selves in the cosmos,
the attempt has to be made to penetrate to knowledge of the
individual. For this it seems necessary to grasp something that
cannot be handled by philosophy as an object fixable in all
its occurrences, in its most important and distinctive qualities

the same, yet endlessly different, and only the same as source of
all our essentially human experiences. The problem of the
appropriate historic object, and whether it is individual or
universal, has been much discussed by modern writers on
"Historismus" and reference to some of their results will be
made in a later chapter.[1] From the present point of view the
central fact for historic knowledge is the individual activity, in
one light subject in another object. The question, then, arises
whether knowledge of this fact in any exact sense is possible.
Whatever the answer to this, a survey of the many efforts at
interpretation of history, whether from a scientific or philosophical standpoint, or from one belonging to history as a
special study, may point after so many seeming failures to a
single clue. From the insuperable difficulty of any general
explanation we return to that individuality itself, which is the
most baffling source of the problem. For we find that to whatever extent the emphasis is laid on other historical categories,
the incomparable distinction of the historic event from all
other happenings of nature, lies in the presence in it of the
qualities of the deed, the work of personality, and the reason
of uniqueness. If it has to be confessed that no universal
philosophy of history is possible, we may still turn to that
which is the root of all historic reality, since for a consciousness
lacking this the endless process of change would be a dream.
This it is which, transfiguring the process with value, makes its
temporal character, its passage as future, present, past put on
the tremendous significance of history, which because it
changes lays upon man the task of persuading the changing
phases to reflect his ideas. This observation is only thrown
out at this point as an indication of the reason for an
attempt which, in view of the general verdict of epistemologists
from Aristotle onwards, may seem doomed to failure. The fact
that history is concerned with the individual has led some
philosophers to reject the testimony of history as to the nature
of things, and many to depreciate the historic categories. The

[1] See Chapter IV.

fact that history cannot be interpreted by means of logical categories, on which account it is charged with irrationality, nor can yield its truths by means of the application of methods adopted in general from the organized sciences, will be further illustrated at a later stage.

Returning to the problem of the nature of the self in relation to history, it should be noted that misconception is encouraged by the practice (difficult to avoid) of discussion of *the self* rather than of *selves*. For this suggests an object, which is in all its instances essentially the same. Or if conceived as the genus, of which the members have specific differences, these differences it is often assumed must be such as to proceed from the genus, or class-notion. This assumption, which appears fallacious, is closely connected with the idea of the soul as substance and object. It would needlessly overload our discussion to illustrate these positions by a survey of the history of theories of the self in philosophy. For the present purpose we might without confusion consider the general idea of the self, as nearly equivalent to Plato's soul (ψύχη), though it is by no means exactly so. When we are reflecting upon the maze of ideas, brought before us by anthropologists, as for instance in the volumes of Sir James Frazer,[1] revealed by primitive beliefs and practices in regard to "the soul", and ask at what stage of thought can soul as self in the modern sense be discovered, it seems convenient to take as a test Professor Taylor's definition of the soul as conceived by the Platonic Socrates. The self then would be "the seat of normal intelligence and character", that "in virtue of which we are pronounced wise or foolish, good or bad". (Socrates.[2]) But more precisely in the meaning of the Platonic Socrates, "The thought is that the 'work' or 'function', of this divine constituent in man is just to *know*, to apprehend things as they really are, and consequently, in particular, to *know* good and evil, and to direct or govern a man's acts so that they lead to a life in which evil

[1] *The Golden Bough, Belief in Immortality, The Perils of the Soul*, etc.
[2] A. E. Taylor: *Socrates*, Chapter IV.

is avoided, and good achieved." (A. E. Taylor[1].) In Professor Taylor's view this is a new doctrine of the soul introduced by Socrates into European thought—wholly other than that of the Homeric psyche or ghost, or even the Orphic psyche with its permanent individuality. It cannot be said that the dawn of anything comparable to this supremely ethical concept of soul can be perceived in those men and women who pass before us in tragic procession in the pages of Sir James Frazer and other students of primitive communities and barbarous religions as types, or as individuals only in so far as their life and fate call forth in the minds of the modern student, irresistible pity which endows them with pathetic lineaments.[2] But as I shall argue, the essential self, if not in activity, is there potentially in beings who had and have the mental experiences involved, who conceived for instance the strangely dramatic ideas of the dying God, the scapegoat with the profound sense of sin involved, who showed in magical practices some recognition of causation, who felt the mystery of death and affirmed an after-existence, however poor in conception. The essentials of the value-experience are not present before the mind can look freely out upon the world relieved from the greater burdens of unspeakable fears and the weight of unquestionable custom. The staggering problem of the lower cultures may, however, be partly met by the interpretation of the potentiality present in all selves, but not to be realized until a certain degree of freedom is reached.

This reference to prehistoric stages is here made as a reminder of the continuity of history overriding the distinction between the prehistoric and historic, whether or not we can trace the links; also of the importance of setting the ideas which arise in different stages of history in relation to the culture to which they belong. That this is true of the more as well as of the less advanced ideas and cultures is not always remembered.

[1] A. E. Taylor: *Socrates*, Chapter IV.
[2] Reference will later be made to the more optimistic view of Dr. Marett in regard to the primitive mind.

The idea of soul or self as subject of experience does not appear to have occupied the place in ancient which it gradually assumed in modern thought. Only in Plato's intense moral preoccupation with the seat of conduct does he at moments seem to pierce through to the principle whose discernment belongs to a later age. This is evident especially in his earnest exhortation in the *Laws* on the honour owed by each to his own soul.[1] (What is the relation, we might ask, here of subject to object, that which honours and that which is honoured?) The concentration on the problem of self-consciousness, expressed by Descartes in the *Cogito ergo sum*, does not throw much light on the nature of the subject which is to provide a principle of explanation of our historic life. In Aristotle's subtle contribution to the doctrine of the soul the notion of form, actuality, ἐντελέχεια, he does not free it from the false metaphysical character it derives from application of the doctrine of substance. Similarly Descartes' more subjective method of arriving at the self is deflected from the path which might have led to a truer concept by the unquestioned assumption that in seeking for something whose existence he cannot doubt he is seeking for a substance. The empirical thinkers, Locke and Berkeley, did not really escape from the idea of the self as spiritual substance, though in Locke's insistence on identity discovered in self-consciousness, and Berkeley's recognition that he has a kind of immediate intuition of himself in activity, there appears an understanding that knowledge of the subject must be of a different type from our ordinary knowledge of objects. In modern philosophy, however, from Descartes to Kant, there seems to be no sign of insight into the truth that for a revelation of the nature of selves they must be examined not primarily as objects of knowledge but in their active historic experience. Whilst rationalism and empiricism contended for the appropriation of soul or self either as intelligible substance or as object of experience, this object under the dissecting analysis of Hume vanished or gave place to the

[1] *Laws*, Book V.

congeries of its elements. Kant's treatment of the unity of
self-consciousness in the first Critique abstracts wholly from
the active presence of the self in events. In the *Critique of
Practical Reason* we meet once more with a kind of intelligible
substance. Now when Hume remarked on the curious fact
that the speculations of his study (or sanctum) appeared to
him unreal, when he left it to enjoy social pleasures with his
friends, was he disturbed or perhaps amused by the suspicion
that there might be something in the atmosphere of the study
extinguishing the self for his perception, if his hunt for it
went on only there and not in the untamed world, where he
might have to face rude storms of unsanctified experience?
It may be suggested that the philosophy of the self was naturally
and inevitably submitted, when its development began in
modern thought to methods which had been elaborated for
the purposes of the philosophy of the world. On this account,
it may be argued, its exponents ignored the existence of much
rich and even indispensable material for its proper construction.
And when at a later stage this subject came to be distinguished
from the departments of philosophy proper as fitted for more
adequate treatment by methods so far as possible similar to
those of the empirical sciences, it was removed still further
from the type of investigation in relation to which resource
might be had to such material. The methods appropriate to
the natural sciences, which are concerned with aspects or
selected divisions of the boundless mass of data in which our
experience is immersed, involve analyses enabling discovery
of elements and properties common to many individuals. At
least the common is assumed, where the closely similar is
observed. Wherever they appear discernible, samenesses of
properties or kinds of behaviour are noted, in order to the
establishment of general laws, explanations which signify the
bringing of the unknown under the categories which give
intelligibility to the known. Such is our intellectual instrumentation aiming at the greatest generality attainable. We
can hardly conceive any other form of understanding in regard

to the external manifestations of the things of our experience. The pain of unsatisfied knowledge, the baffled despair of the seeker suggests to a Kant the speculation concerning an intuitive intelligence for which knowledge would be possible without the categories. But this idea must remain negative, if we cannot know whether that to which the intuition would be directed, that inner being behind the events and laws of nature has a true communion of kind with the mind that intuits. Without such assurance does not the notion of an intuitive intelligence pass into mysticism? Psychology, it has always been recognized (except by the behaviourists), possesses a method available in no other science, that of introspection. But it is difficult to avoid the suspicion that, on account of the enormous influence of methods developed during a considerable period in the other sciences, this inner observation has been in some degree at least modelled on the forms of outer observation. At least a principal aim has been to establish general laws, uniform sequences in the operation of the various functions and their interrelations, the cognitive, affective, conative, these having first been separated from the unity of the active self. The subject objectifies and examines his own fleeting states, which are indeed rather processes than states, at the point of their transition into memory. If he is to gain a scientific understanding of their interrelations, he must abstract them each from the moving whole, and describe them in the language signs which stand for a limitless number of similar data in different contexts. If any of the processes thus observed or caught in the moment of passing is unique, and it may be that all are so, it cannot be recorded in its uniqueness, since the experience of the self to which it belongs is *ipso facto*, in this situation the only and once-for-all occasion of the event. But this would appear to be undiscoverable by psychological analysis.

Reference to the views of Heinrich Rickert and Wilhelm Dilthey respectively on the relation of psychology to history may help to stress this point. Rickert[1] argues that the psychology

[1] *Kulturwissenschaft und Naturwissenschaft*, p. 62.

required by the historian is, if possible, still farther than the psychology of the artist from that of the generalizing science of the soul-life, since it is wholly directed to the once for all and the particular. We rightly, he observes, call poets and creative artists psychologists, for they must be knowers of men in order to fulfil their tasks. But the artist's psychology has certainly nothing in common with the conceptual science of the soul-life, except the name. History he holds to be nearer to art than to science. He points out that we find important psychologists amongst the historians in times when there was no scientific psychology, as for instance Thucydides, of whom Wundt says that he "might serve as a pattern for later ages, in psychological comprehension of the historic process". Polybius, Tacitus, Hume, Gibbon and others were indeed from the standpoint of their times well-trained psychologists, but this only shows that the psychology of their day, which is now superseded, has done no harm to these historians. Not because of but in spite of their psychology were they distinguished historians. We psychologically explain, as Rickert proceeds, the nature of the psychic being when we seek for its general laws, or any other general explanatory concept. But we learn to know the soul-life in history, when, so far as is possible, we live it again, "Nacherleben" in its individual course. Thus we have acquired material in the highest sense essential for a historic presentation.

Dilthey[1] asks for a wider interpretation of psychology. Psychology and anthropology he considers must form the foundations of our knowledge of the historical life. But this presupposes a widening of their scope. He conceives that the method of these sciences might be so modified as to make them capable of showing not only the uniformities of the spiritual life, but also its typical distinctions. "The imaginative power of the artist, the nature of the practical man", should be submitted to description and analysis, and the study of the forms

[1] *Gesämmelte Schriften*, Band I. Erster Buch: *Einleitung in die Geisteswissenschaften*.

of the mental life completed through description of the actuality of its course as well as its context. Thus the gaps which exist between psychology on the one hand, aesthetics, ethics and the sciences of political bodies on the other will be filled in— a place hitherto occupied by the insufficient generalizations of the experience of life, creations of the poet, etc. "Biography", he continues, "is the presentation of the individual psycho-physical unity of life—the fundamental historical fact pure and complete in its actuality. If biography is an important aid to the further development of a true psychology, it has on the other hand its foundation in the state of this science at the time." This last statement hardly seems true of the great biographies, which, as Rickert observes of the great histories, seem to reveal the actuality of their subject, whatever the state of contemporary psychology. Dilthey's view that psychology ought to study the chief types of the spiritual life certainly suggests a method of limiting the generality of the science, and bringing it closer to concrete humanity. Psychology, in fact, is already in our time dealing with certain of these types. But does this give promise of any considerable advance in the understanding of selves in their individuality? Let us assume the artist type as that of men endowed with senses (especially of sight or hearing) much more vivid or intense than those of the ordinary man, this greater intensity being cause at least in part of the ecstasies and agonies of their vision of things and the compulsion they feel to express these emotions, the vehemence of their will in this direction, the difficulty of arousing it in some others. Let other characteristics supposed typical be added to the characterization, suggested perhaps by observation of the living, and accounts of artists in other times. How near have we approached to the understanding of the individual artist B? In one sense we are nearer to the individual with every additional quality that we apprehend as characteristic of that kind of being. But in a deeper sense we are no nearer because the gulf between a collection of qualities or characteristics and an individual is infinite. The individual is in transition, his nature is dynamic. A quality ascribed has changed as we observe him, in some respect slight perhaps, yet meaning some difference in the whole. For the qualities are but such expressions of the self as can be distinguished and named, because we recognize a similarity we call sameness in their occurrence in many cases. The greater, more important, impressive samenesses which stimulate or excite our admiration, alarm, delight and other emotions, have from the earliest stages of culture been singled out, and classified as virtues, talents, passions, vices and so on. These vivid human universals accompany our thoughts of ourselves and our fellows from childhood. They are our ideals, or our dangerous foes. We almost endow them with souls, as did our forefathers, deities for Greek myths, angels, spirits and demons for mediaeval imagination, objects of our aspiration and abhorrence before whom we kneel or raise our shields. Again, it is through an irrepressible psychical tendency that the combination of a group of these qualities as an object comes to acquire for our concept of it an individual character. Yet the individual self escapes the net of these universals, and it is not the real self that we can know as object. This conclusion is also forced upon us by the continual pressure of the experiences of life.

What is the nature of our knowledge of other selves? To deal adequately with this question would be a very considerable task. In relation to the main problem of this work it is of central importance to indicate the answer which seems to be necessitated by historic experience, and ask whether this is consistent with the position to which we should be led by our view of the nature of selves, i.e. the relatively *a priori* ground. With regard to the existence of other selves, our knowledge is (in my view) original or intuitive. The error of the theory that our belief that other selves exist is based on analogical arguments appears to be evident from the fact that in the type of illustrations usually given the experience which is the material for the analogy could not have taken place without previous assumption of the existence of other conscious beings. A leading

example is that of language, the utterance of sounds in which I perceive certain meanings. Such sounds signifying such meanings are directly known to me in my own activity as proceeding from a self, and the inference follows that since they do not in this case proceed from myself, there must exist another self as their source. But I could not have become acquainted with the use of speech, its occasions and meanings without belief in the existence of beings like myself. Going a little deeper, it appears that self-consciousness cannot be conceived to develop apart from consciousness of other selves. If we ask the question of origin, we may find in child-observation that there are no clear indications that the child feels the "I", as "I" before it is conscious of the "Thou", that which appears to it through the face of another. We may agree with Johannes Volkelt that knowledge that there are other selves is *a priori*.[1] The original fact seems to be that the self first feels itself unconsciously to be member of a world of living activities, most vividly appearing in its neighbourhood as those which enter into relations with it, of a beneficent kind. The germ of animism appears to be there from the first. With the beginning of intelligence this instinctive attitude takes on the form of a cognitive principle, in the implied affirmation of the existence of other selves, namely of living activities similar to that which is known in self-consciousness. This cognition is, I think, *a priori* in the sense that as soon as the individual consciously exercises intelligence, he is in necessary possession of it. The solipsistic view, although inconceivable, may appear on first examination not self-contradictory, so long as the self is thought of in abstraction from the universe. It is, however, found on further analysis to involve what I should term a self-contradiction, as contradiction within the self *qua* implicit in the nature of his world. Because since he cannot find in his experience of the universe in which there is *ex hypothesi* no other self-conscious being, a logical order such as his own rational nature demands, there is no

[1] *Gewissheit und Wahrheit*, Abschnitt III, 5, X, 2.

logical system in things beyond his own intelligent activity. But that there should be only a single source of the logical process in a vast experience seems to be destructive of its significance and therefore its validity. In fact there could be no reasoning and no faith in logic for a self who was alone in his universe without other minds to apprehend with him common principles. As it is not necessary to my general argument to prove the self-contradictory character of solipsism since the proof from experience of its impossibility is sufficient, I will not follow out this position further. I merely adduce it since it appears to have escaped those thinkers who suppose that solipsism is incapable of disproof. It would not alone confute the doctrine that there is but one mind, as the universal being in all things. This is elsewhere examined in this work.[1]

The problem whether we have direct knowledge of the nature and qualities of other selves, beyond the general characters inseparable from selfhood, is a different one, and must, I think, be answered in the negative, both on *a priori* and on empirical grounds. From the *a priori* standpoint, it appears that it results from the nature of the self as subject that it cannot be known. To say that what we know must be object, is no doubt a truism. The question still has meaning— Cannot the subject become object for knowledge? In a certain sense it can. Nevertheless, that which we have before us as object-self is not the subject in its individual essence, since this is not only dynamic in nature, it is creative, in its perception of experience at every moment. A living energy can possibly be captured for observation, but not a living consciousness. Consciousness being ultimate and indefinable, this point is incapable of further explanation. I cannot then know even myself directly as object, though I have a peculiar relation to myself which is a substitute for knowledge. That object of knowledge which I call myself, formed from the projection of my subject-self, partly interpreted by analogy and comparison (largely unconscious) with the kind of knowledge I suppose

[1] Chapter XI.

myself to have of other selves, and by those memories which are the substance of myself as past, is better known to me than the selves of others. McTaggart, who holds that in "Reality" we know other selves directly, and in our present experience of "misperception" we know our own self by acquaintance, accepts Bertrand Russell's argument in proof of the latter proposition, though it was later abandoned by its author. The argument was as follows: In any proposition such as I am now aware of equality, I must know that the I which makes the assertion is the same as the I which has the awareness, and since I do not know the former I by description I must know it by acquaintance.[1] From my point of view, the I which asserts and the I which is aware, are in one sense the same, namely, the subject-self which cannot, as stated above, have direct knowledge ("awareness") of itself. I may, however, in another sense contemplate an object which is myself in the act of being aware of equality. Of this object, in so far as it is the abstraction of a single activity, I may be said to have direct knowledge. But in so far as it is the whole self of my specious present, I do not know it in its concrete reality.

On empirical grounds the truth that we do not know other selves directly seems to be based on abundant evidence. The greater part of our social and historic experience is conditioned and permeated by it. Of a world of selves directly known to each other we can hardly have an adequate conception, but we can judge that in the greatest questions affecting human conduct and happiness it would be altogether different from the actual world of our experience. This is well understood by McTaggart, though from a different standpoint, in his argument that between the selves who know each other directly there will be a perfect relation of love.[2] Examples of our ignorance of the inner nature of other selves, their springs of

[1] J. G. McTaggart: Article in *Encyclopædia of Religion and Ethics*, "Personality." *The Nature of Existence*, Vol. II, Book V, Chapter XXXVI.
[2] *The Nature of Existence*, Vol. II.

action, points of view, must crowd upon our memory even from experience of daily life and companionship. From this favourable case we may pass through survey of the lesser relations of human beings in business and the innumerable associations of society groupings small and large for pleasure or convenience, to the great failures of understanding which occur in all kinds of association whether with acquaintances, members of the same community, profession, nation, or with those unfamiliar in type, tradition, race. Or we may turn to historic personalities in biography and history. Do fellow-workers united even in what appear to be the most disinterested, impersonal and widely human enterprises always or usually see into the real motives of each other's actions?—comrades in such great tasks as emancipation of the slaves, legislation on factory conditions, etc. Do they understand the subtle qualities of another's inspiration and sympathies in art, literature, ideals of living? They are nearer to each other in the unpolluted sources of sympathy than a Napoleon to the generals who fought and suffered for him, and abandoned him, or the comrades who remained with him in the tragic monotony of his last years, yet under constant friction with their old hero and amongst themselves. Yet how many of those linked in movements for the welfare of mankind, or the ending of some cruel wrong, have known the secrets of each other's hearts? But illustrations are hardly required of the truth that if a divine knowledge of the searchings of the human soul may be postulated, such knowledge is not for men, even when two face each other in the brightest or the darkest moments in the lives of both. Consider the group of men with whom the "Oxford Movement" began, their similarity in the intensely sensitive devotion to religion and search after a certainty in regard to what has seemed to others differences of belief too subtle to be correlated with differences of truth and falsehood. We may note their purity of life and aim, and tender friendship for each other. Does Newman's record of his religious history show direct knowledge of each other's thoughts amongst these

men, himself and Hurrel Froude, Keble, Ward, Pusey and
the rest of that rare circle? To take one example: "I had from
the first a great difficulty in making Dr. Pusey understand such
differences of opinion as existed between himself and me. . . .
A common friend of ours broke it all to him in 1841, as far as
matters had gone at that time, and showed him clearly the
logical conclusions which must lie in propositions to which
I had committed myself, but somehow or other in a little while
his mind fell back into its former happy state, and he could
not bring himself to believe that he and I should not go on
pleasantly together to the end. . . . Nay at the Commemoration
of 1845, a few months before I left the Anglican Church, I
think he said about me to a friend, 'I trust after all we shall
keep him'."[1] Few of the misunderstandings of history are more
melancholy than those of Pitt and Wilberforce, though the
ties of a great friendship and mutual respect were too strong
for the break ever to be final. But what torture did these friends
not cause each other! Pitt's apparent apathy at times in the cause
of the slaves was incomprehensible to Wilberforce. Wilberforce's speech in the Melville case swayed the House of
Commons to deal Pitt the hardest blow of his career and it
was even thought hastened his death.[2] It seems strange that
Wilberforce did not realize Pitt's terrific strain in England's
almost single-handed struggle against Napoleon in 1805, his
Parliamentary position weakening, the King refusing to release
him, his physical strength nearing its end. Some would say
that the real imperfection was that Pitt did not share Wilberforce's deep religious convictions. But what is this difficulty
but an aspect of the truth that they could not know each other's
deepest selves? For we find in Wilberforce's written impressions
of Pitt fifteen years after, that Pitt was his ideal of a statesman who might have risen "clean above the bounds of circumstance" (Coupland), and infused a wholly new spirit into

---

[1] Newman's *Apologia. History of My Religious Opinions*, Part II
(from 1841 to 1845).
[2] R. Coupland: *Life of Wilberforce*.

the English body politic which would have transformed the
nation.

In regard to the possibility of self-knowledge much interesting
work has been done in modern psychology. If I understand
aright the view expressed by Dr. William Brown, it results
from his discussion of the problem that the self cannot be an
object of knowledge in the ordinary sense. "We can regard
personality as a process but not a product, for it is never
completely produced. It is a process that is creative on the one
side and intuitional on the other. As personality grows, it
produces something new, something that was not there before,
and also brings with it increased insight into the nature of
things, into the nature of the world."[1] With this I am in close
agreement. But if we accept such a theory of personality,
does it not follow that the chief hope of gaining an insight
into the true motive springs of this originative principle lies
not in the investigation of it as an object whether for metaphysics or science, but in the observation of the activities of
selves, and study of their own self-interpretations, in the midst
of life, rather than in the laboratory? By personality here I
understand the self in that most essential part of its being in
which each self is unique.

In some respects I can accept Lipps' view of the nature of
self-consciousness as expressed in his analysis, "Das Ich und
die Gefühle". "I cannot feel without immediately knowing,
that is experiencing myself as that which feels (*den Empfinden-
den*), I cannot imagine without immediately knowing or experiencing myself to be that which imagines, nor think without
immediately knowing or experiencing myself to be that which
thinks."[2] The *I* he holds to be indefinable. "We can only say
if asked what we mean by the word.—Grasp hold of that which
you *experience* together with the experience of feeling, imagining,
thinking, willing, being active.—Lay hold of that which is the

---

[1] *Science and Personality*, Chapter XVII. See also *Mind and
Personality*.
[2] *Psychologische Untersuchungen*, Band I, Heft 4.

point of unity common to all these.—It is nothing else any
more than the light of twenty-five stars is a twenty-sixth
star." The converse holds good. "There is no experience of
consciousness in which I do not feel myself as the experiencing,
feeling, etc.—My existence is this, that I experience myself,
and to speak of any other existence of me has no meaning."
He rejects the method which attempts to find the subject in
the object to draw the thinking *I* out of the thought, the feeling
I out of the felt, as though one were to conjecture that the
eye with which one sees is there where is the visible object."
To this I should only add, from my point of view, that the I
is not merely the point of unity common to feeling, thinking,
being active, etc., it is all these and more, for it includes the
continuous origination of new conscious modes or activities.
Our method of analysing out feeling, thought, and other forms
of conscious experience, and conceiving them in abstraction,
inclines us to forget that they are but modes of a conscious
activity which is the creative unity from which they spring.
In these words I think I am only emphasizing Lipps' meaning,
unless in adding the term creative I am suggesting a more
positive view than his of the conscious subject.

I should also entirely agree that "We can never reduce the
I to an object, or to the 'Not I'. " "To the question, What
am I? the only possible answer to all eternity will be, I am
I." But he allows differences in grades of self-consciousness,
holding that in a certain sense the "*I*-consciousness can be
distinguished from the self-consciousness". The former has
no degree, but I can have a more or less definite or rich self-
consciousness. Here he understands by the *Self*, not the *I*,
but the greater or less intensity or riches of its immediately
experienced activity. The more active I feel myself in a sphere
of objects the stronger my self-consciousness. But this self-
consciousness with its degrees cannot be exchanged with the
I-consciousness. It is possible that his distinction here partly
corresponds with the distinction between the Subject self and
the Object self which it seems to know. But it does not alto-

gether correspond with this, for the self-consciousness which
may have degrees, and various qualities of activity more or
less intense is not to be abstracted (in my view) from a pure
I-consciousness. This would appear (from the passage quoted)
to be a qualityless consciousness, similar to Kant's Transcendental Unity, and Lipps' is perhaps not far from this.

It may be here added that as regards the problem of our
knowledge of other selves, Lipps holds that it is instinctive.
By means of his theory of "Einfühlung" he explains our perception of emotions in another self.[1] On the apprehension of
certain sensible appearances in another individual, we immediately experience certain emotions, anger, sorrow, etc. What
anger is we know only in ourselves, but we feel the experience,
of anger, etc., to meet us in the apprehension of such and such
data or changes in a sense-perceivable body. Thus the perception
and the inner excitement take place in one indivisible act,
although the two experiences come from different sources—
the inner activity or excitement is nothing but a mode of
activity of myself. It is in one word—I. Thus that ensouling
of something which is a process in the external world takes
place—I have infused my soul into it. "This wonderful fact"
is "underivable from anything else." Whether or not Lipps'
well-known theory of aesthetic "Einfühlung" can be accepted,
his interpretation of our knowledge of emotions and states of
mind in other selves by means of it does not seem adequate to
the facts. For it does not explain the experience of otherness
in the qualities and characters of other selves. The fact which
(as I hold) is of such crucial importance to our higher life in
all its forms, namely that of self-transcendence in our knowledge
of others, is simply left out of account, there is no opening for
it, no suggestion of its origin in this experience, through
"Einfühlung". But in whatever form our apprehension of
qualities in another self is explained, it should be noted that
in so far as this takes place and has truth, as is testified by
practical life, it does not carry with it the direct knowledge of

[1] *Leitfaden der Psychologie*, Abschnitt III, Kap XXIV.

the unique individuality from which these qualities proceed
but which they cannot exhaust. It may seem that this conclusion
leads to scepticism in regard to the possibility of historic
knowledge, in any scientific sense.[1] Certainly it would signify
that we cannot find in respect to the more essential experiences
and actions of any individual those general laws of uniformity
which hold good widely for the less essential. Yet we are not
altogether without universals of the activities of selves. These
universals are the principles which hold together in a certain
type of significant sequence all the acts of the individual life.
If the historian succeed in grasping (or intuiting) such a
principle in any single case, the life will be intelligible to him,
however erratic its course may seem to a student following
the guidance of the human sciences. The historian of course
may overcome the strangeness of the portrayal by the exercise
of his artistic gift, and in this sense great history is near to art,
though in history the relation of the author to his subject-
matter is of a wholly different type.

[1] This problem will be further examined in the next chapter.

CHAPTER IV

HISTORIC KNOWLEDGE

MAIN SOURCES OF SCEPTICISM

"Mein Freund, die Zeiten der Vergangenheit
Sind uns ein Buch mit sieben Siegeln;
Was ihr den Geist der Zeiten heisst,
Das ist im grund der Herren eigner Geist,
In dem die Zeiten sich bespiegeln."

GOETHE

OUR examination of the inner reality, or what we may term
the core of history, raises in an acute form the problem of
historic knowledge. For we have seen that history whatever
else it may be is primarily the experience of selves in all their
individuality. It is more than this, but at least this is what is
most essential in the events of history. It has also been maintained that the reality of selves is not in those properties in
which they resemble other selves, but in their more elusive
because unique qualities, beginning with the points of view
which are necessarily different in every individual and determine what the world and his reaction to it in desire and act
must be for him. The problem of knowledge which here
confronts us is perhaps not one for history alone. It may be
that we are demanding of history something which is the
ideal of truth beyond all attainment, as we have to admit in
every other department of knowledge, but which we are
cheated into demanding in history because we think we ought
to know the inner side, the in-itselfness of the constituents of
history. Are they not human like ourselves? The position
arrived at in the last chapter is that, since the chief factors of
history are selves and the self is essentially subject, its inner
nature cannot be known. Hence the true aim of history as we
might conceive it, to reveal the essential course of events in
the experience of selves, is impossible of achievement. From

a more ordinary standpoint this obscurity of historical truth may seem to be confirmed by the nature of many of the difficulties preventing discovery of the facts even in the case of recent events. Lord Morley is said to have observed that "History always misleads. Far more depended on the conversations of half an hour, and was transacted in those, than ever appeared in letters and despatches. No, the truth can never be known. It will never overtake the legend. I have read many books of late dealing with events in which I took some part, and all of them are wrong."[1] Again it may be asked, "What has been the testimony of later years in regard to J. S. Mill's conviction that with liberty of the Press, unhampered dissemination of news, the truth must always be victorious? This question perhaps obscures the immediate problem, for it brings to mind difficulties very formidable in the way of arriving at the facts which have since Mill's day paradoxically increased with the progress of scientific means of communication of news, and which are wholly unrelated to that one invincible difficulty to which I refer—the inacessibility of the inner personal activity to our cognitive faculties. Yet the failure of Mill's hope, and also the experience which Morley records, are not irrelevant to the present problem. For the implication of the position is that if this ultimate difficulty could be removed, all such factors as block common understanding in present conditions, the want of sympathy, rivalry, love of sensation, and other unnamed emotions and desires which bring about distortion of the facts, would vanish. Ingenious talents of misrepresentation, cloudy suggestion and the many technical devices of falsification would not be cultivated. It is not, of course, suggested that true knowledge would reveal all motives to be pure and disinterested. Such a faith would be inconsistent with the view of personality supported in this treatise because required for the interpretation of history and the understanding of the self, according to which the source of evil as well as of

[1] Account of conversations with Lord Morley published in a magazine shortly after his death. (I have lost the reference.)

good has to be found in personality. What is involved in the
view expressed above of the ultimate source of our deepest
ignorance is that, if this were otherwise, if perfect interpersonal understanding could be substituted, history would
offer a field for the unimpeded struggle of conflicting values.
For this conflict issues from the nature of personality which
excludes the manifestation of value as absolute. But in the
actual conditions of limitation of knowledge it often appears
as if the greater the light cast on the externals of the events
that are taking place, the greater the obscurity as to their
inner significance. Otherwise stated, the acquisition of real
knowledge seems at times to be in inverse proportion to the
extension of that for which the name categorial has been
suggested, namely the presentation of events from the standpoint of their external relations. If this impression be justified,
it is in part due to the fact that the interrelations are presented
in forms exaggerating their less essential aspects in default of
essential knowledge, and leaving the way open to misrepresentation by means of false emphasis. We may ask again
whether categorial knowledge or that method which aims at
the general, proceeds by means of classification establishment
of uniformities, etc., is real knowledge in any field? Is it perhaps
the case that, despite the difficulties which surround the
problem of historic knowledge, the historian seeks knowledge
in the truest sense, that type by which all other forms should
be tested? The question touches on the relation of our theory
of knowledge to our metaphysic. Is the real, since it is individual,
and that not in history alone, unknowable by the relational
method, categories and the like? Is Bradley's unwilling, and to
him heart-breaking scepticism justified, in regard to the validity
of inference, the all but overwhelming doubt whether the
logical process can correspond to the real?[1] In that case the
only province in which we might be thought to be making
straight for our goal, though in doubt whether it could ever

[1] *Logic*, Book III, Part II, Chapter IV, "The Validity of Inference" (continued).

be attained, would be that of human events. (I do not of course impute such a view to Bradley.) For although even here we appear incapable of grasping intellectually the individual owing to the nature of our intellectual faculty, we have a form of direct experience of that which we are seeking to know. And in this case alone we can be in relation to the data on the two sides, both inner and outer. It might then be in the province of human history primarily since it is concerned with the individual, and with the human sciences in the second place that categorial knowledge would come nearest to knowledge of reality. It is not impossible that the fact that the arrival at truth in history is so hard, and its achievement so often doubted, only signifies that our ideal and standard here is much higher than in the case of the other departments of knowledge. We may suppose the kind of knowledge we seek in history either not to have any parallel in the other fields of knowledge, or to be in these not only inaccessible, but unimaginable as to its nature by minds like ours. The speculation is admissible, that behind all phenomena there are Monads, or psychic existents, or even that to which James Ward could give the name of persons,[1] but of these it would be a fruitless task for science to seek knowledge, and it is only in human activities that we may cherish the hope of meeting that spirit which is similar to our own.

In regard to the question of the possibility of truth in history tentative suggestions will later be made. I will only here lay down the principle that it is the first act of what may be termed de-egoism which is the opening of the door at once to the experience of the practical life and of knowledge. By "de-egoism" is signified the capacity for apprehension of the existence of other selves, not merely in the primal sense earlier referred to,[2] in which this apprehension is involved in the elementary conscious experience, but fully in our intelligent and emotional nature alike. The recognition of selves as other

---

[1] *Realm of Ends*, Chapter XII, "The Cosmology of Theism."
[2] See Chapter III.

selves is the beginning of moral experience and the entry upon disinterested knowledge. We are not fully awake to the otherness of anything before we are awake to the otherness of selves. By this consciousness of their independent nature is meant a consciousness of them as *egos*, equally with ourselves, no easy matter, for it is the beginning of that spiritual process which is self-transcendence. It appears from history that some of the most famous men have never passed beyond the beginning of this experience if they have even reached it. There is no inconsistency between this principle of the necessity for the historic mind of assertion with all our powers so to speak, that other selves exist as subjects, and the position that we cannot know the inner nature of other selves. The two truths are in fact complementary. In the knowledge that other subjects similar to our own selves are creating experience, and giving meaning to its events, we also know that their ultimate being is necessarily beyond our grasp.

We may now turn to history in the secondary or categorial form, history in which experience is objectively presented, whilst the inner individuality of the agents cannot be exhaustively shown. History in this its more general sense develops from its origin in the saga, the heroic legend, the chronicle, to the great historic works of modern times, with their scientific and also their artistic form. It may be conceived as a creation necessary to the safeguarding of man's distinctive type of life. As memory of his past is necessary to the self, so history to the community of persons. The simile is not exact, for there is no unitary being of the community which partly exists in the past, as the self in its memory. Yet objectively the community may in certain relations be regarded as a single being, it is in fact a category of historic knowledge, or what some thinkers even term a value. As such it implies a history, and indeed requires this to give depth to the concept. The peculiar significance of the idea of nationality will be further examined at a later stage.[1] The question what is the

[1] Chapter VI.

primary object of knowledge in history has been much discussed. According to Heinrich Rickert,[1] who disagrees with the Aristotelian view that we cannot know the individual, there *is* knowledge of the individual in history, though in order to determine the individual we have to draw limits in the continuous flow of actual happening. In his view the problem of historic method may thus be stated: Is an individualizing formation of concepts possible? He recognizes that we cannot have a generalizing science of the soul-life, because this would not give us the characteristic "once-for-all". But he holds that a presentation of individuality through concepts is possible. The individual can be presented, though not in all his unlimited individuality. It appears, however, that since the heart of the problem is exactly here, in this quality of unlimited individuality, any presentation or characterization which is unequal to it must fail to give us the individual. Though we cannot discover in history that a culture has ever been repeated, its characterization by means of concepts cannot demonstrate it to be from its very nature the only one of its kind. From analysis of the notion of living individuality we find that its essential uniqueness continues to characterize the individual so long as the creative originative principle in it is there. But this method escapes our analysis, we are only aware of it in its effects. Rickert, however, is examining the problem from a different point of view, since he assumes that the individual historic object can be found and fully characterized by means of concepts. According to the standpoint I have taken this solution is not adequate unless it can yield a concept or principle which is the law of a continuous series of unique events. Rickert's concept of an individual culture-value would have to be compared with the typical concept of science in order to determine whether it avoids generality. In his view the principle of the dominating cultural value determines which persons and events are important and memorable. But what if

[1] *Kulturwissenschaft und Naturwissenschaft*, pp. 66, 86.

E

a later age reverse the value judgment and find importance in events and persons passed by as indifferent in the earlier selection of principles? It is because the sources and energy of any culture consist in the end of the experiences and activities of selves that we cannot overcome the difficulty of knowledge by treating the culture itself as the essential historic object, that is if we are seeking the object in its individuality. For there lies behind the culture the one force which is irretrievably unique and productive of unique events. This is the *desideratum* of knowledge when we are asking if we can get at reality in this historic world. Rickert's cultural object may well, however, occupy the place of a primary object in categorial history. His own conception of our knowledge of the individual person is as follows: "When we are concerned with a unity of life, as, for instance, of Goethe or Napoleon, we have something that cannot be psychologically explained. This unity does not proceed from the consciousness as the logical unity of the subject, nor from the organic unity of the soul, which makes every *I* a closed connection of content. It rests only on this, that in relation to culture-values, determinate psychic coherences become individual unities which would immediately disappear if they were brought under general psychological concepts."[1] By this I understand him to mean that the principle of the unity is something which psychology could never enunciate as a scientific principle, since in each instance of an individual unity it is only once at work. But he avoids giving it its source in the "organic unity of the soul" by referring it to the "culture-value" for its meaning. The spiritual unity of life which is incapable of generalization is therefore "the unity of the culture-personality which holds itself together in an individual whole with respect to its culture significance". These life-unities of the culture-personalities have nothing to do with the usual opposition of nature and spirit. "The historical unities are not only withdrawn from the contemporary natural-scientific psychology but from every

[1] *Kulturwissenschaft und Naturwissenschaft*, Kap XI, p. 105.

general theory of the spiritual life. So long as we hold fast to this unity of individuality which rests on their cultural significance, their being (or essence, 'Wesen') can only disclose itself to the individualizing historic procedure." From this passage it seems clear that Rickert's doctrine of the individual historic object does not in any way elucidate the problem of knowledge of the individual person, his vision of the world, his thoughts and deeds. Does it throw light on the nature of that which is historically individual, if not as person, as culture or as concatenation of events? The individual unity, it seems, depends on the culture-value. On what does the culture-value depend? If we probe this question, shall we not come upon a concealed circle? The enigma is all the more pressing in view of the examples he happens to select. In reference to what culture-values is Goethe or Napoleon an individual unity except such as are created by the treatment of life or history by these men, certainly the life and history of their times, but given by them such significance as had no being or a different one apart from the ideal genius of Goethe, the demoniac energy destructive and constructive of Napoleon? Elsewhere, however, Rickert recognizes that "The impulses to the creation of new culture-goods almost always proceed from individual personalities."

In some of his uses of the term, Rickert's culture-value appears to be equivalent to what I should prefer to call historic category—e.g. state, religion, science, morality, economy, war—though it is obvious that these terms do not stand all on the same level in respect to the relative abstraction or concreteness of their meaning. At other times he would seem to indicate a more specific set of activities, products of art, group of events, spirit of an age marked out by general interest and by the work of thought as unities in human affairs. Or to quote a picturesque characterization of the "event" by Professor Radl, it is an "island thrown up in the stream of the eternal process, and standing there fast"—referring "primarily to an idea, something which can be understood, but cannot be grasped by the sensuous organ."[1] We must interpret Rickert's view of the culture-value as the legitimate historic object, as belonging to the view of history, characterized earlier as secondary, categorial, objective, and (in spite of his idea of the individual, constituted through concepts) not treating of the ultimate sources of history in their actuality. Yet it would not seem to give to personality its true place in such a scheme. Persons, as I have argued, must remain the chief principles of history, as an objective record of the past. They become themselves a type of categories. This he does not appear clearly to recognize.

According to Ernst Troeltsch, "Every historic concept is a synthesis of natural conditions on the one side and value or meaning or freedom on the other. No selection from the concept of the essential can remove these basic conditions."[2] Again in relation to the selection of the historic object out of the flux of things, "It seems that out of a concealed background, or underground of spiritual life, an individual form of life breaks through, and enters into the form of the physical and psychical apparatus. It is this background, with its constantly surprising forms of new content, which above all distinguishes history from psychology, which investigates only the foreground of psychic regularities. Even a scientific psychology, full of insight, can only hold open the gates for this background. The meaning and content of that which is at any time developing remains exclusively the object of history itself." The essential "charm" and character of the historic life rests on this originality, inner freedom and independence. Further, Troeltsch speaks of the narrower selection which "not only cuts out the object from the process of things, but also within the object, emphasizes only the essential or characteristic features". This is a selection which goes deep into the inner material and in which all depends on the right vision and the fine feeling of the historian. It is first in this way that there

[1] *History without Evolution*, International Congress of Philosophy, Oxford, 1930. *Proceedings*, 1931.   [2] *Historismus*, Kap. I, 3.

results "the transformation of the historic actuality into the historic concept". In these words he raises two questions of crucial importance for our view of historic actuality, and closely connected. These are firstly, that of the selection out of the infinity of experience of those series, or groups of events which are to be the material of history, known and recorded; secondly, the interpretation of the historic content which (as has been argued here) consists preeminently of the meaning given to or found in the events. Is the interpretation to be wholly idealistic so that the history exists only for man, since there is no other being at least within our range who would find in it these meanings and values? The latter question has been tentatively referred to and a provisional answer suggested, but is of such fundamental importance that it must meet us again. "History," again to quote Troeltsch, "is not purely subjective, the historical object as a concrete object of contemplation (*anschaulichkeit*), and in its critical foundation remains the same." The object in its form for perception remains always in the first place a thing for itself and never becomes a mere thing for us. Nevertheless, he adds that the actuality must in the main be referred to the significance and value, even if a purely external process such as earthquake, hunger, epidemic, is in question. These examples very clearly bring out the problem. The main question for history (as I conceive it) is in the state of mind, the suffering and energy of which these physical happenings are the occasion. Thus they become history. Without this never-ceasing building up of the bricks of nature into forms of significance for his mental and spiritual life, man is like the rest of things, a straw blown along in the wind-borne dust, and history has not begun. Turning first to the problem of selection, our whole conception of the place of history in knowledge, its significance in respect to any world-view, the possibility of tracing within history itself in its total impression any principles of order seems in the first instance to depend upon the relation of the selected to the unselected, the knowable to the unknowable. And yet

important thinkers who have treated history from a philosophical standpoint appear to have accepted existing materials
as given without further question. This does not, of course,
imply an uncritical acceptance from the standpoint of the
historian's treatment of his sources. On the magnificent work
of modern students in this respect it is unnecessary to dwell,
and also irrelevant to our problem. For the reference is rather
to the attitude of those thinkers who would base speculative
interpretation of history as a whole, on what Dilthey speaks of
as the mere rags which have come down to us, without examining the principles on which such fragments have been consciously or unconsciously selected. Troeltsch himself is fully
aware of the problem. Writing of the phenomena of the
extension of nature into history, he asks, "When and where
did man appear in the evolution of living beings?"[1] and speaks
of the brevity and scantiness of essential history in relation to
prehistory with its monotonous and primitive implements.
"Here again," he proceeds, "within history, we see the enormous
quantitative disproportion, between nature in an extended
sense, and history—especially when we include reference to
the passing away of culture-periods—culture destructive to
physical and nervous force."[2] It is also destroyed by climatic
changes. For the purposes of the problem at present under
consideration we must think of the outlines of history which
rise so to speak like peaks out of the mist of the past, in
abstraction, so far as this is possible, from the value we find
in the record. We cannot do this completely, for we have to
bear in mind such questions as are suggested by Troeltsch's
own hypothesis of a system of possibilities of meaning which
slumbers in us and is aroused through original study of
traditions of other times and things. He further urges the
necessity of conceiving a development of meaning in humanity
itself, starting from the postulate that no such development is
ever isolated. From the general tendency of Troeltsch's works,
we may understand him to signify by this a heightening of

[1] *Historismus*, Kap. I, 5.   [2] *Ibid.*, loc. cit.

man's capacity for the perception or vision of value, bringing
about a fuller spiritual life. But the doubt arises whether there
is not here involved an illegitimate *a priori*, in view of the
immense *vacua* in history. He admits that in the belief in such
an extension we should go ahead of the facts.

The course of reflection on which we have entered with
Troeltsch suggests difficulties of knowledge in this field, the
investigation of which threatens to lead us to the brink of
historic scepticism. It is essential to survey those that appear
to be the most formidable. The slightest consideration as to
the way in which such knowledge as we possess has been
gained points, I think, to a notion which demands careful
examination, and to which the name chance—*zufall*, *le
hasard*, τυχή—has often been given, not only by the popular
voice. It meets us in the two great aspects of our subject,
knowledge of history and the actuality or substance itself of
history. The latter belongs to the next chapter, but the two
problems are very closely related, and the one has a constant
tendency to pass into the other. In this chapter then, in the
references to "chance" in history, we are mainly concerned
with this phenomenon in connection with the ways in which
knowledge has reached the historian and mankind in general,
but also with certain forms of his interpretation of his knowledge. The former question is raised in a particularly striking
manner by attention to the facts of anthropological and archaeological discovery, through which our information has been
enriched and speculation so keenly stimulated in modern
times. Ages have passed during which peoples, that is individual
experiences as the sands in number, have slept as it were the
historic sleep, from which it might seem later history could
never arouse them. From generation to generation in times
that are historic for us, men lived and contemplated history,
philosophizing about it, speculating as to its meaning, in the
comparatively limited area on which their searchlight could
be cast, supposing this to be sufficient for their needs as students
and thinkers.

"Do you think you can reckon the time which has elapsed since cities first existed and men were citizens of them?" asks Plato's Athenian Stranger[1] contemplating a period he seems to include in civilization. . . .

"And have not thousands and thousands of cities come into being during this period and as many perished?" And his genius proceeds to speculate on the nature of the constitutions and causes of their disappearance. A new age dawns with methods of research unknown to the greatest mind of Greece. Gateways open that had long seemed shut to all possible assaults of man's curiosity. We find ourselves in face of the customs, ceremonies, wars and pleasures of races whose present was as vivid, shining and burning as our own. But in what casual and accidental way does the modern student often happen to knock upon the doors that yield to his pressure! Some of the great archaeologists, Schliemann, Sir Arthur Evans, Sir Flinders Petrie, are led by later history and literature, as well as the flair of their own genius, to the clues they follow up for the revelation of the early forms of cultures known or believed to have existed. Similarly also we may presume the investigators of Chaldaean and Etrurian civilizations. But do we not come upon another class of discoveries, in those of Sir Aurel Stein, in Central Asia?[2] How are we to characterize in relation to the conditions of human knowledge the strange fact that the icy aridity of the atmosphere, itself cause of the destruction of conditions of life and culture, after rivers had dried up or altered their course, was most favourable to the preservation of memorials, even masses of inscribed memoranda on clay, wood, paper in its earliest use flung away as refuse nearly two thousand years ago? Here if anywhere is a salient instance of the contingency that besets the student's efforts to open the fast-closed book of the past, and suffers as it were here and there the fragment of a loose page to be torn out, when there chances to arrive after thousands of years the man brought

[1] *Laws*, III, 676. Translated by B. Jowett.
[2] *In Central Asian Tracks.*

there first perhaps on some other quest and possessed of the necessary passion of curiosity and wonder, of imagination, scientific genius and physical endurance. As an example of "chance" in Bergson's sense (to be later considered), of an event which is *as if* it had been purposed for this end but appears to be quite otherwise conditioned, might be given the discovery of the painted ware culture of Thessaly, characterized by Professor Myres as the most surprising series of discoveries since the revelation of Cretan culture, which has taken place chiefly through the new activity since the occupation of Salonika, 1916, and subsequent opening of Macedonia and Thrace to archaeological activity.[1] If we were to go back further, many instances might be given of discoveries in regard to more primitive cultures, such as the Neolithic culture below the Minoan in Sir Arthur Evans' investigations, culture in Central Africa, and the various penetrations in recent years to the remains of palaeolithic man in burials, the signs of whose meaning the anthropologist interprets, and also in cave-paintings. These scanty references to a vast subject may serve to illustrate what is here signified by the aspect of "chance" attending upon the salvage of data from the immense wreckage of past ages. The testimony of comparative anthropology, as study of primitive cultures surviving in modern times in the expectation that light will thereby be cast on the ancient cultures, is in a different category, but also beset with "contingency" in another form. For in respect to the question of data for knowledge (without entering upon the problem of varying interpretations of the data) we have to take into account their comparative meagreness, the diminishing number of races of this kind, the uncertainty as to the relation of their modes of life to those of vanished peoples and of the ancestors of modern civilized communities. As Troeltsch observes, "The existence of historic investigation itself seems to confirm the view of history as the domain of 'chance' (*zufall*), since it is dependent on the facts at any time handed down or dis-

[1] *Who were the Greeks?* Chapter V, p. 238.

covered".[1] His general view of chance as affecting historic meaning will be referred to in the next chapter.

To turn to the historian in the strict sense, we find that in the view of the late Professor J. B. Bury, "contingency" rather than the general cause is required for the explanation of the great events of history. This is especially the view of his later work.[2] It was a conflux of coincidences which brought about the fall of the Roman Empire rather than a general cause in the Empire. Such a general cause would be found in the decline of the military spirit. He referred to the invasion of the Huns resulting from events in Central Asia strictly independent of events in Europe, Theodosius' death at fifty and the mediocrity of his two sons, as contingent causes. Here it may be observed that a general cause such as the decline of the military spirit might itself be analysed into a concatenation of those contingencies ascribed to chance. The spirit declines. How is this decline made evident? In the minds and conduct of A, B, C, Z, etc. It may be asked, Is this not because of something in the atmosphere they breathe? What is this mental atmosphere, and by whom created if not by these men, or by L, M, N, X— outstanding individuals? The question whether we are to ascribe any such complex of events—as (on account of the tremendous meaning attached to it in itself and the events consequent upon it) we single out as the Fall of the Roman Empire—to "general" or "contingent" causes is one of those on the borderland of the problem of knowledge and of the substance of history. "The doctrine of historic relativity applies no less to his" (the historian's) "own judgments, than to other facts",[3] observed Bury. We might extend the application of this to the historian's intellectual tendencies, as for instance to the rationalistic interpretation which would tend to the search for the general cause wherever possible, and a sense less keen

[1] *Historismus*, Kap. I, 3.
[2] See Introduction to Edition of Bury's *Selected Essays* by Harold Temperley.
[3] *Ancient Greek Historians*, quoted by Harold Temperley.

of the irrepressibly particular and individual factors. Bury himself treats Thucydides as supremely a rationalist.[1] We might perhaps take as illustration of historic rationalism Thucydides' analysis of the causes of revolution, in which from factions of little Corcyra he generalizes to the conditions of revolution universally, "so long as human nature remains the same", and leaves us with the fatal conviction that this is the unalterable truth and it does remain the same. But this is the genius of Thucydides, and what gift is more relative? Or can it overcome the limitations belonging to the burning pity for the human race which is so austerely used and coldly sculptured by the great historian? Bury refers also to the naïf tendency to assume that the ideas which are within the horizon of our own minds are the ultimate ideas to be sighted by men, as, for instance, the present idea of freedom or of nationality. Nevertheless, in his own view, history must depend on the interpretation of our minds. He quotes Macaulay's observation, "Facts are the merest dross of history."[2]

It would appear that in Bury's judgment the historian who (as in Lord Acton's great scheme) should attempt a survey of the development of mankind, as a History of the Idea of Freedom, is not secure from misconception as to the ultimate significance of his principle for human history. Swayed by his ideal, which brings with it suggestion of values of life cherished and powerful in his own experience, he perceives the historic process in its light, in the forms history permits as forwarding or obstructing the growth of freedom. The rest fades into unimportance and insignificance. But in this example of the idea of freedom there is surely high promise of the introduction into history of a category or principle capable of bringing intelligibility into the tumultous disorganized movements of peoples akin to ourselves, at an earlier stage of civilization—barbarians destroying the Roman Empire, civil wars of early modern times, struggles of many kinds for political or social freedom, in which hampering restrictions are

[1] *Ancient Greek Historians.*   [2] *Selected Essays.*

swept away. Yet we may ask, Does the word mean the same
thing in Ancient Athens, where freedom of the spirit found
an expression, which added for all time new worth to human
existence, though slaves were near at hand, and in twentieth-
century England half disenchanted after a thousand years
pursuit of her most precious ideal, and again in modern India
demanding the same gift, in the midst of a caste system which
appears to the Western mind wholly alien to freedom? Whatever the answer, it may be agreed that the idea of the growth of
freedom can be intelligibly used to bring some degree of order
and meaning into our arrangement of large and complex series
of facts and many different phases of national life. "Some
degree of order"—yet we must not be deluded by any such
noble formulae, as that of the History of Freedom, into the
belief that if this could be definitely traced in the sense intended
by the historian in popular institutions, in signs of awakening
mind, and unrestricted expression of thought in literature and
speech, we should be near to the real history of the peoples
concerned in more than a very partial or fragmentary way.
Freedom is essentially a state of mind and sense of favourable
conditions for the activity of personality which is not extensively attainable unless certain institutions exist to which
therefore a perhaps disproportionate importance is attached.
But even a true conception of the growth of freedom in this
respect in the minds and lives of a people would correspond
only to a section of their history. We are as it were presented
with a drama on a stage, supposed to give us an epitome of
the lives of a large crowd behind. Only a very small proportion
appear on the stage, and even of the lives of these actors we see
but a slight extract. This example has been dwelt upon as a
reminder that even in the interpretative use of one of the
great historic concepts, which is also a great value, the inevitable
relativity of the category to the historian's point of view
becomes as it were a ground for obtrusion of chance into the
history in the preservation of some events with underlining
and emphasis, oblivion to and slight notice of others. This is,

of course, an illustration of Croce's principle that all history is contemporary, or that which is not contemporary in his sense is irrecoverable. The relativity of the historian to his own age is brilliantly brought before us in Dr. Gooch's survey of the stages through which historical science has passed in its growth in modern times. How should a Buike who realized the debt of every age to its predecessor, a Voltaire who despised the past and held the "Middle Ages no more deserving of study than wolves and bears", and a Rousseau who hated the present, perceive the same historic truth? To the historian of the rationalist eighteenth century, and the historian of the romantic movement of the early nineteenth, how different the relative importance of events and their meaning! Of great interest is Dr. Gooch's characterization of Ranke's qualities as a historian. He is the "greatest historical writer of modern times". But "His tranquil harmonious nature made him to some extent blind to great outbursts of passion, to the heroism and tragedy in the lives of men. The 'Reformation' conveys little of the wild exaltation of the time. In dealing with individuals and nations alike, he was most at home in the middle regions of human experience."[1] With great penetration Dr. Gooch thus brings out the relation between the historian's temperament and the possibilities and limitations of his vision. However disinterested and impartial his spirit, and highly trained his method, his character, his emotional nature and, we may add, his experience must help to determine his selection of facts or events, his sense of their relative importance, above all his understanding of men and the aspects of their nature which are perceived by him. Guizot, as Dr. Gooch also observes, has been "accused of presenting laws instead of life, abstractions in place of men and women". It might be more justly contended "that he makes history appear more orderly and rational than it is".[2] Chance then, it may be urged, has

[1] *Growth of Historical Science*, Cambridge Modern History, Vol. XII, Chapter XXVI.
[2] Ibid.

brought it about that this historian X lives in this particular age, and sees through the categories of his own generation those past men in whom he is interested, their activities, the question whether the great personalities of the time were all-powerful in the determination of the values and the obscurely but ceaselessly swaying and changing heart and face of the people described. Even the spectator of all time and all existence must stand on his own look-out tower. If we push this line of doubt as far as it will go we may conceive the idea of an absolute vision and judgment as perhaps itself the last infirmity of finite mind, the last relativity. Can even the principle that each age must be judged by its own standards of value, which Troeltsch announced in the admission that it is not possible to escape relativity, be realized?[1] How can one age penetrate through to the standards of another? We may know that they are other than our own, but we cannot know them except *through* our own. And it is in the valuations of this that inevitably we find our absolute. For each individual subject his present (as follows from the idea of "the present" given in Chapter II) has a power incommensurable with that of any other phase of time. This is, of course, a truism in regard to the present as experience. But it is also true of the present age objectified for knowledge, the specious present of history, whose limits in the past and the imaged future vary in relation to the depth and power of present meaning. Thus the contemporary for a Wilberforce includes the history and eventuality of his struggle for emancipation of the slaves, for a Newman the Tractarian Movement up to its issue for him whether in reconciliation with his own Church, or refuge in Rome.

Let us attempt to sum up the chief conditions of the limitation of our historic knowledge, as so far briefly discussed, together with another factor not yet examined as such and which may be characterized as "Animism" in history. These limitations might be viewed from Bacon's standpoint as

[1] *Historismus*, Kap. II, 5. Cf. Introduction to Troeltsch's *Christian Thought*. Baron von Hügel.

"Idols", εἴδωλα, if we do not press the analogy too close. With Bacon, we may distinguish those that are more inescapable by the human mind, such as ultimate relativity, from those which can in some degree be controlled, and their illusion or fallacy-producing tendency restricted, or relativity in a secondary sense. Such would be the character of the historian and his times. In the first place there is the great divergence to which attention has already several times been drawn, between the conceptions both of the historian and of the ordinary consciousness as to the subject-matter of history. By this we are reminded that history in the original and primary sense, as a true record of the conscious experience of mankind, is not possible. Objective history exists, history, namely, as giving certain aspects of the events of the conscious process, under or by means of categories which have appeared to the historic mind as most important. In connection with this first limiting condition there is to be reckoned the fact which has been adduced of the immense vacua or empty stretches in our historical data, in recognition of which it seems impossible to avoid the suspicion that our empirical knowledge can give no clue as to the general tendency of the process as a whole. Whether an *a priori* is possible in this sphere is a problem for the philosophy of history.

The second of our *idola*, which may variously be viewed as the second great stage in the search for historic truth, or the second source of the deepening of the problem, appears in consideration of those categories of objective history which condition the historic object. How is this object itself to be conceived? Our discussion of Rickert's view of the cultural value seemed to confirm the impossibility of knowledge of the real individual, whether as person or as event. The ideal of a true type of knowledge proper to objective history then emerges. This, though not impossible, and claiming at least the validity of other forms of knowledge, presents difficulties of its own, whilst not obviating the difficulty of the restricted nature of the data. The latter difficulty seems to be diminished, however, in so far as in the chief historic categories such as race, nation and the institutional forms constructed by man's activity, we have substitutes for the individuality of the unique agents which cannot be reached. The validity and adequacy of these categories may, however, be called in question, and even concerning those that have most commanded the interest of man's historic intelligence doubts may arise with respect to their relativity and ephemeral character in face of the immense ages of human experience. The third "Idol" or stage in the advance of the problem confronts us in that which has been described as the element of chance or casual aspect in the vocation of the historian, and in the preservation of data for historical interpretation. This does not signify that the notion of chance is applicable to the choice of his vocation by the historian, for it may be held that if there is anything absolute in the construction of history it is in the necessity of such a task to the personality of the worker. But in relation to the form of history which results, the principle of the selection of data, it is chance or contingency that A rather than X is the recorder, however wide the range of his historic interest. It will be evident that all these points of view for the distinguishing of Idols may be said to depend on relativity, but relativity to the age in which the history takes its form for knowledge may be added as a fourth of these limiting conditions. It may here be observed in enforcement of this point that it ought to be well understood by those who have had living experience of the change of values affecting our thought about history in passing from the Victorian era to the age succeeding the European War. Those of us who have actually known both periods have had an experience of the reality of such changes, the more impressive because of the peculiarity of the Victorian outlook which gave to its values the appearance of a stability perhaps seldom before felt, and seeming to point to a continuous increase in the direction of an achievement of the greatest realization of the same kind of value. The contrast of this with the outlook of the succeeding era is deepened by the distinctive quality of present feelings in regard to dominating values which gives them no similar security, but rather an instability threatening to become greater. This change involves a profoundly changed outlook upon history as a whole.

Turning to the fifth "Idol", with its attendant wave of historic scepticism, the nature of *Animism* in our historic concepts must be examined. Closer attention to this seems necessary, inasmuch as it is less easy to realize and has been less noticed than the other grounds of doubt. In the course of study of the recognized phenomena of history, especially those groups of occurrences which possess a special significance in general, and come to be regarded as historic events in a capital or major sense, we frequently come upon traces of this animistic tendency. Now in the last analysis of objective history the ultimate element appears as the event. Persons as the principal sources of events are, it has been argued, the chief constituents of history. We cannot, however, take them, in so far as they constitute the leading categories, as the only constituents of the history we know and share with other experients. This is because of that other factor which has to be recognized, as a kind of blind force outside personality, indifferent to the drama of value and disvalue, although as element in the whole event it contributes to historic value. Further analysis of this factor of the "Other" must be postponed to the next chapter. Now the strange fact which meets us in our interpretation of the event which we were first inclined to regard as impersonal is that we tend to endow it if not with personality, at least with some personal features. This tendency, obvious in ancient and mediaeval thought, persists, if for the most part unconsciously, in modern. What is the nature of the life or activity which we attribute or lend to the event, or the object in nature or in art, and even to manufactured things? If we survey forms of animism in general, we find the personification to be of many kinds. The living presence may approach the type of the self, or it may be something foreign to our own intimate experience (though not, of

F

course, absolutely foreign), yet having tendencies sinister or favourable to human beings. It may have feeling, thought, will, or be incomplete in function, like the wan shades of the Greek Hades, or those many varieties of beings half-human, yet soulless, first conceived by the imagination of primitive man, and later glorified by genius. History shows some of the phases of this play of the mind which is indeed a serious play, in the creations of imaginative peoples, and ages of moral and religious allegory. When the stream becomes a nymph, or the tree speaks, thought and feeling appear to be only very vaguely ascribed. In more complex cases there is personification of a form of human activity or culture, elaborated round some scheme of life, as in the ancient mythology a goddess of hunting, a god of war. The Greeks also personify moral virtues and other excellences, and at times add to the concreteness of the notion, by attaching to it the image and character of some actual individual. There appears to be hardly any aspect of life or art which the Greek effervescing imagination could not personify, delighting as it did in an ideal world peopled with beings more interesting, vivid, above all definitely significant, their meaning identical with their being, and more unexpected in their activities than those of the ordinary human world.

The construction, of course, had its remarkable aesthetic qualities. But we are here primarily concerned with the mental or spiritual need, of which animism is the manifestation and satisfaction, and the problem of its influence on knowledge. Is it of the nature of that need in which, taking the form of Einfühlung, Lipps finds not only the secret of aesthetic experience, but also (as we have noticed)[1] of our perception of emotions, and passions in other selves, and further of the chief category of scientific knowledge—cause?[2] In aesthetic Einfühlung the self as subject, identifying its own activity with that of the object viewed, strives in the striving of this. Perceiving a striving tendency in the falling stone, the line, it *is* the line or the tendency, or force. Or in my contemplation

[1] Chapter III.   [2] Lipps: *Ästhetik*, Band I, pp. 190, 226, etc.

of the rock, I feel its activity, striving against weight; subject and object are one. Lipps here points to an undoubted experience, which though he seems to exaggerate its potency, yet makes an important contribution to our mental constructions in several directions, and we may add to those aspects he treats its effect in connection with historic animism. This seems to be the result of peculiarly subtle processes, though the outcome may be simple. For an object does not become a historic object unless it is already charged with meaning. It is only history for subjects who have experienced activity and the making of events, the giving a content of meaning to the process. Did the event as we conceive and know it take on in the active experience the type of a personal order, which related itself to us as having a character beyond all our deeds, and compelling them to its own form?

The conception of historic animism developed in these pages appears to be, although independently arrived at, in essential harmony with the view expounded by M. Bergson in his recent book in regard to the personification of events. He refers to this view in illustration of his interpretation of primitive religion in its function of a defensive reaction against fear. With this I am not at present concerned. After an example of the instinctive personification of an earthquake (quoted from William James' *Memoirs*), M. Bergson gives as illustration of animism his own feeling in regard to the event of the declaration of war by Germany on August 4, 1914. Since his childhood in 1871, the idea of another war appeared first as imminent, then as probable, and at the same time impossible. On August 4, 1914, "J'eus la sensation soudaine, d'une invisible présence que tout le passé aurait préparée, et annoncée à la manière d'une ombre précédant le corps qui la projette.— C'est pour intervenir à ce moment, en cet endroit, qu'il c'était mêlé à toute mon histoire."[1] If this were a constant experience, our active life would seem to take place in the midst of a

[1] *Les Deux Sources de la Morale et la Religion*, II. *La Religion Statique*, p. 168.

company of beings, namely of events, which are either other than human or partly more and partly less. It is the phenomenon itself, according to Bergson, to which a soul is imputed. But the experience is not constant, unless in a very dim and faint sense. It is rather that certain of our less ordinary experiences, especially those in which every aspect is heightened by emotion or intense striving, and in particular if there is a feeling of historic importance in what is happening, are attended by this sense of the presence of a being not ourselves. This sense may be present in any degree rising to the height of the idea expressed in Hardy's *Dynasts*, in which the human beings are mere pawns of the blind overruling will. It is doubtful, however, whether in Hardy's conception the experiencing agents or puppets would have any consciousness of the will of which they are the instruments, unless there should be amongst them any who even in the midst of absorbing action can still exercise contemplation.

It ought perhaps to be pointed out that animism in our historic knowledge, as I conceive it, is not identical with that kind of animism which Professor Stout finds in common sense.[1] By this he means "The tendency to find mind in nature generally, and not only in the form of individual minds, connected with particular bodies such as those of men and animals." Whereever we find "force, stress, strain, power, energy", as signified in ordinary language, on the observation of a chip swept along by a current, "we are reading into the merely sensible phenomenon some analogue of what we ourselves experience in active movement and in making efforts against resistance". But the myth-making shown in belief in gods or spirits, "in some way actuating or controlling objects", "becomes discredited with growing insight into the systematic unity of the material world".[2] Any tendency to personify the objects of experience, Professor Stout regards, of course, as fallacious, and characteristic of a less advanced stage of thought than that to which the type of animism which he considers valid belongs.

[1] *Mind and Matter*.   [2] Ibid., Chapter II.

The animism to which I refer might perhaps be described in
Kantian language as belonging to the schematism of the
imagination. For there is certainly in normal experience no
conscious belief in personal beings behind objects and events.
We only discover it by unravelling mental processes whose
operation is too subtle and delicate to be ordinarily noticed
and classified. Kant's imagination, we may remember, operates
as a blind but indispensable faculty of the soul. It is not a
magical activity transforming the facts into myths, but its
work prepares the data for categorial knowledge. The process
underlying historic knowledge, which I describe as animistic,
is not less of the highest importance to the seemingly immediate
decision of our conscious activity as to what are the events of
our actual world. It affects more or less deeply our selection
of those phases in the process which are to be permanently
remembered and affirmed as events, whilst the rest fade away
into indifference or nothingness for history. Somehow these
events greet us in a personal way. This seems, as noticed above,
to have some affinity with that which Bergson means in his
notion of personification as a defensive reaction of the mind
in the face of fearful events, familiarizing them, even though
as malicious beings, yet in this guise less terrible than implacable
necessity. As regards Bergson's interpretation of the place of
animism in primitive religion, I would only make the com-
ment that this religious use of animism presupposes the
tendency in our mental activity. These pre-rational sources of
meaning in events, it must be observed, may also have effects
less beneficial to man, since they are liable in crises of practical
life to overwhelm the rational structure based upon them.
Examples are obvious, such as that of the national idea in
certain phases with its animistic core. This potency of
irrational invasions of the cultural life does not exist in the case
of Kant's schematism, for he is only concerned with the
bases of scientific knowledge. The question may, however,
be asked, Is not all hope of truth in history cut away by the
admission of this "Idol", this profound animistic tendency at

the basis of our recognition of events? We are at present
dealing with the chief sources of doubt as to historic truth.
Yet it is possible that the apparently blind tendency in
question (here resembling the schematism of Kant's system)
is not altogether fallacious in its results, and may even mark a
stage in the discovery of historic values. There will be further
reference to this aspect of the problem at the close of the
chapter.

Returning to the question of the nature of the personification, it seems that the beings which appear in our concepts of
"French Revolution", "Reformation", "Great War", etc., are
not completely personal, but a sort of monstrous creatures of
will and force.

"The French Revolution", said William Wallace of Oxford
in almost his last lecture before the sudden and tragic arrest
of that great teacher's career, "has been made to stand for
many movements which could not pass through those narrow
portals." He was, I suggest, indicating a result of the animizing
process in our concept of a tremendous event. The category
can more easily as it were gather into its compass a large
complex of happenings, if it is thus felt to represent a unitary
vital being. We may turn to personifications which single out
some great character of events in our interpretation, all-
powerful for human interest, such as "Fate knocking at the
Door" in Beethoven's Fifth Symphony, or some universal
and supremely impressive event—Death as addressed by so
many poets—"O eloquent, just, and mighty death" (Raleigh).

> "What seemed his head
> The likeness of a kingly crown had on."
> MILTON

"Sleep—Death's twin brother", or stages of life, "Youth",
"Manhood", "Old Age". I think we can trace in the ordinary
not only poetic imagination of such presiding genii, so to
speak of comprehensive, and arresting events or series of events
the more definite and vivid form of the basic animism on which

I have been dwelling as it intrudes into the illuminated region of consciousness. If we examine the concept of Destiny, that which is personified appears to be a certain mode in which the events of a life or of a group of lives or even the totality of human lives is conceived to take place. On the one hand, the creative originative quality of personal action is withdrawn, and whatever active force is felt to be present in the total sequence is attributed to a numinous being. But destiny itself is destined, there is indeed no creative force left in the process when conceived under this notion. Some element of personality nevertheless appears to attend or haunt our representation of the power which determines the whole process in only one direction to one end. In a sense we are paradoxically personifying the very absence of personality. The tenacity and insistence of the animizing tendency could hardly be more forcibly illustrated. The puppet or marionette view of man's situation belongs to this order of ideas. To Hardy's immanent will blindly operating, reference has already been made.

As an illustration of certain vagaries of animism natural and artificial might be taken a passage in Vernon Lee's study of musical attitudes. In criticism of the hero-worship of the composer by a certain class of musical enthusiasts, she speaks of the "unsuspecting interpretation, the personification of the music and its effects into a composer". These people transform "the happenings of the music" into "the composer and his drama". "As a divinity is made up of nine-tenths of the hopes or fears of its votaries", so here "The composer is made up of the loveliness and majesty of his music, and the irresistible impulse to thank for them."[1] In this curious analysis Vernon Lee seems first to assume an impersonal composer, or the music without the composer, and then to trace the invention of the composer, who is hero-worshipped in the personifying process of his worshippers. It is an interesting example of depersonalization in order to presume the reverse process. The author's intention is doubtless to suggest that the composer

[1] *Music and its Lovers*—"The Imaginary Composer," pp. 321 et seq.

who is exalted in the devotion of the music is an unreal being, not the actual Mozart or Beethoven. This seems a somewhat arbitrary interpretation, but it doubtless fits a certain kind of attitude to genius and so far illustrates a species of animism, in which it is the music which is personified, or at a second remove, the "spirit" of the music. But when she proceeds, "The great abstract reality, Art or Thought, has forced the artist or the thinker to feel, to shape, to think in one way, and no other", there is a half-concealed personification in the ideas of Art and Thought, more fallacious than the personification of the music as the composer which she deplores. If these realities *were* abstract, they could not bring to birth in the artist that unique process of feeling, imagination, thought issuing in the shaping which is his work of art. Also the suggestion that the artist is forced in any sense but that of undergoing a supreme and wholly individual concrete experience, or that there is any necessity except the inner necessity of expressing the highest value he experiences, seems false. The problem of the personification of ideals and values will however meet us later.

The illustrations given have been chosen to exemplify animism in relation to experience of events, as events, not as entities, but as the ultimate elements of history. In relation to events, and complexes of events, as historic concepts, the greatest example is found in the personifications of history itself, which culminate in the philosophies of history, or the spirit of history as a kind of universal being. Of these Signor Croce's system is the best representative,[1] since it comes nearest to the identification of the Spirit with history. The idea of manfestation of mind or spirit in history does not appear to attribute to history itself a soul. This latter notion would carry out to its fullest implications a widely prevalent mode of thought in the ordinary consciousness, traceable in the sayings that "history teaches", history will show and the like, or at a higher imaginative level, "The history of the world

[1] Cf. *Philosophy of the Practical.*

is the judgment of the world", "Die Weltgeschichte ist das Weltgericht", Hegel's very questionable aphorism.

As to the problem whether this animistic root at the basis of our historic ideas confounds all hope of arriving at truth in any sense in this field, a few observations may be made in conclusion. It has been admitted that the ideal of truth in history cannot be realized. But there is a great range of knowledge which is historical in a secondary sense taking the form of a panorama of persons and events comprehended in a system of categories or schemes which seem to arise from their interrelationship, the *dramatis personae* of history, races, nations, civilizations, institutions, political, military, cultural and religious modes of being, etc. The persons and events of the panorama are themselves concepts or categories rather than unique individuals, but the individual subject contemplating history interprets them on the basis and by means of the forms and qualities of his own real experience. The historic intelligence, like Bergson's intellect, does not penetrate to the dynamic reality. But it is not as is the intellect for Bergson, pragmatically conditioned. It does not construct its panorama merely in the interests of practical life. The objects of historic knowledge must have meaning and value. Now it is not incredible that the animistic tendency should as a preliminary stage, and belonging to a barely conscious stratum of the mind, but not solely in the "childhood of the race", serve as preparation for the construction of those concepts of value in which our original experience is expressed or objectified. Strange though this process may appear as introduction to a valid conception of the system of history, it might afford a basis for insight into historic significance better than any unmeaning procession of bloodless events.[1]

[1] Suggested by Bradley's "unmeaning ballet of bloodless categories".

CHAPTER V

THE SUBSTANCE OF HISTORY IN ITS FACTORS

A

THE EVENT AND THE PERSON—THE OTHER OR BLIND ELEMENT—CHANCE, CONTINGENCY, THE CASUAL

"To consider the world in its length and breadth, its various history, the many races of man, their starts, their fortunes, their mutual alienations, their conflicts; and then their ways, habits, governments, forms of worship, their enterprises, their aimless courses, their random achievements and acquirements, the impotent conclusions of long-standing facts, the tokens so faint and broken of a superintending design, the blind evolution of what turn out to be great powers or truths, the progress of things as if from unreasoning elements, not towards final causes, the greatness and littleness of man, his far-reaching aims, his short duration, the curtain hung over his futurity, the disappointments of life, the defeat of good, the success of evil, physical pain, mental anguish, the prevalence and intensity of sin, the pervading idolatries, the corruptions, the dreary hopeless irreligion, that condition of the whole race so fearfully and wonderfully described in the apostle's words, 'having no hope, and without God in the world'—all this is a vision to dizzy and appal, and inflicts upon the mind the sense of a profound mystery which is absolutely beyond human solution."

JOHN HENRY NEWMAN

LEAVING the problem of the conditions under which the foundations of our historic knowledge are laid, we now turn to consideration of the content of history as a great expanse of country there for our possession, whenever we desire further knowledge of it, and are willing to gird ourselves for the journey with the equipment of students, in the spirit of those who follow well-accredited guides, or venture into the less-known tracks observing the general rules of experienced explorers.

This simile is used to indicate the standpoint of this chapter—no longer that of the adventurer who does not yet know whether his America exists, whether namely there is an object of knowledge there the same for all who seek, but that of the realist who examines undoubted fields of knowledge and asks concerning the main contours, laws, or principles, the nature of the content. The problem of knowledge then is no longer prominent, though it may not be always avoidable. The position has been taken that although the principal sources of history must be selves, it is impossible to treat history as consisting solely of the experiences of selves. It is therefore more in harmony with the general character of objective history to assume its ultimate constituents to be events. For this type of history cannot present the ultimate individuality of selves. This is not, of course, inconsistent with the inclusion of many distinct aspects and forms of history. Such are the histories of nations, civilizations, wars, religions, or of history viewed through more abstract categories, economic, legal, etc. What is involved is that the content from all these standpoints is found under analysis to consist of events. The position still holds good that in the events the most distinctively historical factors are deeds, the expression of personal activity, those changes which have been termed "creative", in order to emphasize their dependence upon the meaning and ideas brought by human will into the process. But since the greatest difficulty in the rationalization of history has its root exactly in the fact that the series and concatenation of events can seldom or never be understood simply as the outcome of human actions, it seems necessary to take the events as our central historic constituents. This may seem a dark saying to those who hold the view that it is on the contrary the factor of human activity itself to which is due the difficulty of presenting a rational or scientific scheme of history.

"The great man", says Bury, "is not only an accident but an unforeseen and extremely disturbing accident. His exceptional brain might be scientifically explained, but such explana-

tion did not supply us with a calculus for the future. Even
in domains where generalization is most fruitful (as in economic
and social history), he may prevent it from being wholly
subject to general laws." "The heel of Achilles in all historic
speculations of this class has been the rôle of the individual."[1]
It is no doubt unnecessary to observe that Bury himself would
not aim at minimizing the rôle of the individual as source of
events with a view to the interpretation of history by general
laws. The reference, however, will serve to illustrate the position
maintained in this book, that the ideal in historic interpretation
has to be sought not in the systematization of the process by
means of general laws, but in the discovery of the special
type of order belonging to history in the realm of human
values. From this standpoint the obstacle to the attainment of
its proper ideal which appears irremovable is the obtrusion
of other factors into the process than those determined by
the activities of persons.

Let us first attempt to indicate the nature of the problem by
further consideration of the notion to which reference has
already been made, namely the "other" in the Platonic sense as
opposed to the principle of the "same" ($\tau o\ \dot{\alpha} \upsilon \tau \acute{o}\ \kappa \alpha \grave{\iota}\ \tau o\ \ddot{\epsilon} \tau \epsilon \rho o \nu$).
M. Emile Meyerson takes this opposition as a text or a symbol
in his brilliant analysis of the nature of the "irrational" confronting science in its efforts to reduce all provinces of knowledge to intelligibility, by means of the principle of identity,
"the same".[2] From this standpoint the opposition can be
exactly applied, though whether his distinction is strictly in
accordance with that of Plato may perhaps be questioned. It
is rather to Plato's meaning in the opposition of the same and
the other that the present reference is made, since this seems
broader and capable of application to the spirit of history, as
well as that of scientific knowledge as understood by Meyerson.
The form of the application in the two realms respectively
is of course very distinct, since history demands a different

---

[1] Selected Essays. Quoted in Introduction by Harold Temperley.
[2] De l'Explication dans les Sciences.

type of explanation, and without individuality and difference it is destroyed. The principle of the "Other" then is taken to include all those elements in the process of events which are not the outcome of the personal activity which is present, or certainly not clearly analysable into this, not purposed, not foreseeable from experience of the human factors. The intention of the agents does not work out as planned, and their actions seem as it were to be entangled in a network of unmeaning hindrances. The effect is again to obscure the operation of value and disvalue as it might be seen apart from these disturbing factors, in the idea of history (as for Acton) as the conflict of good and evil. They are not necessarily the cause of evil. It may happen that they appear to be a hindrance to evil as well as to good. They are a-moral, or indifferent to value.

It may here be observed that it is possible that my treatment of this subject would have been influenced by Professor Whitehead's illuminating *aperçus* on the nature of history in his last book,[1] if I had had the advantage of reading it before the problem had taken shape in my mind. My own standpoint is essentially different from that of Professor Whitehead, since I cannot treat the interpenetration of history by ideas in the objective manner which is consistent with his Platonic affinities and his doctrine of "eternal objects". But his felicitous statement of certain great impressions which arise for us on the study of history must be especially welcomed. And amongst these is his view of the subject at present under discussion. This dual characterization of all processes in which human action is implicated, which I discuss as due to the pervasion of events by the "other", the factor foreign to the personal principle, blindly working, Professor Whitehead speaks of as the "senseless side of history", referring to the "dichotomy", by which the history of ideas is dominated. Thus he characterizes the inrush of barbarians into the Roman Empire, and the introduction of steam in modern times, as "senseless agencies driving their respective civilizations away from inherited modes of order".

[1] *Adventures of Ideas*. Introduction. See reference in Chapter I.

With these he contrasts democracies in our time and Christianity in the Roman, as illustrating beliefs issuing from and into aspirations. The latter would in a very broad sense stand for agencies proceeding from the creative activity of personality, but would demand (in my view) further analysis, since they cannot be shown to work without serious intermixture of the alien factors. Professor Whitehead also, however, recognizes on the other side intermixture of "brute necessity" with fragmentary intellectual agencies. I think then that in respect to this problem my view is consistent with his, so far as it can be expressed in these general terms.

An illustration from a social development of recent times, superficially unimpressive perhaps in relation to history, yet widely ramifying in cultural effects, may help to render more precise what is signified by the intermixture of factors indifferent to value in a course of events which appear to be initiated freely by individuals with special ends in view. Such factors may be seen partly or in major proportion to deflect the process into channels unintended or bring about results unlooked for, as though the whole course were affected or even dominated by a power the opposite to that conceived in Hegel's doctrine of the craft of reason (List der Vernunft), turning to irrational ends that which was intelligently planned. The question then may arise, Are we seeing an epitome of the historic process? Does all history happen like this? The most salient examples do not occur in joint efforts or movements for a "common cause", though the features above indicated often appear in these in a minor degree, but in the rise and growth of some unlooked for, unprepared for social development, the outcome perhaps of invention or a combination of scientific inventions made use of to produce a new kind of utility or means of pleasure. The illustration I would choose is that of the growth of the cinema industry, not because I know it to be more productive of deleterious than of beneficial social results, but because the drawbacks attendant on its development appear to be so obviously due to that blind character in the process of which I speak. Reference may be made to the extraordinarily vigorous and rapid development of the "industry", outrunning any expectations that might have been formed, the large prizes it has offered in wealth to those engaged in it, the financial necessity of appealing to the largest possible numbers of the public, causing a lowering of the standard of production as regards art and education, overshooting its mark in the lowness of ideal rather than running any risk of diminished popularity. There have also entered in interests of industries such as the electrical quite irrelevant to the main interest and even effects of speculations on the New York Stock Exchange. Again on account of the Great War, the cinema industry in the United States gained an immense advantage over those of other countries in its high organization. Ideas of life still more foreign than those of Europe in relation to Oriental and African civilization have been presented by the cinema all over the world, with incalculable results in misunderstanding. Contributory causes of what may be called from the standpoint of any ideal intrinsic to a form of art or quasi-art aiming at social pleasure, an irrational outcome of much of the highly intelligent work put into cinema production might be pointed out. These lie partly in what may be summed up as the material conditions, partly in conditions which may be grouped as irrational, although they are classifiable as psychological or psychical. They have their place in the complex interlacing series of antecedents and consequents amongst the numerous fragmentary motives of action, which have unintended effects on the value or disvalue of the event. Such are the interest in some particular "cinema stars", jealousies and rivalries of writers, managers, actors, etc. The need of livelihood, the desire for wealth and fame, the passion for power may be included here, but these belong to the more fundamental sources of human action. The struggle for power in particular (often absorbing that for wealth) is, from the standpoint of this treatise, the corruption of the intrinsic personal striving for self-transcendence. The point of importance is that many motives which had no such purpose enter into the stream which issues in a value or disvalue. In a certain aspect this kind of development corresponds to that which Troeltsch brings under chance. In one of his references to this (*zufall*), he describes it as something which always results from the crossing of various heterogeneous systems of laws, having no common root, interlacings, which now advance, concentrate, stimulate, now break up, causing uncertainty as to the historic meaning. He includes also conflicts of value-tendencies with natural happenings, as for instance the submerging of talents, sudden death before completion of a work, hunger or epidemics which destroy a culture. "All these chances play an appalling (*ungeheure*) rôle in history, so that it has often been regarded as the domain of chance."[1]

The example of the history of cinema production was chosen to illustrate especially the principle that as in this case (at a certain phase of its development) evil may seem to result from the event rather than from the willed deeds as individually purposed, or the work of persons as central determinants of the event. Unforeseen effects, some good, some bad, on schools, homes, social habits, grow as it were with the exuberance of nature in tropical growths, like fungi spreading round about the effects intended. The examination of the presence of the "other" in a little historical fragment reveals that this fact in many of its occurrences may be otherwise regarded as chance, meeting us as a kind of objective character in the historic process. We find that history may be conceived as "the domain of chance." This is the spectre which stalks through history as viewed by Troeltsch in his unceasing labour to discover great value tendencies, if not unmistakable signs of universal purpose. It may seem that M. Bergson's definition of chance gives the reverse interpretation. "Le hasard est—le mécanisme se comportant comme s'il avait une intention." If the rock falls on a man loosened by the wind in a storm, the physical effect is fully accounted for. It is not this, it is the human significance of the effect, the death of a man, which demands

[1] *Historismus*, Kap. I, 3.

explanation. This significance is not contained in the physical cause, the cause is not equal to it. It seems to belong to another type of order, teleological; there appears to be required, then, an intention, as though the rock or the tile had chosen to fall.[1] The point of view is different, but there is no real inconsistency. It is our unconscious animism in the interpretation of all events which impels us to find this "as if" of purpose wherever in the process of nature an occurrence has special significance for many minds. Here is Bergson's chance. *Le hasard.* But from the standpoint of *Historismus*, with its principle of historical interpretation of all events, it is the ever recurring factors of interference with any coherent interpretation through historic values which are conceived under chance. "Chance plays an appalling rôle in history." Let us consider this proposition in its widest implications. Perhaps if for chance we substitute contingency, meaning by this the dependence of human history in general upon, or at least its close interrelation with, conditions which from the standpoint of our developed value judgments are not intrinsic to its essence, we shall be less committed to any special theory, and more unrestricted in reference to relevant aspects of history. Contingency for this view is by no means identical with Bury's contingency or determination by the particular rather than the general cause, for this particular cause (as the great personality) might be the proper source of the event and its value. We are, in fact, returning to the further consideration of the dualism of history, which as noticed above appears to be closely similar to Professor Whitehead's dichotomy. In an estimate of the factors which ought to be included in that alien or other element which compels recognition of the dualism, we have first to remember the conditions of the environment of human activities, and their change from age to age and race to race, nature, climate, geography, etc. Also for each generation in the cultural ages and peoples as it enters upon its task or historic vocation,

[1] *Les Deux Sources de la Morale et de la Religion. La Religion Statique*, pp. 152 et seq.

G

the humanly constructed or artificial conditions may be the most important part. Consideration will be given at a later stage to the significance of institutions from our point of view and the problem whether man whilst achieving continually greater freedom from necessities of the natural environment, does not forge for himself in some of his organizations a new kind of force alien to freedom, which again becomes a source of dualism.

The civilization into which an individual is born determines in vital respects the mode of action possible for him, the standards of conduct which it is difficult for any but a moral genius to dissent from, oppose, or rise above. This appears to outline limits to the absolute freedom of personality. Consider the differences of the environing limitations for the man of the fourth, thirteenth, seventeenth, or twentieth century. It must not, however, be forgotten that the material setting itself gains a meaning reflected from the principal meaning which makes the event, as though the relation were that of soul and body. In order to form some impression at least definite, though it cannot be comprehensive of the immense incidence or presence in history of that other element, which sometimes oppresses the student as universal contingency, we may take a few salient illustrations. The first will belong to the relation between the inanimate environment and the crooked course of human development, and the delicate balance between the needs of man's life and its values. Next we are confronted by the stupendous problem of the animal world, and its claim to a place in history. Finally, at stages in history at which it might be expected that having experienced the glory of his own creations of culture, and the loveliness of human relations in their higher forms, the principle of personality could assert itself in man victorious over the dualistic factor, we must observe the breaking out of this in the very arcana of human relations themselves, its irruption into history from personality.

The important place of the geographical factor in the beginnings of human culture has been abundantly recognized from many standpoints. In relation to the origins of the Greek type of civilization, it has seldom been more vividly presented than by Professor J. Myres.[1]

"The question who were the Greeks", he says, "is at bottom *a geographical problem*" [italics mine], "in which interaction amongst human agencies has been rigidly directed and restricted, by non-human factors, of a peculiar and rather complicated kind." The effect of his treatment of the subject is to produce the impression that geographical and other material conditions were favourable to the realization of genius potentially present in members of the Greek peoples. Going further back to the distinction between the "natural society" which has not got beyond the task of the maintenance and the continuance of life, and the society which is human in a more essential sense, he shows how in becoming a tool-making animal man finds that he has ideas and ideals of his own to express. Beyond the need of making something, there is "the aim of enhancing the work, so that it approximates to some standard of perfection present to his consciousness".[2] The threshold between animal and human was passed when certain of the primates, instead of wandering away in the Ice Age in search of easier conditions, began the attempt to conquer nature, making fire and clothes. Here is indicated the germ of human creativity, the independent attitude to the process of change, conscious effort directed upon this, the foreshadowing of will.

The close relation of the political creation of Greek genius, the City-state, to the geographical structure of their land, with the divisions caused by the barriers of mountain ridges, has often been pointed out. By Professor Myres the significance of this fact is brought out with peculiar force. "We learn to know the Greeks, as exponents of a Greek view of life based on the mode of life imposed on them by the rigid conditions of their geographical surroundings, but rationalized, and

[1] *Who were the Greeks?* Chapter I.
[2] Ibid., Chapter VII, p. 464.

thereby idealized once again into an outlook on life commensurate with their aspiration, not only to live, but to live well in the fullest sense." The recognition of this "aspiration to live well", which could not come out of the geographical and climatic conditions plus the necessities of living, without the presence of other implications in the nature of the living being, distinguishes Professor Myres' treatment of the problem from nineteenth-century accounts of the evolutionary development of the human manner of life and cultural activities from the standpoint of natural evolution. There is no such over-simplification of the problem, as in that interpretation which assumes that a complete knowledge of all the factors in the situation analysed would provide an answer to the question of the ultimate source or emergence of the ideal interests. But the questions why having reached a certain stage, many races proceed no further, or why in the environment of Greek life Greek genius only appeared once and endured in its splendour for a comparatively brief period remain unanswered from both standpoints. The assumption, however, that the capacity for the higher type of existence is potential in all human life (omitting for the moment consideration of the animal problem), whilst its realization is dependent upon a thousand conditions which remain contingent seems less irrational than any which supposes this capacity suddenly to emerge or to arise if sufficient time be granted out of an origin in which there is no seed of it.

"The half-men of Neanderthal", says Professor J. B. Haldane, "chipped flints in a crude way, and possessed fire, but though they inhabited Europe for scores of thousands of years, they have not left a single work of art. Only by a perhaps misplaced courtesy do we call them men."[1] The art of chipping flints and making fire may not appear to contain more promise of a spiritual type of life than the art of the nest-building and songster bird. But we must not risk departure from the universally recognized distinction of man as *Homo sapiens*, the specific

[1] *The Inequality of Man and Other Essays. Is History a Fraud?*

type to which all branches of the human family alike belong.[1]
And by this it is implied in the present context that a beginning
of intelligence, the capacity at least to objectify experiences
in the form of images which are almost ideas is necessary to
the essential personal life, though it does not always summon
this into existence. Are we therefore compelled to deny to all
living things below *Homo sapiens* any vestiges of the experience
of value? The admission that man can only possess the quality
thus indicated in the form of intelligence as known to us, and
also that without this personality could not achieve its function
of giving meaning and worth to existence, need not exclude the
possibility that the germ of personality lies concealed in some
of the animal beings. With reference to this problem, it may
at this point be said that if it were necessary to choose between
denial of the presence of a transcendent element in human
personality, transcending namely the conditions realized in the
passive natural society, and the alternative of ascribing it
potentially to all living things, the second horn of the dilemma
would appear less far from the probabilities. This would
signify the ascription of such an element to life universally
as implied in the capacity for a creative beginning. And at
least it seems to be against the evidence to suppose the events
of all non-human lives to be totally devoid of value, apart
from pleasurable feeling in the satisfaction of biological needs.
Before this presumption could be accepted attention would
have to be given to the following considerations. In the first
place there are many signs in the animals of emotions and
interests akin to those of the higher human experience. Here
come in the indubitable capacity of some species for affection,
loyalty, self-sacrifice, the constructive activity of others, and
apparent aesthetic enjoyment of sound and colour, the curiosity
and seemingly disinterested interest in unfamiliar objects
shown in several species. In the second place the view of the
philosophical biologist von Uexküll is one that ought not to

[1] R. R. Marett: *Faith, Hope, and Charity in Primitive Religion*,
VI, p. 99.

be ignored. According to von Uexküll, not only is the world of every human subject unique and unshareable, but this must also hold good of the whole animal world. It is the neglect of theory of knowledge by biologists which has led to those amateurish experiments in which the attempt is made to investigate an animal's intelligence by setting it to deal with human implements and to learn to use these as would the human being. "If we tried to change the point of view, and look at things from the animal's mind, we should suddenly find ourselves surrounded with the animal's appearances, which have no connection with our own."[1] We are thus reminded how profound is our ignorance of the nature of animal experience, and that in the countless varieties of this there may be values unimaginable by us. Or, regarding the problem on the other side, from a more realistic standpoint it may be asked, Are we justified in a dismissal of all the brilliant achievement of the natural world of living things, in its immeasurable variety and beauty, the innumerable forms of struggle for life and self-defence, the endlessly curious and ingenious devices for continuance of the species and protection of the young, as though these qualities were not to count in our view of the ultimate nature of conscious activity, or as though they were only there for our enjoyment?

Any attempt to orientate ourselves towards the problem of the beginnings of distinctively human history thus makes unavoidable some glance beyond to the environing animal life. In relation to our present subject, the effect of this lengthening of the shadow of history ("cast before") appears to be as follows. The significance and range of those conditions in the great event of history proper which have to be brought under the class of otherness is indefinitely increased. In the facts of animal life we find an adumbration of some of those human experiences or emotions which are the very texture of history. Are we constrained to enlarge our concept of that illimitable

[1] J. von Uexküll: *Theoretical Biology*, Chapter V. Translated by Doris Mackinnon, D.Sc.

event which is human history, in view of the multitude of
sensitive and conscious beings who appear as subjects of
experience to have a claim to a life of value? In the ends of
introducing order into this tremendous array of facts which,
on an idealist view, cannot be denied some relation to man's
experience, and his place in the cosmos, it seems that we should
have to form the conception of the history (in our sense) of
living things as a whole. But in a conception of history thus
widened, the place occupied by the activity of beings experiencing and creative of value as it is for us would be proportionately
narrowed, unless we indulge in ungrounded speculations as
to the unknowable kinds of value experienced by the animal
species. From this avenue of thought, however, we must turn
aside if we are to hold fast to the principle that history is
constituted by the experience of selves; and though we may
be driven to admit fragments and simple phases of experience
similar to our own beyond the limits of personal experience,
we are not justified in a resort to these fields for light upon that
historic world of which we have direct experience. Philosophic
idealism cannot intrude into the sphere of "natural" history,
whatever the fascination for philosophers of the speculations
of the philosophic biologist. The fact, however, that the authentic
voice of history does not speak in halls of the cosmos silent
and dumb, but raises itself above murmurs innumerable which
sound at times like its own voice and in tune with this, has to
be reckoned with. These great currents of sensitive life which
in relation to our knowledge must remain irreducible to the
current of creative experience determining historic events, are
preparatory to history. History arises out of them, and the
dualism of history, in the essence of its events as the deeds of
selves, shows the kinship of man with all living nature. In
this light, all history, even in the strict sense, becomes contingent,
since it is inseparable from a foundation whose relevance to
the higher life may be guessed at, but which remains an im-
penetrable mystery. That there should be history at all as we
have conceived it would be no less contingent than the rise

of Greek genius under special geographical conditions. The dawn of human history upon the animal world, as we have seen, is conditioned by a series of physical changes or convulsions, climatic, geological, etc., which are of major importance for scientific investigators examining the facts as far as possible in abstraction from all human valuation. They are general causes. The same physical phenomena, however, when conceived in relation to the changes of habit and kind of life amongst the ancestors of man to which they give rise, involving entrance upon the toilsome path of resistance to nature, the foreshadowing of creative control, are contingent. It is an instance of Bergson's chance, on a gigantic scale, the effect in its significance has no equivalence with the cause.

At a further stage, if we ask how what is called civilization began, we are referred by Professor J. B. Haldane to plant genetics.[1] Civilization, he points out, "is based, not only on men, but on plants and animals. . . . If it can be determined where cereals and cattle were first domesticated, we shall have gone a long way towards tracing civilization to its source".

But let us pass on from the problem of the beginning of the simplest culture and that of the beginning of the path to civilization, in regard to which there must be a larger element of speculative interpretation in the result for knowledge than in ages of recorded history. If what we have spoken of as seeming chance and contingency, conditions that are stumbling-blocks in the rationalization of history, appear to preside at these beginnings, what of the later stages? Do not these conditions become less insistent, once the historical being takes control of his existence? As soon as this suggestion is thrown out, and we turn to history on the great scale, we are confronted by the fall of civilizations after a course of general progress to a state which seemed stable, and perhaps permanent to their members, the causes of the decline or "loss of nerve" still remaining mysterious to the modern student. Or the principal disaster of history so far as known confounds our hopes,

[1] *Is History a Fraud?* op. cit.

the failure of every civilization steadily to advance in the development and enrichment of the higher life, so that all factors which appear unfavourable to this within the series of events, all alien elements are progressively controlled.

The problem we are facing may be brought more within our grasp for consideration if we ask the question whether those obvious factors of contingency, in relation to the values of culture and civilization, to which special reference has been made, drop away or are discarded as human races advance and approach nearer to the condition which is more intrinsic to history, since we conceive its essence to be determined by the activity of selves. We may remember Sir Henry Maine's often quoted dictum that the progressive races are those which pass from the condition of status to that of contract.[1] That there is perhaps an over-simplification in this saying is suggested by the work of some modern anthropologists. Or that the distinction may be looked at from a different angle is shown in Dr. Marett's extraordinary subtle and novel treatment of the opposition between static and dynamic in relation to primitive and advanced societies. "To cover the whole range of human history, we need", in his view, "two conceptions of progress—one as movement along a line, the other as movement in a circle." And he points out that the latter kind of progress would be presumably the only kind available once we had reached "Heaven". It is an "eternal round of activities", smoothly accomplished, a "beautiful continuance" for which the savage asks. In his very difficult life, his "Practical Wisdom" lies in maintaining the static society in existence, though some novelties are permitted.[2]

Whatever the adequacy of the conception of progress, as applied to the more primitive or static society, our immediate problem is whether to the degree in which society becomes more "dynamic", it sloughs off, so to speak, the more tyrannous

[1] *Ancient Law*, Chapter V.
[2] *Faith, Hope, and Charity in Primitive Religion*, Chapter VI, "Faith".

of those conditions which clog the free expression of human activity and its realization of value. We may return to that factor which we have seen to be so incalculably potent in the first emergence of forms of life that can be called human, and in the determination of the type of a civilization, as pre-eminently in the case of Ancient Greece. "Geography is the basis of history", says Sir J. R. Marriott,[1] a principle which he abundantly illustrates in his *Evolution of Modern Europe*. "The effect of geography upon history is irresistibly suggested by a glance at a physical map." Here it is not pre-history, or what might be termed from the standpoint of our knowledge, where there is no memory or record, sub-history. which is in question. The proposition refers to history in every sense or at every stage. We may perhaps allow "geography" to stand for all those impersonal factors, environment, climate, means of subsistence, which provide the material to which value may be brought, but which at the same time more or less rigidly limit freedom, and determine within degrees relativity of value to the age, the race and its local background. From the stand-point of the "barbarians", their invasion of Italy might be said to be due to general causes. From the standpoint of Roman civilization and its decay, certain of the invasions may appear to the historian, as for instance to Bury, to be due to "contingent" causes. In relation to the position of this treatise, the causal conditions in both aspects must be conceived as contingent, in the sense that the vast significance of the effect is incommensurable with the importance of the assigned causes. The process from those changes which we classify as causal to those which have to be regarded as effects is far from any analogy with the willed course of action of rational agents progressing towards a result through means belonging to the same order of events.

Coming nearer to our own times, Sir J. R. Marriott speaks of the geographical revolution following on the discovery of America and the results on the great highways of commerce,

[1] *The Evolution of Modern Europe*, Chapter II.

the importance henceforth of the Atlantic overshadowing that of the Mediterranean, the changed position of Venice. "The geographical revolution found England unprepared to assume the rôle which nature seemed anxious to assign to her." But in co-operation with other conditions history gives to this almost the chief place amongst the causes of the new power and activity of England in the sixteenth century. To the special gifts of the people, energy and thirst for adventure, the geographical revolution had to be added. The contingent factor or "chance" is surely here again. For the fact that men with a genius for adventure were amongst the explorers does not affect the essential nature of the process of events, the inter-mixture of the impersonal factors with the personal principle, the dependence of a development of high importance for the character and history of people upon "geography". This is indeed Sir J. R. Marriott's thesis. "Nationality itself", he writes, "is largely the creation of physical geography." He illustrates this in the case of England, and also argues that the effect of geography on political development can be seen as mainly determining the parts played in history by Spain, Italy, the Balkan countries. The significance of "nationality" from our standpoint will be considered at a later stage. The tremendous importance of this principle in history, whilst nevertheless from our point of view the nation cannot be regarded as an ultimate fact, makes it necessary to subject it to special examination. The problem of the relation of geography to history raises in an urgent form the question of the nature of historic idealism, and its contrast with the idealism of knowledge. But this problem cannot here be examined, since its treatment would take us too far away from our immediate subject.

At the point now reached it seems necessary to go a little deeper into the basis of our thought in the use of this notion of chance or accident in the process of history, in relation to which it is the results that appear to our interest in the progress of mankind and our estimate of the value of human experience to be of greatest importance which are subject to "chances" of many kinds. Necessity, uniform laws of causation may be postulated at all stages of cosmic development, and in this sense the order and regularity of events be vindicated. But it is not upon the assured working of these that the existence of history as we have conceived it depends. We have indeed argued that there would be no interest in the discovery of these uniformities that they would not even be sought out and formulated by the abstracting, categorizing intellect, were it not for the ideal of another type of order. This is the type more originally and essentially required by the human mind, since it is personal, the order in which certain values would be supreme. And to this the value of uniform law in nature is subordinate. The process, however, by which realization of these values is conditioned appears perpetually dependent on those factors which to whatever order they belong are irrelevant to the historic values. This indicates the presence of the Other in events, the "contingency" of history, the advent of the great things of the spiritual world as by "chance". Such we find to be the aspect of the beginnings of human culture and the entrance upon civilization. And when we turn to the later stages, in which we might expect the true character of history, as experience of selves, creative work of personality to be manifest, the process unrolls itself as still in the main deeply dyed with the same qualities from this standpoint. At moments we may even ask whether the human interpretation is not a great illusion, or at least the belief that it steadily affects the form taken by the next stage in the changing process. This would signify a despair in regard to the actuality of freedom in history, the sign of which we seek as the supremacy of the *deed* in the *event*, a doubt whether, whatever may be the success of individual lives in the control of circumstance, such success can conceivably attend on the attempts of the human race to control its course. The advent of intelligence amongst the causal conditions of living activity would be found to hold no promise of its final supremacy. The profound impression created by such work as that of Sir James Frazer,[1] of the torments suffered by man in the dawn of conscious reflection on the great events of life, birth and death, would point to the truth that reason is always too weak for the task of giving to human society that supreme worth of which it enables the individual to have some visions. Overwhelmed by a host of fears unknown to his non-rational fellows, the mental endowment of the savage seems to increase his slavery rather than to set him on the road to freedom. In Dr. Marett's[2] view, a more optimistic interpretation of primitive life is justified, and hope rather than fear regarded as the chief gift of religion, from which he sharply distinguishes "magic". M. Bergson's interpretation of the real significance of primitive religion as the "defensive reaction of nature"[3] against the disintegrating effects of intelligence on man and society is a distinct type of theory. In this perhaps we may trace the idea that in the primitive society at least any exercise of the abstracting intelligence (which is not the whole of intelligence) in the affairs of life requires control by more concrete principles, emanating from the whole individual. But whatever the interpretation of primitive religion and of magical practices, the fact remains that dawning intelligence, though it increases man's power over nature in some respects, restricts his freedom in others. The problem for those who conceive history as determined by man's discovery and creation of value is whether this characteristic of the interrelation of selves with their environment is ever left behind. By what experience and arguments based on our postulate, it may be asked, can it be shown that in reality the higher civilizations rise superior to this situation or can show hope for such a victory in the future?

What then is the ultimate significance of this factor, which in relation to our view of history operates as "chance"? From

[1] *The Golden Bough* series. *Belief in Immortality, The Dying God, Spirits of the Corn and of the Wild, The Perils of the Soul*, etc.

[2] *Faith, Hope, and Charity in Primitive Religion*, op. cit.

[3] *Les Deux Sources de la Morale et de la Religion. La Religion Statique.*

the objective point of view which dominates in the present
chapter, it appears that throughout its incidence in every part
of existence, "chance" as we find it must in the end be the
outcome of the infinity of the real. The grandest expression
of this doctrine of infinity is given by Spinoza, though for him,
since human valuations are false, being due to the limitations
of the modes, there is no chance.

"To those who ask why God did not so create all men that
they should be governed only by reason, I give no answer but
this: because matter was not lacking to him for the creation
of every degree of perfection from highest to lowest, or more
strictly because the laws of his nature are so vast as to suffice
for the production of everything conceivable by an infinite
intelligence as I have shown in Proposition XVI."[1]

"From the necessity of the divine nature must follow an
infinite number of things, in infinite ways, that is all things
which can fall within the sphere of infinite intellect."[2] For
Spinoza, this principle was of the highest value, because it
was essential to his conception of the nature of God, or substance.
From the standpoint of this work the meaning and value of
history cannot be saved unless there is an ultimate significance
in the initiative and creative effort of selves. For as regards the
environment of their activity it must be agreed that no limits
can be traced to the variety of processes, *qua* affecting the
value of existence. In other words, experience does not testify
that laws of value can be laid down necessarily realizable in
existence, thus limiting its indefinite variety. We cannot on the
basis of experience assert that the principle that value ought
to be has a cosmic validity. Within the known process of
history, including pre-history so far as we possess evidence of
its nature, we are not for instance entitled to say on empirical
grounds that such and such conditions, geographical, climatic
and others were present because required for the life of the
Greek people and their peculiar genius, or that the hour had
come for the decline of Rome and a principle immanent in

[1] *Ethics*, I, Appendix.   [2] *Ethics*, Part I, Proposition XVI.

history brought the barbarians to her gates. The poverty of this type of interpretation is evident in the numerous striking examples of "casual" events, through which a great hope has been destroyed, or a great disaster brought nearer. A group of these is assembled by Mr. John Buchan in his lecture on *The Causal and Casual in History*,[1] including the death from a malignant fever of Henry, son of James I, whose rule, instead of that of Charles I, would have given a wholly different course to history; the bleeding of Napoleon's cheek from a scratch on the 19th Brumaire, which, suggesting that his life was in danger, turned the ebbing tide in his favour; the monkey's bite which killed Alexander of Greece in 1920, and so led to a series of events of which the success of Turkish nationalism under Kemal was the outcome. For Mr. Buchan these are accidents, small things which determine great events, not to be explained by reference to great causes, not easy to rationalize. One more reflection on this aspect of history may be quoted. According to Cournot, chance, *le hasard*, asserts itself everywhere in nature as in society. "It is the mutual independence of several series of causes and effects which meet accidentally to produce such and such a phenomenon, determine such an event, lead to such an encounter", which is therefore qualified as fortuitous. "The true function of history", as Sée defines Cournot's view, "is to distinguish the necessary and the fortuitous, the essential and accidental. If these two elements did not coexist, there would not be history at all."[2] Here by the accidental Cournot would appear to mean the fact that an event of important significance for history proceeds from the confluence of various series of happenings which in their indifference to each other, and irrelevance to the historic meaning, constitute a process as unlike as possible to a purposive sequence. And Sorel observes that "Politics are a conflict of which Chance seems to

[1] Rede Lecture, Cambridge, 1929.
[2] Henri Sée: *Science et Philosophie de l'Histoire*, Chapter IV, "La Conception critique de l'Histoire, Cournot."

be modifying the whole course.''[1] History is the peculiar arena
for the struggle of categories of interpretation from the standpoint of value. Here if anywhere, where the appropriate form
would be that which we know in ourselves as the essential
form of human activity, the striving for value, we might
expect to find teleological causation supreme in the event-
process. But overlooking the fact that the issue should be
decided in history first, philosophic thought has been more
constantly preoccupied with the problem in the field of nature
outside man, in the belief, perhaps, that if the purposive principle
can be detected as at work in this wider sphere, the problem
would be less intransigent in the province nearer to human
interest. For Aristotle (it seems) it was less difficult to conceive
the agency of desire for the good in nature than in the seemingly
lawless world of human affairs. He can state the ideal of perfect
harmony in ethics and politics, but when it is his concern to
show the character of actual cities, we are presented with the
cynical analyses of the worse states in the *Politics*. When he
refers to nature apart from man he can raise his thoughts to
the movements of the stars in circles each presided over by
its own first mover, the realization of a perfection, after which
even natural things on this earth may strive though very far
off. Or so we may perhaps interpret him. For ''nature strives
for the good''. Reference to a striking observation of Professor
Stout in regard to the Concept of Teleological Animism may
throw light on this aspect of the contrast. ''If from the point
of view of physical science we attempt to account for teleological
order, as we find it at present, we can only do so by going back
on past history. We must trace the present concrete situation
to prior concrete situations, and these again to others more
remote. Their historic regress could have a limit only on one
assumption—viz. of ultimate laws which are principles of
organization, so that however chaotic the initial distribution
may be, the cosmic order which we now find must arise from

[1] Quoted in *Recollections*, Viscount Morley, Vol. II, Book IV
(Heading).

it. But the fundamental laws of physical science, gravitation, conservation of energy, are not teleological. They are in themselves indifferent to teleological order, and cannot ultimately account for it."[1] Professor Stout does not appear to consider the full implications of this admission, in relation to the validity of animism in his view, in its indication of the presence of mind in the universe. For the force in ourselves on analogy with which we ascribe force or striving to things in nature, is a force teleological in character. It may further be observed that the teleological order we seem to discover in nature at present is pre-eminently found in the individual organism. So striking is the suggestion of purposive order here in harmony of parts, co-operation in the achievement of an end or wholeness, that the perfection of the single organism has been the favourite type for the concept of the whole, in groups of organisms, species, races, or for logical coherence in Hegelianism, or the harmony of the aesthetic ideal. But does the process of nature show a cosmic interest in this perfection? Nothing, it may seem, is more determined than the striving of the individual to attain its type. Through all discouragement and obstacles it forces its way to realization of that form which the seed has the sleepless impulse to become. No turning back, no choice of degeneracy, no denial of life's value such as occurs in the human species, "sicklied o'er with the pale cast of thought". It will, so far as nature's force will go, regenerate or remake the lost limb, or invent something that will take its place. But it has also to be noticed that the processes of nature in the environment, though they may be favourable, may also seem to care nothing for the individual or the type.[2] Without taking into account the enormous waste of individuals necessitated in the constitution of living nature by the very laws of life, climatic changes

[1] *Mind and Matter. Teleological Animism.*
[2] "So careful of the type? but no.
    From scarped cliff and quarried stone
    She cries, a thousand types art gone.
  I care for nothing, all shall go."
                    TENNYSON, *In Memoriam*, LVI

H

and many other conditions undermine and cut short the life of the species, and magnificent types of primaeval beings have vanished. If we charge with meaning the life of plant or animal, we must recognize that the worth of their existence is not less subject to contingency than that of man's. According to Cournot, as we have seen, chance asserts itself everywhere in nature as in society. Professor Hans Driesch's highly interesting attempt[1] to trace the principle of "wholeness" (Ganzheit) in all the great orders of nature up to human life, in the end of establishing it as a metaphysical principle, cannot succeed, as he finds, without an appeal to principles not supplied by experience. He concludes that signs of a real evolution, corresponding to that of the growth of the individual to its goal in maturity, cannot definitely be traced within experience either in the development of the species or in history, whether of the animal race or of humanity as a whole.

As regards the credibility of historical teleology, or belief in an immanent principle working in history towards the realization of some great good, experience in modern history provides few phases of event more difficult to interpret from this point of view than the so-called industrial revolution. For this came about at a time when it might have been expected that after the humanitarian rationalistic and cosmopolitan movements of the eighteenth century, mankind would be prepared to use well for the common good the extraordinary new powers which scientific invention put into their hands. Instead of this, a number of conditions which, as we may say acted as blind forces, overwhelmed the movement with factors alien to value, deeply unfavourable to the personal principle. "Unless these new forces could be brought under the control of the common will, the power which was flooding the world with its lavish gifts was destined to become a fresh menace to the freedom and happiness of men."[2] As Drs. J. L. and Barbara Hammond show

[1] *Wirklichkeitslehre*, II, 6, A.
[2] J. L. Hammond and Barbara Hammond: *The Town Labourer*, Chapter I.

in their penetrating analysis of the conditions which made these great new agencies of material civilization for several generations a curse rather than a blessing to the majority, the most formidable was the prevailing system of ideas.[1] "A fatalist view of the condition of the working-classes came to dominate politicians." This resulted mainly from economic theory, the doctrine of "enlightened selfishness", and the Malthusian theory of population. Reference is made to this subject here because the singular fact that the ideas themselves ruling a progressive age may contribute to a retardation in the most important matters, "a catastrophe of civilization", seems on any teleological view a problem of baffling difficulty. The course of the industrial revolution illustrates in a remarkable way the fact to which reference has earlier been made, that with growing freedom in relation to nature man frames new systems to which he may become enslaved in another perhaps more deadly form. But further consideration of this phenomenon belongs to the following chapter. It seems then that the facts of experience whether in nature or in history do not afford sufficient basis for the presence in the course of events of that teleological principle in relation to human valuations which is most contrary to "chance". The variety in events wholly "accidental" in its effect upon value processes, or results, is, at least from our standpoint, limitless. "Everything happens in the lapse of ages"[2] as the first historian discovered, and the events in which we find value must also happen with the rest.

I have set the teleological principle over against chance, because this seems to be at least for what Bosanquet would call "the first look", the greatest opposition in respect to order in a process, relatively to the human point of view. But the disjunction is not exclusive as regards the world as a whole. We are not driven into a world where chance alone rules,

[1] J. L. Hammond and Barbara Hammond: *The Town Labourer*, Chapter X.

[2] Herodotus: *History*, Book E, 9. Rawlinson's translation.

because we have to abandon cosmic and even historic teleology. The personal principle brings with it the demand for a universe in which value can be realized. This fact cannot be explained from any state of affairs from which value was wholly absent. Because value is not already realized except in a low degree, there must be a process towards it. This follows from the principle intrinsic to value that it ought to be, as we know in our consciousness of it. If there were no factors alien to value it would already be fully realized. Again, if the process towards it were universal (teleological principle of the cosmos), the world must have been perfected long ago. From this consideration it is evident that there must be elements hostile or at least alien to value and inexpugnable in the nature of things. But it is not implied that the principle from which value proceeds may not increase to a degree to which limits cannot be set, its control over these alien elements. There appears no theoretic reason excluding this possibility. The chief obstacle lies in the nature of personality itself. As we have seen, it is the source from which disvalue as well as value proceeds. The problem of the greater efficacy of this principle is mainly a problem of freedom. An attempt to consider it in this light will later be made.

There is then a principle in the nature of things superior to chance and independent of this. In theory everything could result from chance with the exception of that principle which could not even flash, like a falling star through a world in which chance alone ruled; the principle of purposive striving to realize value. For once it were admitted that chance could give birth to this no limit could be set to the amount of purpose which might by chance be produced, and a wholly teleological world might one day be the result of chance. Otherwise stated, If we include in the unlimited variety of possible events a single purposive event, we must logically include purposive events of all kinds and degrees, and one such event must at some point occur, which would be a universal purpose. A little grain of purpose admitted into the universe of events whose original nature is chance would in the end transform the character of the whole. Neither could chance come forth from purpose without threatening its intrinsic nature. If then both are present together in a world, their origin must be distinct and they are mutually irreducible.

Spinoza's exclusion of purpose is necessary in a reality which is timeless and eternally perfect. Chance equally with purpose is inconceivable or meaningless in a non-temporal universe. Necessity can be conceived as the nature of the extended timeless substance. Bergson's conception of *le hasard* involves causal temporal sequence and the opposition or crossing of the two kinds of sequence, distinguished by the presence or absence of an element of value. If we conceive the world primarily from the standpoint of universal necessity, the occurrence of value is chance or in the end illusion. Meaning and value are only found by individual selves, and the degree and kind of the value depend upon qualities in the selves which cannot be objectified and included in a system regulated by universal law. The death of a starved man would only signify the result of natural law, and similarly his martyrdom for a cause.

Yet it must not be forgotten that this very concept of natural law would not originate, if it were not for those subjects who introduce all the factors which cannot be interpreted in the abstract formulation of necessary law (which they also introduce). Roses as beautiful roses can never be identical instances, and the differences are unpredictable and indefinable. Nor can love of beauty in the different selves be identical, though the love may be treated as identical for the purpose of organizing protests against ugly advertisements. In the world of necessary law a moment of the process becomes chance (*le hasard*), if as it occurs for the human subject it reverberates in a world of meanings, which may seem everlasting to a continuous succession of selves. The very idea of the eternal world may arise as chance in this sense, for its arising cannot be interpreted from the standpoint of the process alone. The process of things theoretically limitless reveals nothing of the eternal. But this concept is required as soon as the process is transformed into history, for the historic mind demands the eternal once the significance of the transient is perceived. This transience has become tragic for the dramatic view of life, irretrievable for the ethical sense and thus the beginning of remorse and conscience, a beauty which the aesthetic perception cannot save, except by an appeal to the eternal beauty. For knowledge it is an idiot's tale or a wholly inaccessible truth unless thought can find in it universal and enduring principles. But the concept of uniform law to which the activity of the spirit gives birth grows in strength, and since the spiritual process though producing it cannot acknowledge it as supreme in history, history remains outside and appears of small value to those philosophers who find in scientific law a nearer approach to the concrete universal of Hegelianism.

"History is a hybrid form of experience incapable of any considerable degree of 'being or trueness'. The doubtful story of successive events cannot amalgamate with the complete interpretation of the social mind, of art, or religion. The great things which are necessary in themselves become within the narrative contingent, or ascribed by most doubtful assumptions of insight, to this actor or that on the historical stage. The study of Christianity is the study of a great world experience. The assignment to individuals of a share in its development is a problem for scholars, whose conclusions, though of considerable human interest, can never be of supreme importance." Bosanquet therefore regards "Social Morality, Art, Philosophy, Religion", as taking us "far beyond the spatio-temporal externality of history".[1] This is of course an interpretation of history almost wholly contrary to that given in this treatise, since it treats the most important constructions of human experience as though they were objective realities apart from the selves. The reference to Christianity is a remarkable

[1] Bernard Bosanquet: *Principle of Individuality and Value*, Lecture II.

example of this interpretation. Contingency in Bosanquet's sense cannot be avoided since the "great things" cannot be shown to proceed from universal law. Even within its own peculiar province, the broken, mixed and fragmentary character of purpose makes it an uncertain and sometimes deceptive category of interpretation of the individual life. It is not always adequate as a supreme moral category. Hence the doubtfulness of the Aristotelian method, as will be brought out in the ethical section. The view that purpose provides the key to the nature of the ideal in life must not be accepted as more than a hint of the direction in which to look. According to the interpretation which is more in the spirit of Platonism, the good life manifests the presence of the ideal throughout, in all the interconnected series of means and ends (though in my view this would be otherwise expressed). In the special purpose informing any series of deeds, the mode of expression of this ideal is objectified. The inner essence of personality, the strain to transcendence of the limits within which chance, contingency, the alien processes offering hindrances to the realization of value prevail, cannot be sufficiently expressed under the category of purpose, though this is one of its chief practical forms.[1]

[1] See Chapter VII

CHAPTER VI

THE FACTORS OF HISTORY

B

SOME GREAT HISTORICAL CATEGORIES: INSTITUTION, FORCE, ORGANIZATION, NATION AND WAR

History is "an immeasurable, incomparable profusion of always new, unique, and hence individual tendencies, welling up from undiscoverable depths, and coming to light in each case in unsuspected places, and under different circumstances. Each process works itself out in its own way, bringing ever new series of unique transformations in its train, until its powers are exhausted, or until it enters as component material into some new combination."

ERNST TROELTSCH, *Christian Thought*

"No man takes light from his brother till blind at the goal he stands."

ALGERNON SWINBURNE

HISTORY is defined by Seeley as the "life of States".[1] This, as Dr. Gooch observes, is the exclusively political view of history. The individuals who are the sources of history are swept along in the stream of events in which the life of states takes form. This is the great paradox which is discovered by thought upon the life we know in our own experience and contemplate in the record of history. Viewed objectively, in the forms of order which seem to be shaped by events themselves in man's struggle towards civilization and which become categories for historical knowledge, states or nations, institutions, political, social, religious, etc., history acquires a certain intelligibility. At the same time the present activities of individuals, based upon and grouped in these traditional forms, fall into certain types and relations which provide the order, some degree of

[1] Quoted by G. P. Gooch: *Growth of Historical Science, Cambridge Modern History*, Vol. XII, Chapter XXVI.

which is the essential basis for freedom. The kind of rationality which historic actuality thus gains is, as we have seen, imperfect both from the standpoint of the scientific demand for uniform law and from that of the demands of the order of value which seems essential to history in its original nature. The imperfection is due in both cases to the same factor differently conceived according to the difference in the respective ideals of order. The principle of individuality which cannot be admitted into scientific history makes demands upon any form of history which aims at giving it full scope which cannot be fulfilled. History cannot be unrolled as a history of selves in their inner nature and their interrelations. Recorded history is more than this and it is also infinitely less. In the last chapter we examined from various points of view the factors which, together with personal activity constituting the process of events as history, confer upon it that character which appears in one aspect as a kind of necessity (ἀνάγκη) rather than freedom, in another as chance rather than purpose, in another as contingency rather than ordered development according to laws of value. In all aspects we may speak of the presence of the "other", or blind agency in the historic process. The difficulty of any forecast in regard to the possibility of an advance beyond this character which seems inherent in history, an advance namely which is not merely an advance in a single civilization but permanent and general, lies in our inevitable ignorance in regard to that power which must remain the chief source of history, since, if it were less than this, humanity would sink back into the unhistoric existence. Is an increase conceivable both in the power of personality over the alien conditions attendant on its activity and in the capacity to pierce and penetrate to the reality of other persons? An answer to this question will be hazarded at a later stage. In this chapter some consideration will be given to the nature of those great constructions which are, as it were, the *dramatis personae* of large-scale history, growths of man's genius as a maker of history, at once unconscious and conscious, irrational and rational, practically necessitated and intellectually stabilized, proceeding from dynamic sources, but tending to static formation. The most common type of these structures is that of the "Institution". The most important fact about them is that though created by men they become in some respects limitations of freedom. They take the place of individuals in history and mould these in their form. As in the case of primitive man natural conditions, geography, climate and so forth, so at a later phase of development these human or cultural structures dictate to some extent his form of life. But in this case men themselves have forged the engines which are in part their instruments, in part their masters. They have done this urged by an irresistible combination of impulses. The value of the institution depends on the question which of these impulses preponderate. The institution usurps the place of men in major history. Only a small proportion of unusual men seem to equal the institution in the making of history. These men as we see them in history appear in some degree depersonalized, impersonal, though they may be giants in their egoism. Only thus can they meet the institution on its own ground or work with it. Ordinary men and women, however, are required for the activity of the institution, and it is these who are shaped by its forms to the degree in which it becomes the main thing in their lives, so that they are not creative of value outside it. Thus the individuals may be lost in the institutions which they and their predecessors have in fact endowed with life as the coral insects in their reefs.

A brief reference to the effect of institutionalism on the history of the greatest of the movements inaugurated by personal creative force will serve to introduce the problem of the relation of the individual struggle for value to the institutions in which attempts are made to preserve it in enduring form. If we ask whether there has been any instance in history of an event or series of events in which the power of personality as the fundamental historic principle was intensified and displayed in so high a degree that it might reasonably be expected that its supremacy would be established over all irrelevant and

alien forces, the answer must be that if at any time known to
history, this occurred in the beginnings of Christianity.

The greatest attempt at the transformation of history into
an actualization of experience of the highest value in personal
life was made in the introduction of the religion of love. The
only aspect of this subject to which I shall refer as necessary
to our problem is the ethical. I will assume that if what we may
call the absolute ethic has ever been put before humanity,
we may judge from the nature of the Christian teaching that
it is to be found in this. The ideal to which all experience of
selves in their interrelations points was presented with the
greatest possible force, on account of the perfection of the
Founder's life, the incomparable beauty of the teaching, and
the moral genius of the group of His immediate followers.
The problem with which we are concerned is that of the
extraordinary vicissitudes in the history of Christianity in
respect to the central moral ideal of the brotherhood of human
beings. Why was the power of the absolute ethic so comparatively
weak, when it had been given so sublime an opportunity to
work upon human history? It may be said that the answer is
plainly written in any history of Christianity. The beauty of
the life of the early Christian communities on the whole is
well known and has been protrayed by many modern scholars.[1]
But when Christianity was nominally accepted by the Roman
Empire, this acceptance was not real in any spiritual sense.
It did not take place through a moral conversion or transformation of individuals except in a minority of cases. Also
the passions and antagonisms of the men who were making
history, individuals dominated by unlimited craving for power,
semi-barbarian races invading the Empire, together with the
disintegration of the Roman rule, created conditions too unfavourable for the progress of a new moral ideal. Above all
the Christianity that Constantine's Act made into the great
ecclesiastical organization of the Roman world was an institution that already exhibited characteristics alien to the original

[1] Cf. Dobschütz: *Christian Life in the Primitive Church.*

teaching, priestly power and organization, the requirement of exact agreement on dogmas and rites, tendencies to persecution.[1] As regards the ethics of love, this no doubt prevailed in many individual lives. But it is not this which could be actualized in a great institutional organization. Such an organization must inevitably become like other institutions of the world in which it was founded. It is, however, to the profounder problem which remains after such general causes have been cited that we have to draw attention. This is the failure of the greatest moral ideal of history presented with unparalleled power, to bring about a defeat of the alien forces which do always take from the historic process the character of manifesting value in its purity in the conflict with disvalue. "The development", writes Dean Inge, "of the Church into a great political corporation may be explained by historical causes which make it in a sense inevitable. Writers like Loisy have argued that since the Church was compelled either to transform itself in this manner or to perish, and since we must assume that its Founder did not wish it to perish, no further justification is needed for the political methods which were thrust upon it in the struggle for existence. The conditions were not made by the Church, and had to be accepted by it."[2] The Dean observes that this argument begs the question whether the spirit of Christ is permanently incarnated in an institution, a position which could only be upheld if the society *ex hypothesi* divine manifested in its actions the spirit it claimed to embody. His own terrible indictment of the Roman Church reminds us of evils associated with that ecclesiastical organization which have been amongst the worst that mankind has suffered. The religion of love was in name made responsible for horrors of persecution amongst the greatest that have been experienced, including persecution of the mind by threatenings of eternal punishment. Dean Inge speaks of the Inquisition as the most

[1] Cf. Gibbon: *Decline and Fall of the Roman Empire*, Vol. III, Chapter XXI.

[2] *Christian Ethics and Modern Problems*, Chapter IV.

ghastly chapter of human history, but persecution was by no means confined to the Roman Church. He does not allow that "in regarding nearly the whole of Church history as an aberration from the intentions of the Founder" he is "surrendering the citadel". It is not, of course, the purpose of this reference to consider the significance of Church history, but to call attention to the apparent failure to overcome the relativity of all human values to the historic situation even in the case of this sublime presentation of the ethical good. The example is the more impressive because of the depth of the failure, the degree of lapse from its own most exalted virtues of love and pity, shown in official Christianity. The *odium theologicum*, it may be urged, has no portion in true Christianity. But how did it obtain an entrance into institutions created in the process of the Christian movement? This is not a question of historical causes. It is a question that concerns the relation between the spirit of man and his institutions, tested in the most crucial of all cases. According to Loisy, "the conditions were not made by the Church and had to be accepted by it". Here seems to be the fatal limitation of the free movement of a great ideal in men's minds, that which ought to be creative of something new in history. The conditions which have to be accepted bring in the deadly change. Dean Inge reminds us of the long ages to which we may look forward for the nearer approach to the Christian ideal. "Two thousand years are a very short time in the history of humanity." Yet it seems that less than a few hundred years are long enough to show that the Kingdom "that is within you" cannot be founded in history. In the saying that we must "render unto Caesar the things which be Caesar's, and unto God the things which be God's", the Founder of Christianity gave utterance to a great historic truth, and Caesar has continued to be the chief creditor of history. Our ideas and ideals must be enshrined in institutions. This is the grandeur of history, but it is this that produces its chief departure from the presentation in clear outline of the drama of good and evil. Thought is objectified in the institution, but history carries it forward to another age in which another type of thought arises. The institution was to express a set of ideas, to keep them in activity and give their inspiration to the next generation. The splendour of its ordained laws, and regulations for observation, its organized system within which men are to work, each in his appointed place in the traditional spirit of the institution, may be expected to capture the minds of the new age and draw them into the old circle of thoughts. Something of this kind does tend to take place in less or greater degree in the experience of many. The very nature of the self is partly constituted (as we have seen) by memories, some of which may be inseparable from these experiences connected with honoured institutions. Yet it seems also true that the spiritual force and quality of the founders which had its expression in the institution cannot pass on without change to another generation. It may continue to manifest a high energy and vitality, but this proceeds from the spirit of those who follow and are led to find in it a symbol of their own best sources of inspiration which are never identical with those of their predecessors. The essential significance of history cannot therefore lie in the history of institutions any more than the essential life of selves in the operation of these. As already emphasized, all the meaning and reality possessed by institutions is nevertheless contributed to them by the experience and work of selves.

The institution has its symbolism in civilization in the erection of houses and cities, buildings and temples dedicated to and expressive of the effort of man to rise above nature for the purposes of his higher life. The human being belongs to nature, but his potentiality for a greater freedom than nature permits can only be realized through the construction of an environment which he can inform with his own ideas, first in respect to the immediate needs of life, later with reference to other needs that, with the development of individuality, drive him to invent his own forms of living in kind transcending what the natural life can offer. Ideally and essentially the institution does not need a bodily form. It is an ordered set of principles and laws, modes of action and co-working in the mind of a group of persons, expressing an idea or set of ideas. In its proudest development, most crushing to the free soul, it includes set creeds, dogmas. Its objectivity in the Hegelian sense consists in its expression of the mind of a people or a group of peoples. In my view there is no such common mind and will, for the ideas of each member associated with the institution are individually his own. But plans directly realizable as methods of action may be common and regulated by the rules on which all members have determined together. The material edifice adds an influence, partly unconscious, to the force which the institution exercises, or—to speak more exactly—the emotions, thoughts and practical aims which the idea of it stimulates in the minds of its members. It may thus greatly assist in arousing similar ideas in the minds of later generations. Thus the material side of civilization moulds our spirits in some degree in the likeness of that which was its original soul. This is especially so where the constructions of a genius attempting to express the highest in the spirit or ethos of his own age or race possess that beauty which subdues our imagination, suggesting ideals that are greater than our own. The institution having its own material form comes to be animistically contemplated, in the manner suggested in the fourth chapter. It is felt to have a soul, and though this may be other than the soul found in its original construction, it may be no less an object of love and inspiration, no less a historic power sweeping men to deeds of immense effect, good and evil. The significance of the notion, "historic force", will be later considered. The men thus affected may be in ignorance of its meaning which has changed from age to age. "As well might one hope to stop the earth's course in her orbit", wrote Lord Bryce, "as to arrest that ceaseless change and movement in human affairs which forbids an old institution suddenly transplanted into a new order of things from filling its ancient place and serving its ancient ends."[1] The individual, indeed, may suppose himself to be working for, defending, glorying in something that has absolute value, the eternal in the changing, the Imperial Power in the eternal city, when there may remain only the outer semblance, and even this marred and defaced, in which each still finds some idea which appeals to his reverence or his pride. This is in part due to the need to objectify, which obtains some satisfaction when that which is precious in the subject's own intimate experience appears to be reflected in the external form and even perpetuated, so that it can be found again when the first experience seems to have gone beyond recall.

In contrast then with those historical factors which are not only impersonal but in weighty respects unfavourable to the control of circumstance by personality, the institution appears originally as a free creation of personal activity, an instrument fitted to its needs, necessary to the higher life. But not less than those conditions which are in themselves unfavourable to freedom, it may become an oppressive or even tyrannous restraint. The most signal cases of this development occur when a new source of distortion and corruption has entered into it, namely its use not for ends allied to its original purpose but as instrument of the passion for power. In the immense complexity of the strands out of which human history is woven, this motive-force is often inextricably mixed with others even in a single mind, and the institution works for both good and evil. But where it is chiefly used in a conflict for power the evil results of the values on human existence are predominant. The history of the "Holy Roman Empire" as treated by Bryce presents a fine illustration of an interpretation of a phase of history as mainly determined by the dominance, mutual relations and conflicts of institutions, representatives of tremendous ideas, each attempting to control the course of events by means of these. Bryce sets forth a system of ideas which seems to have been constantly growing and decaying

[1] *Holy Roman Empire*, VII.

from the fourth century to the sixteenth.[1] He enquires concerning the influences which made "the empire itself appear through the whole Middle Age not what it seems now, a gorgeous anachronism, but an institution divine and necessary, having its foundations in the very nature and order of things". All that remained to represent the empire of the elder Rome had long perished, only a "turbulent and profligate rabble" the Roman people remained. He finds the explanation in the state of the human mind in those centuries, dominated by the two great ideas which "expiring antiquity bequeathed to the ages that followed—those of a world-monarchy and a world-religion". The Roman dominion had made the first possible, since it destroyed the idea of the necessary diversity of races, and Christianity the second. The idea of the community of all the faithful proceeded from the first lesson of Christianity as love. What seems remarkable from the standpoint of the relation of ideas, the question of their affinity, is that the concept of unity should proceed from that of love, and be enforced by the "growing rigidity of dogma and importance of the sacerdotal order". Tendencies seeming very far from anything that could follow from love are contained in these developments. The historical psychological complex of ideas does not depend on their affinities, whether according to logic or in the order of value. In Bryce's view metaphysics also contributed, realistic theory suggesting the "idea of humanity as a universal being into which all individuals are gathered", as a basis for the doctrine of a universal monarchy. The chief question for us is the effect of such ideas on history. As regards the institutions, the later conflict of Empire and Papacy, with its results for the peoples dragged into the strife, revealed that there was no vital principle of unity drawing individuals together in recognition of each other's personality. The Institutions were not used to express a spiritual principle of first importance by those who made of them instruments for individual ends.

[1] *Holy Roman Empire*, Chapter VII, Note. "Theory of the Mediaeval Empire."

"At no time", again to quote Bryce, "has theory pretending all the while to control practice been so utterly divorced from it . . . there has never been a purer ideal of love nor a grosser profligacy of life." By the ideal of love he means no doubt that enshrined in writings, expressing the Christian principle, and pervading the lives of a few saintly men and women. These are outside the stream of history as history of states and institutions. The figures in the foreground who occupy the stage of history use institutions and other men as means to their own attainment of power and pride of life.

As regards the theory of the institution, we cannot then agree that it is "objective mind" in Hegel's sense. But in a sense it may become an over-self for every one who asks for connection with it. Apart from it he may be a freer personality, but his freedom is indefinite and its efficacy may seem to him infinitesimal. Except for the great creative personality, a life that in the sphere of culture refused the aid of institutions would be as one without the habits of a regulated existence. But entering as member into the life of an institution, the individual suffers as it were its brain to dominate his own, and present the thoughts and feelings on which he has to act. Its brain seems to contain the ideas of those who originated it. Yet those ideas have changed with time, and a member now taking an important part in its activities will accelerate the change in proportion to the value or force of the thoughts he brings to it. Most favourable examples of this are seen in the history of educational institutions, when the new-comer feels himself to enter into a tradition to which the ideas and work of a succession of personalities have given value, as in a college or school. Although the good felt by the last new student cannot be identical with that discovered by his predecessor, there is a continuity of value due to the peculiar character of the educational ideal in its true form, stimulating those who perceive it to appeal to the essential self in all individuals with whom they have to do. The best type of educational institution is thus near to the kind of Utopia in which the

personal principle has, so to speak, a free field, with least
hindrance from those alien factors in history which have been
discussed. This is because it is partly abstracted from the
concrete stream. But that even ·here these factors enter in
and mingle with the purely personal will probably be agreed.

Newman's curious doctrine of the Angels of Institutions
gives a vivid expression to his view of their mixed character.
He considered that there was a "Middle race of spirits, δαιμόνια
—partially fallen, capricious, wayward; noble or crafty,
benevolent or malicious, as the case might be. They gave a
sort of inspiration or intelligence to races, nations and classes
of men." Thus he explains why the actions of bodies politic
and associations is often so different from that of the individuals
who compose them. States and governments, religions, communities and communions "were inhabited by unseen intelli-
gences".[1] His method of accounting for the factors which
interfere with the real progress of the institution, even though
its individual members may be progressing, is simpler than that
which I have attempted. The notion of beings with a great
deal of good in them, yet with great defects, who are the animating principles of certain institutions, seems to over-simplify
the problem of the obstacles to the spiritual history of a movement or the production of the intrinsic value at which it aims,
which often seem inherent in the attachment to an institution.
It is to be noted that the insistence of the Tractarians on the
separation between Church and State (or their opposition to
Erastianism) may be taken to express the belief in the possibility
of a purely spiritual institution. In my view it is impossible
from the nature of the institution as such that it should express
in purity the creative activity of a spiritual principle. This
seems to be confirmed with overwhelming evidence by history.

Institutions are at times characterized as historic forces,
and the significance of this category demands consideration.
The subject of the historic proposition, it may be argued,
must be dynamic, if there is to be understanding of historic

[1] *Apologia pro Vita Sua.*

knowledge as a form distinct from that which is in general regarded as scientific in the strict sense. For it has to be shown how in this field events can be understood to succeed one another through relations which cannot be analysed into relations of like kind with those of the sciences whose ideal is the static system. The notion of force seems then required to provide the relation. Accordingly our historic world is by some conceived as though it were largely at least a theatre of forces, which determine events and profoundly affect human deeds, whether as immanent in these, or externally compelling, or as powers against which the individual struggles. In his study of Lord Acton, Bryce thus describes a discourse of Acton's, expounding his idea of a history of liberty. "The eloquence was splendid, but greater than the eloquence was the penetrating vision which discerned through all events and in all ages the play of those moral forces, now creating, now destroying, always transmuting, which had moulded and remoulded institutions, and had given to the human spirit its ceaselessly changing forms of energy."[1] Bryce himself speaks of "This roaring loom of Time, these complex physical and moral forces playing around us, and driving us hither and thither by such a strange and intricate interlacing of movements that we seem to perceive no more than what is next to us, and are unable to say whither we are tending."[2] In these passages we probably find a description of something not far from vivid impressions we have ourselves received in the reading of history or directly in the experience of our own times. International problems of many unpredictable forms, unforeseen economic entanglements, vast numbers of men asking for work, which is more and more being performed by non-human instruments— are these phenomena produced by "forces" whose operation is ill-understood, since they have not been willed by men, and are yet of incalculable human significance? Must they not be due to some active power like that of man, but greater and impersonal? The origin of the notion of force seems to be in

[1] *Biographical Studies*, pp. 396–7.   [2] Ibid., pp. 156–7.

our own inner experience. Acton's notion of forces which had moulded institutions and "given to the human spirit its ceaseless forms of energy" seems therefore an inversion of the truth, unless our view requires reinterpretation in the light of a greater or wider truth. All lines of our argument converge on the result that force originates in and proceeds from a person. This does not exclude the conceivability of a supreme personality, source of all historic forces. But the character of history seems to preclude this interpretation, unless such a supreme origin of these supposed agencies is to be thought of as working irrationally from our standpoint (an intolerable paradox) or to wholly unknowable ends. A different significance is given to the term force in Mr. and Mrs. Hammond's vivid presentation of the growing sense of the labourers in the Industrial Revolution of impersonal forces working against them.[1] Force must pass from the living to the living. But the feeling of impersonality was a true reaction to the fact that the agents in a sense worked blindly, not foreseeing or desiring all the results of the series of events they set going. It may be said that their own personality was not in the action. They did not know as selves the persons on whom the organization would take effect. Thus the conception of "forces" for those students of history who have made use of it includes at one extreme the moral or rational power, employing the efforts and aims of men for greater ends than those to which they were consciously directed. At the other it suggests a blind or senseless agency which they may dimly feel to be hostile. In Acton's view some objective power acting upon men from a transcendental source would seem to be implied. Bryce's words give eloquent expression to the sense that men are not freely facing issues they can comprehend, whilst yet the struggle is no mean one. His language is vague and might be interpreted in accordance with the view of the dualism of events. A realistic facing of the facts seems to point to a more subjective interpretation of the idea of historic force than that implied by Acton. It cannot be given a foothold in

[1] *The Town Labourer.*

history except as an experience of selves, whom we may conceive as driven by forces in so far as desires, passions, fears which lead to action are aroused in them. It is natural to attribute the moving power or force to the object or institution which serves as stimulus of the emotion or desire, and the instinct seems a true one if the source of the stimulus is another self. When a writer speaks of the forces of the modern world, in their effect on a primitive race,[1] these forces include all that system and manner of life which are introduced through commerce and travellers, the arrival of articles procuring new pleasures, Western education, mechanical devices, etc., which belong to institutions of a more advanced civilization. The force seems more precisely to signify the stir of mind and feeling, the new ideas and disturbance of traditional points of view which result.

It may be held with qualification that the concept of forces moral and a-moral is a category of value in objective history. It originates in the inner experience of the self and corresponds to something actual. But detached from its origin, abstracted as a cosmic entity, it is a fabrication of the historic understanding, an aid to intelligibility, belonging to the content of history only in a secondary sense.

In a striking passage of his *Realm of Ends*, the late James Ward admits the difficulty which arises on the pan-psychist interpretation of the world-process, on account of what he designates as "physical hindrances". In these would seem to lie the chief obstacles to overcoming the dualism of the spiritual or personalistic and the naturalistic types of event. These physical hindrances, in Ward's view, consist in the "actions of inferior—sentient it may be—but still irrational monads. The disaster would be none the less appalling on that account, nor is its possibility for that reason seriously diminished".[2] A parallel but even greater problem arises within human

[1] Margaret Perham: "Nigeria To-day." Article in *The Times*, December 29, 1932.
[2] *Realms of Ends*, Lecture X.

history in regard to the dualism, not of personal activities and the hindrances of the phenomenally material world, but of the purely personal principle and the principle of organization which man has himself created, which belongs to the structure he rears for his environment above the structures of nature. These organizations at times seem to combine the nature of the blind or "senseless" factor in history with that of the intelligent and purposeful, just because they embody intelligence directed to a special instrumental service abstracted from the concrete vital movement they are intended to subserve. On this account they are liable to action devoted to their own subordinate end, detached from the vital developing needs of the whole. They become in fact machines, the peculiar material creation of practical man, intended to be the perfect instrument of his purposes. They work on their own path, according to necessity, their relation to human activities borrowed, so to speak, from the methods of natural law, but fixed, without possibility of variation whether beneficent or maleficent. They are therefore prone to behave in a more purposeless way than the things of nature, if for a moment the overruling purpose of the whole system to which they belong vacillates or flags. An extraordinary example of this type of event is supplied in Mr. Winston Churchill's account of the circumstances immediately leading to the Great War. I am here hazarding an interpretation of his interpretation. In a brilliant passage he shows how the point was reached at which the prescribed war plans of the German and Russian Empires and the execution of the successive stages of their mobilization became the overpowering theme in both countries. In fact, whilst the main issue, the question whether or not war must follow, was still under discussion, and therefore the ultimate end for which the military organizations existed did not yet demand the successive movements of the machines, the perfection of the machine dominated in the circumstance of the imperfection of the purpose it was to serve. "Military reasons cut across and dominated every diplomatic situation. Immense efforts were made, led by Sir Edward Grey, to retrieve the situation. But none could regain control of the purely technical measures which the leaders of armies demanded and took. A situation had been created where hundreds of officials had only to do their prescribed duty to their respective countries to wreck the world. They did their duty."[1] For James Ward's action of irrational monads, we have the action of rational beings as members of an organization not free to use their full reasoning powers. The organization must trust for its highest reason to a personality or personalities beyond. This is necessary for its utility. If these fail, its action for the very reason that it is half-intelligent may be pregnant with a more positively irrational product than that of the force of nature. Where the human brain has provided the forms of behaviour, the result, if not guided by higher intelligence, may be comparable to the effect of madness. The natural force is not insane.

Organization is an essential category of objective history, for it is necessary to the state, and in some degree to all individuals as members of the state. Mechanism in which appeal cannot be made to the whole intelligence of the members is its danger or even disease, but does not appear an essential or leading aspect of the higher organization. The gift for practical organization on a great scale is exercised by the statesman of genius. He creates as it were new frameworks within which the lives and personal activities of men can move, whether with more success in the business of frictionless living or on a higher plane for the personal infusion of meaning and worth into experience. Both in the theoretic and the practical sphere the category-giving intelligence works through classification, or the grouping of the terms or individuals, by their external relations. Individuals enter into the systems constituted by practical genius for the better ordering of a community, in virtue of the significance of their function in the organization. The practical genius of the more ordinary type is fascinated

[1] *The World Crisis*, "The Eastern Front".

by the system, its adequacy for the fulfilment of a certain purpose, its success in making the members perfect instruments for that purpose, by abstraction from all their characters except those that are relevant. The greatest practical genius, however, has and retains an insight into the uniqueness of the individual members. He cannot lose sight of their peculiar differences. He knows that the men are more than the organization. The lack of this insight prevents the greatest organizing work from attaining its highest value. Thus Napoleon did not realize his soldiers as personalities, as is evident in many incidents of his career. Of him Mme de Staël said: "He neither hates nor loves, for him no one exists but himself, all other people are merely number so and so. A great chess-player, for whom humanity at large is the adversary he hopes to check-mate."[1] In Egypt he yearned for the power of the ancient ruler, "whose dreams were fashioned by his slaves with their myriad feet".[2] Similarly his grandiose schemes for the reorganization of nations were not guided by understanding of the true nature of these peoples. Dr. Gooch points out that the reaction of the Germans from Napoleon's experiments in remaking the map of Europe showed itself especially in the new impetus to interest in their own history, together with nationalism.[3] With regard to Alexander of Macedon's attempt to realize the unity of mankind—if, as Dr. W. W. Tarn argued with immense learning in his British Academy Lecture,[4] it is to Alexander that this idea, wholly original in his historic epoch, owed its origin—from what is known of his career he seems to have possessed that understanding of the reality of other selves which was lacking in Napoleon. We may note that he appears to have experienced that true affection in friendship which the enormity of his egoism made impossible for Napoleon. Thus the non-Greeks for the first time ceased

[1] Quoted by Emil Ludwig: *Napoleon.* [2] Ibid.
[3] *The Growth of Historical Science. Cambridge Modern History*, Vol. XII.
[4] Raleigh Lecture, 1933: *Alexander of Macedon and the Unity of Mankind.*

to be "barbarians" to the Greek.[1] Once more the truth that the organizing genius is incomplete, and will fail of the highest success, unless to the intelligence which can group, classify, arrange the moving map of humanity in such wise that the linked men as pawns will perform the most admirable evolutions, is added the mind that is aware of the individual, is again illustrated in the history of Louis XIV. This monarch, "the best actor of majesty that ever filled a throne",[2] showed high gifts for practical reorganization. But in later years, in addition to his growing lust for territorial aggrandisement, "more sinister was his deeper superstition and his ever-increasing anxiety to be master, not merely of the goods and bodies of his subjects, but of their consciences and souls".[3] Thus, since he was aware of his subjects only as tools in the fabrication of his own power, or automata with brains into which his own dogmas might be forced, the life departed from his organizing schemes.

As was suggested in the last chapter in the reference to the early course of the industrial revolution, the most tyrannical of the organizations which man creates for the achievement of his own advancement in civilization may be the organization of an ideal system, ideas and beliefs about the powers, resulting from unchanging laws of his own being, physical, psychical, moral, which have to be reckoned with in his life and social arrangements. Just as the inner, spiritual force from which ideas arise is the strongest thing in the selves and inseparable from their creative function, so the ideas it produces and objectifies, if they are not continually renewed and in so far as imperfect transformed, may be the source of a slavery, the greater because it is unconscious in those who are the chief believers. In the case of the industrial system, the workers who were the sufferers from it, and most oppressed, were in a sense less enslaved to the ideas which upheld it, because

[1] Cf. D. G. Hogarth: *Alexander of Macedon.*
[2] *Bolingbroke*, quoted by J. R. Marriott.
[3] J. R. Marriott: *The Evolution of Modern Europe.*

either ignorant of these or not accepting them. "The fatalist view of the condition of the working-classes came to dominate politicians—the educated classes built up an edifice of gloomy error."[1] In *The Town Labourer* it is shown that "Neither Malthus nor Ricardo really taught the dogmatic despair which was generally received as the lesson of their philosophies. . . . Their ideas when adopted by other minds hardened into a rigid and inexorable theory . . . that was a stubborn barrier to all social agitation."[2] It is obvious that such a system of ideas may be far more obstinately intrenched than a tyrant in his passionate selfishness who appeals only to physical, not to intellectual forces. The peculiar importance of this type of human construction for our subject is in its illustration of the truth that the blind factors in human history may partly proceed from the minds of men themselves. If there could be banished from the process of events all that we have discussed under chance—the casual, the contingent in the guise of concurrence of circumstances and movements irrelevant to each other, or in the environment of nature— there remain in the very sanctuary of history the creative mind itself, possible sources of impediment to freedom in human progress.

The direction in which we may look for a solution of the problem in this most insidious aspect seems again to be in the truth that progress in a world of persons can only be through the work of the whole person, recognizing the reality of his fellows, and their freedom, not as "number so-and-so", not as factory worker alone, or living being subject to implacable law. It would appear that a similar state of affairs in respect to the rule of fixed ideas has been illustrated in Russia, for a period of years sufficient for reference, though the outcome is not yet determined. In this case, however, the system of ideas has evidently been inculcated in the majority not so much by appeals to theory as by methods of enforcing acceptance,

[1] J. L. Hammond and Barbara Hammond.
[2] Ibid., Chapter X. "The Mind of the Rich."

which even on the hypothesis that they are entirely psychological resemble in type those of physical force.

"What really appalled me was the absence of human friendship, of simple human relations to which I had been accustomed. Formerly when you met others of your kind, you spoke to them spontaneously; if you were sad they sympathized with you; if they suffered you condoled with them. In the madhouse in which I was now living I found that there was a complete lack of natural feeling. Day by day life was growing more official, more egocentric. Even my own home was becoming a sort of 'administrative department', although I do not know how it came about."[1] I have quoted this passage, which expresses the feeling which would be especially keen in an artist, because, simple as it is, it hints at what is from the present point of view a standpoint and condition of society most hopeless for amelioration, showing the denial of personality and personal relations. To the artist mind the world without personality was a "madhouse". The beings who go about in fear of open speech, in anxiety whether their actions will be misinterpreted, not daring to utter to each other their inmost thoughts, do not live in a personal world, they perceive outer shells of their fellows, not their true selves. "This was the sort of thing", writes Chaliapin, "that froze and deadened our souls, laid waste our hearts, and sowed the seeds of despair in the minds of all." The economic effects of the Soviet system are irrelevant to the present problem. Also the question whether the institution of economic communism in itself in any way excludes the possibility of a society developing a high form of culture and of social relations.[2] I am only referring to an instance of communism as a system which aims at standardizing thought, destroying its individuality and freedom, and imposing a set of ideas or dogmas. Such systems may be observed in history as having at the best consequences unfavourable to the finer manifestations of the human spirit, at the worst

[1] Feodor Chaliapin: *Man and Mask*, *Memoirs*, Chapter XXII.
[2] Logically such exclusion does not appear necessary.

deadening to these. But is it possible for mankind to escape them? Do we not always live under them, with imprisoned souls, even when we suppose ourselves to have attained freedom, as did the most sincere believer of the nineteenth century in unmitigated *laissez-faire*? Possibly we are touching on the first and last problem of human history, which—according to some authoritative descriptions—begins in the painful labour of the savage to fulfil the thousand and one imperatives which his unpractised brain discovers as embodying demands of the mysterious beings who control his life. The greatest question of history would then be whether it points to a final release from slavery to the systems of ideas to which the mind gives birth, and a free attitude over against them. Further reflection on this question must be postponed.[1]

Let us turn to what would be regarded by many as the greatest of organizations—if it is an organization. The idea of the nation appears to stand alone. It is more than the organization, both in its necessity and in its significance, more than the institution in its roots, more than both in its power and its ideal. From the standpoint of this book it must in the first place be asked, Are we to conceive a national movement as a movement whose energy and spirit are the energy and spirit of many selves, co-operating as friends, possessing interests, experiences and standpoints which are closely similar in many broad aspects of life? Or must a power so strong as this proceed from a source which is one in its wholeness? Are we driven to believe in an over-personal being active in history when we follow the course of any such division of peoples as the British, for instance, or the French? We may observe the manner in which free institutions came gradually into being in England and ask, What is the true meaning of the historian's observation that—"In England—the national will found expression in a parliament"? In France "King and people found in the feudal noble a common foe".[2] Or of the active

[1] See Chapter X.
[2] *The Evolution of Modern Europe*, Chapter III, "The Making of Nations".

part played in some at least of the great events of European
history, by peoples who feel themselves to be striving for some
ensouled principle greater than they. Are we not confronted
with movements which would not have been initiated and
carried through had not each participant been conscious
of some super-personal unity working in him and his fellows?
Such an admission would not seem consistent with the standpoint of this work, or only to be made so by the assumption
of a great and powerful illusion at work in all such cases. I
do not propose here to examine those theories of a "general
will", or a national personality which imply a real being in
the union of the selves, thus named. We must, however, here
enquire whether the most important facts of which the core
lies in the idea of the nation can be seen to be consistent with
a conception of the co-operation of selves never absorbed in
any oversoul. Is it possible on these lines to explain such a
phenomenon as the exaltation or enthusiasm in which all
the individuals concerned may seem to enter into a new life,
and momentarily at least to be hardly conscious of vivid
separate existence? Can this be interpreted to signify only the
intense, individual emotion and striving of each, deeper,
keener, because he has fellow-workers intimately akin in
feeling and aim?

> "Draw near together; none be last or first.
> We are no longer names, but one desire;
> With the same burning of the soul we thirst,
> And the same wine to-night shall quench our fire."
> HENRY NEWBOLT, *Mukden, 1905*

This represents an experience that cannot be ignored. What
does it mean? It would be strange if that heightening of the
emotional being which carries with it intensification of the
striving nature, rendering the individual capable of efforts
beyond all he has previously found possible, should be at
the same time a sinking and loss of the self, the one being
that can creatively act because of thought and feeling. Are
we not liable to be confused and misled in our interpretation

of the extraordinary experience in which the last vestige of
egoism seems gone from our emotions, and "selflessness" is
complete? Selflessness does not imply negation of the self,
but the fading away of all divisions produced by separate
interests and wants. The mystical experience of pure contemplation is distinct from what is here considered. The way to
a right interpretation of these facts does not, I think, lie in a
denial of a special character in the experience distinguishing
it not only in degree, but in kind from more ordinary experiences
of co-operation. Some aid is afforded by the distinction which
has been insisted upon between the reality of selves as subjects
in their essential uniqueness in original experience and their
place in history viewed objectively, the established form of
historic knowledge, shareable by all minds. For the purposes
of history thus conceived the national being must be taken as
one of the most important categories, at least in the modern
world. And the individual student of history, since his attitude
to history cannot be purely theoretic, his knowledge being
knowledge in which the knower is himself active in a historic
process, strongly inclines to impute to this concept of the
nation something found in his own current, so to speak, of
ideal selfless experience, his love of other selves in the present
and admiration of those of the past. Thus arises the idea of
an objective being most worthy of love, and capable of action
which will increase the bonds of love in the community or
organized society. Thus the nation, comprehending all such
ties and interpersonal values, source of a unique kind of fellowship, is posited, as direct result of certain experiences, combined
with historic knowledge. It symbolizes numberless facts which
emerge in life and action together and are difficult to express
simply with precision. The realities which it appears to express
proceed primarily, however, from history. In the first place,
each member of a society of selves is a self in virtue of the
passage of past into present experience, and continuing to
belong to his past finds in memory other selves inseparable
from this, meeting them as though he could directly enter

into their remembered past. Secondly, he is both as emotional and as cognitive being constrained to construct the past beyond memory on a similar type, as consisting in a long process of the succession of selves in their activity intimately interrelated. On account of these experiences it is that the national community seems to possess so great a reality. To the unity of the historic basis many other factors contribute, affecting imagination and life, place, language, institutions, culture, etc. Thus the historic bond seems the most important source of the reality of the nation. But since as an entity it only belongs to the objective view of history, since there can be no unity of a national subject, and all that content and value which each subject contributes to it he contributes as individual, the category does not possess ultimate reality.[1] That it is not inseparable from human experience in this form is evident from the course of history. The idea of the nation as we know it has not existed for any great length of time, though other types of community have in some degree occupied its place in former ages, as would be expected from the importance of that historical principle which is certainly one of its chief sources. The idea of our country, J. R. Green's idea of England, for instance, seems to be a vision of some supreme good, objectified from its source in innumerable subjective experiences of high value. As such it takes on the character of a Platonic idea or form of value possessing a similar beauty or power. From the feeling in Rupert Brooke's sonnet *The Soldier* arises the same ideal.

But the national idea certainly has not worked on men's minds, so as to affect the course of events always as a pure value, and it seems necessary to go into its roots from a somewhat different standpoint. Ought we not, it may be said, to conceive the tremendous force of this principle, especially in its more sinister effects, as resulting from ultimately biological factors made more powerful by the sympathy, imagination, etc., which are human dispositions? Is it necessary to point to the

[1] Cf. T. H. Green: *Prolegomena to Ethics*, Book III, Chapter II.

presence in man of a self-activity underivable by evolution from the nature of all living things? There is nothing, it might be argued, in the high development of the sympathy and imagination exhibited in the national idea, and already fore-shadowed in animal qualities, which is not explicable through the increased capacity of the brain. I shall maintain, however, that the immense historic significance and efficacy of the idea of the nation results from the following facts.

It is the meeting-point of two principles, the one transcendental, the other empirical. The emotion which is felt in the consciousness of similarity in points of view, feelings, thoughts, attitude to life, culture and ideals is projected, as we have argued, into the idea of the nation. The special nation itself becomes an object of value; this value seems to be immanent in every individual member. A feeling akin to love may be aroused for each one as representative of the nation, at least in times of keen national consciousness, when all the contributory currents of emotion are at their height. The passions of life, self-preservation, inseparable from preservation of the tribe, prompt the desire for solidarity, unity. This is the lower side. In respect to the social impulses of this kind, it is easy to argue that some common force, universal in the group, the tribe, the race, dependent on our nature as living beings holds together all the members. Is there not here a basis for mass-psychology? There are many phenomena difficult to interpret without admitting something like a "herd-instinct", though we may agree with the late Graham Wallas that "the co-operative action of men in society is due not (as the early Darwinian sociologists supposed) to simple and mechanical instincts of Imitation, or Sympathy, or Suggestion, but to the stimulation in each human being, by his relation to his fellow-men, of many varied and interacting dispositions".[1] The "herd-instinct" does not cease to be the instinct of an individual. Graham Wallas recognizes, however, "the peculiar exaltation of feeling and action which is caused by the sensible presence

[1] *The Great Society*, Part I, Chapter IX.

K

of large numbers of our fellows".[1] This peculiar exaltation appears to me (though I do not think he would have agreed) to be due certainly in part to the causes analysed by the social psychologist, but in part or at times also to causes dependent on the transcendent nature of the self, enabling that peculiar consciousness of the reality of other selves to which reference has been made. When we observe or study accounts of human beings in a panic, and turn from these to the observation of a number of men in unison "as one man" volunteering for a difficult or dangerous task in the saving of life, we feel that the interpretations required by these two types of common action are different in kind. It seems reasonable to admit different principles at work upon men, in "common" movements, the one arising out of laws of the higher animal world, the other out of the essential principle of personality. The higher national principle does not infringe upon the free creativity of persons. They may willingly subordinate or sacrifice themselves to a purpose similar for all in a seemingly identical spirit which is in reality, however, individual in each.

The distinction suggested, even though it allows of the presence in the same action of both principles, the ideal or spiritual and the biological-racial, is probably too sharp, and requires the qualification that always in humanity there is the potentiality of the personal principle, and that it may be present in a "common" action, in which no trace of individuality is evident, and the social psychologist supposes himself to be observing a mass of men whose behaviour he can liken to that of a swarm of bees, or an ant-hill, a favourite simile for some social thinkers. Further light may be thrown on this aspect of the problem by a brief reference to historic groupings other than that of the nation. Sir Alfred Lyall, in his account of the *Formation of Some Clans and Castes in India*, writes of the forms, remote from those of Western Civilization, in which principles connected by us with such names as "fatherland, mother-country, patriotism, domicile", are dimly suggested.

[1] *The Great Society*, Part I, Chapter VIII.

The European observer does not meet with "great governments, nationalities, religious dominations, widespread races", but "various and manifold denominations of tribes, clans, septs, castes and sub-castes, religious orders, and devotional brotherhoods". Lyall thought that he had found here the survival of a very rudimentary state of society.[1] A Rajput chief would introduce himself by naming clan and branch, family and lineage, going back to an eponymous ancestor. The question of the state to which he belonged would be a far less important matter. Here the historical thread is all-in-all.

In a strongly contrasting case a boy might be noticed by the roadside who, an orphan handed over to a religious mystic, acknowledged no ties except that of his fraternity. No other account of him is required. It is "the combination and crossing of two fundamental ideas, Race and Religion", which "have worked out in India, perhaps the most singularly complicated pattern of society that exists anywhere". From the point of view taken in this book, the chief question which arises here concerns the part played by the mind of the individual in weaving these principles into the forms in which they become great values, of immense efficacy in the history of humanity. The answer must remain speculative. In some accounts of human progress a chasm seems to be left unfilled between the ages in which forces only biological in kind govern the behaviour of the group, sympathy, loyalty, etc., being interpreted as social forces necessary to its survival, and the age in which the bond of race has become a great idea for good and ill. The latter state has evolved from the former, but how the later spirit emerged is unexplained. According to our interpretation of the relation of the self to historic development, the value of the higher experience is potentially present wherever there are selves, conscious of each other as selves. Here there is the capacity for free or self-originating activity, though it may

[1] *Asiatic Studies*, First Series, Chapter VI, written after Lyall had become acquainted with Rajputana, "a country possessing a very rare and antique stratification of society" (1882).

not yet be exercised. From the surveys of the customs of
primitive races presented by Sir James Frazer, we often gain
an impression of behaviour so predominantly controlled by
fear that small scope would remain for the exercise of individual
self-prompted activity. A different interpretation is made
possible by Dr. R. R. Marett, who conceives the religion of
the savage as biologically a manifestation of the will-to-live,
and hope as "the prevailing tone in religious feeling".[1] Terrorism
is always a morbid symptom.[2] Also he points out that there is
something which proceeds from man's own consciousness.
"The other animals just live; but man has superfluous energy
enough to say to himself as he lives 'Here I am living'."
Throughout his analysis of the motives in which primitive life
and action finds its inspiration Dr. Marett presents us with
individuals. We are not confronted with men merely as members
of a group. Whether they hope, or fear, or educate their youth
by the harsh discipline of initiation, or insist on severe preparation by austere and fearful rites, before an individual may be
set aside and entrusted with the function of guarding sacred
lore they have spiritual qualities, they are not without vision.
Considering the custom of savages, to huddle together, "it is
somewhat amazing that in the mechanism of social institutions
elaborate provision should be made for those in need of a time
of spiritual retreat".[3] This view opens the way to a dispelling
of the mystery of the beginnings of value in its higher forms.
It is already present in the ideas that dominate primitive
human life, the early stages of culture. The individual is at
work, interpretations of experience proceed from men as
individuals, not from the mass as a group imposing ideas,
whose origin as ideas seems unintelligible. Also the possibility
need not be excluded that in all cases of the development of
custom and law in primitive history there has been active
from time to time in the long process the influence of the

---

[1] *Faith, Hope, and Charity*, Chapter II, "Hope".
[2] Ibid., Chapter III, "Fear".
[3] Ibid., Chapter III, "Curiosity".

unusual or extraordinary individual. "To borrow Carlyle's words", says Lyall, "the perplexed jungle of primitive society springs out of many roots, but the hero is the prime source out of which in a great degree all the rest were nourished and grown." "It may be difficult to overrate the impression", he adds, "that must have been produced by daring and successful exploits in the primitive world."[1] Lyall's profound study of Hindu religion convinced him of the immense part played in past and present by the feeling for the impressive personality in all the diverse forms of popular Hindu belief. For he noticed the religious genius of the Hindus, both in its more advanced and more simple manifestations in his own experience, continually creating new forms, but always preserving this intense consciousness of the significance of personality, the religious leader, seer, mystic, the astonishing individual who was deified even in contemporary history.

The roots of history as "the life of states" may be found in the groupings of men by race and religion. These primal categories are not merely constructs for the objective interpretation of history, they have their origin in a stratum of experience which affords material for the higher history. These groupings are already human, and something to which the name of personality may be given has been at work in conveying to them their essential quality. There are also foreign impersonal factors belonging to the element which is "other". These seem originally to predominate. The beginning of history is not, however, merely a struggle for life amongst groups who gradually develop some self-regulation, blindly striving for social preservation, but from the first other principles of explanation seem demanded. An important fact on which Lyall's treatment of the bonds of race and religion throws much light is that here, where these are all-powerful in determining the groupings, we find a system which is in certain respects preparatory for later ages of national history. It must, however, be remembered, as already indicated, that we are not entitled

[1] *Asiatic Studies*, First Series, Chapter VI.

to assume that the national principle and category is more intrinsic to history than that of the city-state or any other form of association in which numbers of men have found a principle for a historic process in which they all acknowledge certain regulations of life, institutions and ideals, and share similar standards, views and purposes in relation to conduct in various matters important to all. It is evident that if our contention in regard to the presence of higher elements in the national idea is justified, history in relation to this must take a different course in the future. These higher elements would bear witness that in national life, especially on account of its historic basis, certain values of personal relationship and activity were best expressed. Yet the value of personal relations has been in one great aspect of history ignored and denied in these modern times in which the national principle has grown strong, not less perhaps even more than in ages in which other forms of the grouping of peoples were in the ascendant. "The national spirit", says Sir Philip Gibbs, "is less generous than the individual, more greedy for wealth at the expense of its neighbours, more intolerant of criticism, less inclined to charity, and totally destitute of any sense of humour."[1] The difficulty of estimating the part which has been played in modern history by the national idea, of striking the balance between the value of its effects in the sphere of culture amongst the several nations and the immense disvalue of the rivalries of peoples which it has stimulated, is partly due to the great complexity of the elements which constitute it. There are its origins in the groupings of race and religion, the ideal qualities contributed by the personal principle, the forces alien to this proceeding from the barely human factors determining mass movements, the blind instinct and desire to feel, think and do like all other members of the tribe. If we consult works on modern history, we find that the larger portion of the period, say between 1453 and 1932, may be treated by the political historian almost

[1] *Ways of Escape*. Quoted in Review in *Sunday Observer*, March 26, 1933.

entirely as a history of wars, the preludes to these, and their
results on those aspects of life which seem open to the gaze
of the student of history. There have been wars in which all
the factors we have indicated as combining to produce the
national idea have been concerned, including that which was
called transcendental. But a feature inevitably qualifying the
state of mind engendered by war is a loss of the sense of the
reality of selves in the opposing peoples, as this sense or conviction has been earlier described. The almost perpetual
occurrence of wars and dread of their recurrence, the conditions
which make this possible, seem indeed to present a threatening
difficulty affecting the whole philosophy of the selves in history.
We may advert to the argument (in Chapter III) that direct
knowledge of other selves in their qualities and their ultimate
nature is impossible, and that this truth, which can be understood from inspection of the nature of selves, is abundantly
confirmed by history. Knowledge, however, that other selves
exist is direct and implicit in consciousness of self. The greatest
prophets and teachers of practical ethics have striven to arouse
in individuals such knowledge of the qualities and inner being
of other selves as would be the salvation of the world, working
for this through all the avenues which lead to the kind of
knowledge which though necessarily indirect is full of life,
a function of the complete person. The view that in times of
war the members of the nations engaged are blind to the
personality of their opponents, I find to be in striking agreement
with Max Scheler's view expressed in the following passage:

"Why is death in war (and in duelling) no murder? In the
case of death in war, in the first place the person is absent.
The person is not given in that being who is called the enemy.
Only as a member of the collective being 'the enemy', a complex
of vital power, is the individual given. The foreign state may
be object of hate, of vengeance, and so forth, but not a person
belonging to it."[1] There is a play, L'homme j'ai tué, in which
the shattering effect on a soldier, of sudden realization of the

[1] *Der Formalismus in der Ethik*, Teil II, V, 6, (c).

personality of the man he has struck down, is expressed with singular insight.[1] The soldier devotes his life to an effort to make atonement. What then the interpretation has to explain is the staggering fact that history, and here in particular national history, which in its essence is constituted by the meaning which persons bring to it, yet consists to so great an extent of events in which the value or even the fact itself of personality is by implication denied. It must be granted that the conception of blindness to personality seems to imply the feebleness of the principle, if not in the vision of meaning and value, at least in the power of this vision to work upon the events. The weakness of personal deeds, the preponderating influence of the alien factors in the course of events, and even within the deed itself, produce that impression which Newman characterized as one "to dizzy and appal". One might reflect on the problem on the lines of Thomas Huxley in his Romanes Lecture.[2] Better perhaps from our standpoint than his parable which contrasts nature in the wild untamed forest, in which the forces of evolution by natural selection were unchecked, with the gardener's little plots protected from the fierce competition of the stronger plants, would be a parable distinguishing between sheltered and unsheltered waters in the stream of history. Our ethical and philosophical interpretations of human existence as a "vale of soul-making", a scene for the conflict of good and evil, the manifestation of personality, the achievement of freedom, and so forth, would be appropriate to the comparatively quiet pools, formed by jutting-out rocks at favourable points in the turbulent river. But the dominating type of history would be found in the main torrent, raging past and over all impediments, and from time to time drawing the partly sheltered waters into its current. The principles, moral laws and ideals set up for the community as in the tranquil secluded pools would then be swept away. So Thucydides in his famous reflections on the horrors of revolution, engraved in unforgettable strokes the

---

[1] Maurice Rostand, translated by R. Berkeley.
[2] *Ethics and Evolution*.

distinction between the sheltered and unsheltered condition of affairs. "In peace and prosperity both states and individuals are actuated by higher motives, because they do not fall under the dominion of imperious necessities, but war which takes away the comfortable provision of daily life is a hard master and tends to assimilate men's characters to their conditions."[1] His words in the whole passage from which this is an extract may serve not merely as an indication of the historic qualities and violence of war, but as symbolizing the contrast between the general impression of the history of past ages, and those interpretations in which the moral issues are uppermost, and the question how to attain the highest values, the main one for every individual. It will be argued in the chapter on Ethics that the general trend of ethical discussion has been to turn our minds away from the setting of ethics in history. Nor is it enough to test the view of the relation of persons to history, maintained in the present work, by illustration within any selected range or circle, a little space of family peace, a brief progression of generations in which the successions of birth and death pass with moral and aesthetic beauty, the life of a small community under a chief or leader who is father and friend of his people, Aristotle's best city of friends, the early Christian Society. We must not rely on these Utopian fragments, though they also are illuminating, but face the experience and doings of the human race throughout the ages so far as known to us. Not that ethics is not concerned with the ideal. But the problem is whether in the light of history, the interpretation of the meaning of human existence which is a necessary basis for the ideal, is not swept away or set aside. The general answer to the problem in this form, which can be offered on the basis of our position, will only fully appear after a further considera-tion of the function of personality. There is one consideration, however, bearing upon it in an important way which may be adduced at this point. It may be urged that the weight attached (often unconsciously) to the mode of necessity, in relation to

[1] *Thucydides*, Book III, 82. Jowett's translation.

the total sequence of past events, has a deceptive effect upon us. Now as regards the idea of necessity, it is the problem of a necessary or unchangeable character of history in the realm of value, with which we are here concerned. From the point of view which we have taken, the question of the prevalence of uniform law in all those departments of experience with which the sciences of nature deal is not the issue. It has been recognized that the postulate of the deterministic universe is one which science finds requisite for its procedure, whilst the derivation of the scientific ideal of order from the original demand for order in a universe in which we are to find value has been pointed out. On the other hand, the attachment of the notion of necessity to the type of order which science posits does not appear to be justified, since the scientific categories have no title to pronounce upon the ultimate nature of individual things. The ultimate source of the idea of an unchangeable character in the nature of the historical experience, however various the moulds in which it may be cast, appears to be human experience of the passage of present into past, the unalterable form in which the event is immediately fixed, in contrast to its previously undetermined character. The fact that events have occurred, and are fixed in an order which henceforth is eternal, appears to give rise to the idea of their necessity which first comes with the emotional force of the Greek ἀνάγκη. But as has so often been argued in logical treatises, experience cannot prove this necessity. From Hume onwards, however, philosophical logicians have been chiefly interested in the basis for confidence in regard to the relation of inductive enquiry to our expectations of the future. We need not examine the position of that form of neo-Hegelianism for which the future is equally necessary with the past as a corollary of which the time-series may be conceived as reversible.[1] From this point of view, history with the temporal process becomes unmeaning, except as a confused misperceived form, through

[1] F. H. Bradley: *Appearance and Reality*, Chapter XVIII, "Temporal and Spatial Appearance".

which we gain a certain awareness of some universal principles. But this way of thought points to a corresponding, though opposed principle, namely, that the characterization of the series of future events as free implies an identical characterization of the past events. Though from our situation in the present the past is unalterable fact, we must recognize that it has no other necessity but this, together with the fact that we shall be able as before to bring by means of the categories, in certain abstract general aspects, past and future series together as correlative. But it is with the ultimate nature of subject selves that we are concerned, when we enquire whether the forms which the relation of selves to the series of events (which in this relation put on the character of history) has hitherto taken must everlastingly recur. The problems lying behind the enquiry are that of the possibility of a greatly heightened worth in experience on the whole, and of the persistency of defeat in the sphere of human efforts in this respect. Since, as has been argued, there is no logical ground in the nature of the temporal series for the conclusion that its actual sequence is necessary, this result must be applied to the past as well as the future. In correspondence with the practical view of freedom in the future, there is needed a realization of the possibilities of freedom in the past. The importance of this standpoint for our conception of history as a whole can be seen from the following considerations. In the first place, although it cannot lessen the impression of the tragic character of past history, it removes a serious obstacle to the vital belief in freedom for the future. For unless we keep alive a well-grounded conviction that our consciousness that the "gates of the future are open" was equally justifiable for our predecessors in their present, the present belief is liable to grow weak and to fail of the tremendous import it has potentially for our action. The tendency of the irrevocable fact to take on the aspect of necessary fact leads to the attraction to its likeness of the yet unborn event.

A doubt may, of course, be raised in regard to the assumption that we *are* conscious of inner freedom at least within limits in our facing of the future, our attitude to the plans and purposes of life. The subject of freedom will be more fully examined later. A consideration which appears to be of great importance, since our whole conception of history really hangs upon this thread, namely on the view of the relation of the self to history, which could not be reconciled with determinism in regard to the experience of value, is the following. However limited freedom has actually been, in the major events of history, in proportion to the possibilities, however unconcerned in respect to human good the cosmic process may appear, there is no iron law to forbid our free conception of history, as including other possibilities which might have been achieved, on the condition of a higher personal energy occurring not once or twice in the length of ages but continuously. If it be objected that this is only to push the problem one stage further back, I cannot offer a direct denial of this, nor is it necessary to my position. For this only professes to offer an interpretation of certain of the more baffling aspects of historic experience which refuses to ignore any of the facts. It belongs to this aim to point out that we are prone to find grounds for despair in deductions from admitted facts which do not necessarily follow, and may even be fallacious.

CHAPTER VII

HISTORY AND ETHICS. FREEDOM

"The Mind is its own place and in itself
Can make a heaven of hell, a hell of heaven."

JOHN MILTON

IF man is a historical being, the necessary counterpart to Spinoza's great principle, enunciated from the standpoint of the contemplative nature—*sub quadam specie aeternitatis*—must be accepted in all its bearings and significance as the clue to his practical situation, *sub specie temporis*. The question how to transcend his purely temporal situation may be the fundamental question for the good life as for the life in its aesthetic aspects, and in its search for knowledge. But these value activities have their character for human selves, as activities in history in a process of change which without them has no meaning. It would appear to be of the first importance that we should approach the problems of the practical life with its values that are universal in all forms of experience from the historical standpoint. By this it is meant that the good for the individual is his good as member of the long historical process. The nature of his ideal, therefore, as well as the true significance of his activities, their scope and limitations, will not be understood without realization of the nature of his relation to events, the tendencies of his development in history, the problem of changes in values from age to age and its bearing upon that principle of absolute value of which the greatest moral teachers seem to have been conscious.

It has indeed been held that in view of the brevity of life and the enormous burden which is laid upon each individual by the past out of whose influences he can with difficulty raise himself, as also the ever repeated failures of past struggles for permanently nobler forms of existence, the best hope of new creative movement in ethics lies in an ignoring of the past so far as possible. We ought to contemplate the universe for action as now open before us, and endeavour to realize such good as our vision can discern, allowing past experience to suggest methods but not ideals. This may be a practical rule for action, which is needed in many cases and situations. It does not, however, affect the historical point of view as I conceive it in application to the true understanding of the ethical principle in life as a whole. History cannot be forgotten since the self, its activities, the question whether they can achieve any real change or creative action, are all bound up with the actuality of history, which is only actual for selves. If we deny the significance of history we deny the significance of selves. The forms which history has taken hitherto have then to be at least reconciled with the possibility of creative activity in the present, and this implies, as was argued in the last chapter, that there was the possibility of such activity in the past, however slight the results achieved by the principle.

It results from the historical standpoint, in the sense indicated, that the unreality which attaches to some ethical systems is due to their abstraction from history. It seems that such problems as that of the "Good" with all the questions attendant upon it would be better grappled with if approached by minds not detached from the historical outlook, but steeped in history. History exists for us because the men and women of the past, like ourselves, have continually worked in events under some particular idea of what is good, though they may not have been aware of this meaning in their actions, and though their springs of action may often seem to us contrary to the good. The history of ethics suggests that the problem of "freedom of the will", as framed in moral philosophy, is insoluble, and the final result of the attack upon it in the most important recent work in ethics, that of Professor N. Hartmann, is that while it is morally necessary and ontologically possible, the facts are not adequate for a proof.[1] But it may appear in a

[1] Nicolai Hartmann: *Ethics*. Translated by Stanton Coit, Vol. III, "Moral Freedom," Chapter XIX (f).

different light if we consider it as part of the larger problem of the relation of human personality to its historical world. Is it not of primary importance to observe what is the function of personality in this relation, and how, since the process, if there *is* history, is charged with the effects of personality, it has there worked, what it has created, in what manner it has transformed the process in giving meaning to it, changing events into the likeness of this meaning? Whether the question of freedom of the will can be asked, and what significance it has cannot be finally determined without reference to the fact that however pitiful in relation to the standards which the personal principle itself has discerned, their flickering light may be in the course of events, it is personal experience which has created history out of the senseless movement of natural things.

The course of our argument hitherto has then brought us to the position that history is not only unintelligible, it is not anything without the creative energy of man. This does not decide the specific problem of freedom of the will, but the latter cannot adequately be examined in abstraction from this truth. A single quotation from an eminent historian of ancient civilization may be given in emphasis of the standpoint.

"Why did such a powerful and brilliant civilization, the growth of ages, and apparently destined to last for ages, gradually degenerate? *In other words why did the creative power of its makers wax faint?*"[1] (Italics mine.) The greatest historic problems then depend upon the positive nature of freedom. The question whether the will is free is secondary to the question what this freedom means.

From the assumption here implied we may turn to the problem of personal freedom, and attempt to estimate the form in which it arises. A few more references to history will remind us where we stand. The question has been suggested above whether the history of Europe under Christendom does not

[1] M. Rostovtzeff: *A History of the Ancient World*, Vol. II, *Rome*. Translated from the Russian by J. D. Duff.

in the main lack entirely the features it ought to have on the postulate of this work. I speak of "political" history. Is it enough to reply that this great impression is due to the fact that political history cannot treat of individuals in their functions as individuals in personal relation to each other? It is (as I have argued) primarily concerned with certain categories, in the first place states, and men collectively viewed as representing or at times for the purposes of the history identifiable with their states, and with all those interlacing and intercrossing functions which have grown out of the interrelations of those states. Within the states it refers mainly to general aspects of the lives of those individuals, legal, economic, etc. It is not concerned with persons except in so far as their actions affect some public interest. In this respect at any moment it may become personal. Certainly the public action and interest of the individual cannot be sharply separated from the private. Alexander was not less acting as an individual when defeating the Persians with great loss of life than when slaying Clitus. Only his own vision of the deed appeared to him *toto caelo* different in the two cases. But in the historian's history it is the people in some general character, and individuals as standing for some interest of a people, party, etc., which constitute the subject-matter. This of course does not imply that for the imagination of the great historian this category of "the people" is not continually vitalized and enriched by his vision of the individuals to whom the category refers. It is only to indicate the function of political history as such. Also, in modern history especially, we may seem to have considerable knowledge about the individuals as individuals, because we have more details in regard to all those modes of their action in which the general qualities are diversely expressed. There are many biographies, also autobiographies, in which the individual strives to show how personally he was motived in great events. But if in recent history through the abundant channels of seeming knowledge, and through living experience of our contemporaries at least at a little distance second or third hand, we are brought to believe in the reality of some degree of creative energy in selves, its presence and its passing away, which assists us in the interpretation of the rise and fall of civilizations, can we maintain this faith except in relation to special stages of civilization? We are once more brought up against the fact of long ages of human existence of which the record hardly permits the conception of history as constituted by the value found in events by selves. Since we cannot accept with McTaggart the "easy" division, though not "cheap" (for the price is heavy), between a real world in which selves are existing in timeless and perfect interrelations and the illusory world of apparent experience, it may be objected that the view involves in a new form the Spencerian doctrine of the culmination of evolution in a stage of Absolute Ethics. The hope of arrival at this, however, seems inconsistent with the whole process of human history, as in Spencer's philosophy with the process of natural evolution. A brief restatement of the position in reply to such an objection may help to clarify it. One important contrast with the Spencerian scheme is that no goal is here assumed in which the ideal in human relations is necessarily to be attained. The main theme is an interpretation of the nature of the self in relation to its historic situation. We found that human history, which is the essential type from which natural history is an abstraction, essentially means the course of events as it is for selves. This meaning intensifies to value and disvalue to the degree in which the self is active. From the comparatively scanty knowledge we possess we cannot assert that the course of things tends to a greater and greater actualization of value in the future. There may have been ages and peoples unknown to us in the past in which creative personality was actualized more perfectly than in any known period.

Having recalled this main point of view, let us refer again to the problem of those ages of which we have some knowledge, but chiefly as monotonous records of events, often brutal, whose existence seems inconsistent with our standpoint. A comparatively favourable instance would be the era of the barbarian invasions of the Roman Empire. The invaders on the whole had advanced well beyond the first stages in culture. They had had experience of settled habitations, of pastoral, if not agricultural life, of some forms of government, in certain cases a democratic constitution.[1] The spirit of Roman civilization captured to some extent many who came into contact with it. The facts we have to face are those that point to an intelligible explanation of such a phase of history on its own ground, as history of the movements, migrations, wars, etc., of peoples in search of the means of life. The explanation looks to causation by "natural forces", not different in principle from the forces which drive hordes of creatures of other animal species to wander on a similar quest. Pressure of population, necessity of food, lack of experience in agriculture —such are the incentives. Now the interpretation I am maintaining does not deny that we have here a portion of human history. But it holds that it is primarily history in the human (i.e. the original) sense in so far as later men give a meaning to it. It was also significant as history (whether consciously or not) to the individual men of those wanderings in so far as the events had some meaning for them, beyond the fact that they made life possible. For instance, with the lay or saga in which there is some commemoration of a past deed (however mythicized) genuine history as historic experience has begun. It is said in the review of a recent book by Otto Cerbach[2] "Races of men like hives of bees have their swarming periods." Following his author, the reviewer refers to those European races who were lucky in swarming early, and are now distributed over a great part of the earth. The plausibility of these large-scale views and speculations concerning the material of history is undoubted. Whether the behaviour of the human species is brought in the way above suggested or in some other

[1] Cf. Bury: *Barbarian Invasions of the Roman Empire.*
[2] *The Open Door, Sunday Observer,* March 19, 1933.

form, under categories applicable to animal life generally, the interpretation testifies to the fact that as a member of nature man is subject to "natural history". The term history is here used as if it had significance in abstraction from history as the process of events informed with value, and as though natural history with all the wealth of meaning it has for man could exist prior to or apart from his advent. The fact that these racial movements and many of the mass activities of humanity in the temporal process can be described in terms of causation by physical needs and changes in the forces or agents of the natural environment, need not conflict with the position that essential history proceeds from the interpretation by man of his experience together with the changes with their meaning which he is capable of introducing into it as a result of that interpretation. These changes are limited by the material conditions of existence, and the striving against these limits is one of the distinguishing characteristics of the human individual. This striving is always motived by his nature as individual rather than as one of a kind. The ultimate and inextinguishable faith of man, inspiring though without full consciousness of it, all the efforts that proceed from the self is that within indefinite degrees he can enlarge his range for free activity. If the individual interpretation of his behaviour and that of his fellows is wholly lacking, it is hardly possible to define his doings as genuinely human, but the potentiality is always there, however prevented by environment from realization. It is evident that in this sketch, the factors discussed in Chapter V, under contingency and the "other", are pervasive in the events. From this point of view, nevertheless, we may understand why the reality of human history must lie in the history of individuals of which the history of groups can only give abstractions more or less adequate for certain purposes of knowledge. If for example it is argued that the age of discovery of new lands for European peoples came when expansion was needed, and when after many centuries of a tolerably settled existence they were stimulated to strive for the greater prosperity of which they were now capable, the truth of these propositions makes no difference to our interpretation of the spirit of the discoverer. Of first importance is the meaning he found in that expectation of new worlds, and its "wild surmise" qualified by all previous history of human search. For this not only enhanced the deed, as the prehistoric man's sense of shape the value of the useful pot he fashioned,[1] but determined in considerable degree the forms taken by the expansion.

From these considerations it may be seen that the all-essential condition of the achievement of reality in human experience as history is freedom, and that the creative energy of which Rostovtzeff speaks as belonging to the makers of Roman greatness is a high manifestation of the same energy or freedom. The term which has been so variously and ambiguously used both in categorial objective history and in relation to the subjective experience, in political and in ethical issues, must not be lightly adopted. It is not, of course, any particular category of freedom that is implied, legal, civil, political, etc., though these may be important corollaries or even essential conditions. It is nearly akin to that freedom of the mind of which the clearest conception was given by Greek thinkers in spite of the limitations in their view of its scope. Something more positive is, however, required than the Greek idea of a mind which remains itself, unaffected by professionalism or too close a cleaving to any pursuit which through habitual influences contracts the outlook. For this imperative enlargement of the concept we have, as is implied by the tenor of our argument, to go to the great impressions, as well as the inner meaning, of history. But, as must be noticed again at this point, it appears to be held by some thinkers that a method which treats ethics in close relation to historic actuality involves a renunciation of the freedom of ethics in the affirmation of its ideal, if need be against all actuality. This seems to be implied by Professor N. Hartmann in a

[1] Cf. Myres: *Who were the Greeks?*

passage in which, after expressing the idea of an advance continuous since the breaking away of ethical thought from mythology, he affirms that with the ideal as guide man potentially can attain the highest. "Everything must and can be achieved by effort." He proceeds to refer to the history of the human mind so far. Together with progress it admittedly shows retrogression. "But here historical experience cannot be decisive. The creative element in man is necessarily in opposition to it—mankind must do what is in its power to transform its downward movement into an upward course. For historical experience cannot dispute the possibility as such."[1]

This must undoubtedly be recognized. The position of this work, however, implies that in spite of all the ground for pessimism which seem so strong in history historical experience in the deepest sense can be brought in to support the view that greater freedom and more ideal history is at least conceivable in the future. In any case history cannot be ignored. If it is unfavourable to the hope of the future, the explanation of this must be sought. It is not enough to turn our back on history with Nietzsche or Hartmann and declare that the creative spirit of man is necessarily opposed to it. If this is a true proposition to-day, it must also be true of all our yesterdays, and in asking what better forecast of the days to come can be made, we cannot blot out history. For as has appeared from the previous arguments, man is within history and history his own inner being. The philosopher inclines to contemplate history as something past and superseded, as though in entering upon life in accordance with an ideal system of ethics man can enter upon a new order of existence free from the alien factors in events. It seems essential, however, if we are to understand the relation of the moral values to actuality, the moral genius of man to the history for which men have at least in great part been responsible, to attempt some analysis of history into its elements, in order to discover, if possible,

[1] *Ethics*, translated by Stanton Coit, Vol. II, "Moral Values," p. 337.

how those that are alien to progress have entered in, and what is their relation to "the creative element in man". Again, when Professor Hartmann observes, "The value of the disposition is not commensurate with the greatness of the work intended. The value of the work is irrelevant to it. It remains what it is even in cases of outward error and failure"[1]—he utters a profound truth. But in stating it thus he omits to notice that he has touched to the quick the problem of ethics and history. Here we find the failure of events to justify our postulates in regard to creative personality. For if the value of the disposition were throughout history incommensurate with that of the work, either ethics or human life itself becomes a dream. Or there is a metaphysical chasm such as appears in Kant's distinction between the noumenal and the empirical realms and the doctrine that we cannot know whether freedom has been actual in experience. But this mystical view is the last retreat of freedom and steals the jewel of life from common humanity.

In the history of ethics the significance of freedom has been too much restricted to the specific notion of moral freedom as freedom of the will. The question so often raised in varying forms, whether the will can act in spite of all motives, appears to pose the problem in a misleading way. The terms of the argument take up their positions for our reasoning on the pattern of the generally accepted analyses of processes in nature. We think of distinct motives as it were separate causal sequences, reinforcing, counteracting, balancing each other, each motive being a cause we can abstract from its setting and suppose to work in broadly the same way in any character into which it enters—e.g. ambition, sympathy, desire for wealth, etc. Such a scheme, however, appears to be mythical. Obviously freedom has been excluded in advance. In theories of "self-determination" it is recognized that the motive is individual in any self, the self being a unity, and each motive

[1] *Ethics*, translated by Stanton Coit, Vol. II, "Love of the Remotest," p. 329.

what it is for that self alone. This view seems true as far as it goes, but the question arises as to the source of the conditions which make the self what it is, and the original problem arises at another stage. For those who take their stand on the indestructible conviction of self-consciousness, which reasserts itself, after every apparent undermining, the belief in freedom must be based on an *a priori* or intuitive principle, superior to scientific argument and acknowledging neither the authority of uniformity of nature, conservation of energy, psychophysical parallelism, etc., nor of the logical metaphysical principle of wholeness which does not allow of any real individuality in the distinct elements of the whole. From the standpoint here maintained, the intuition of self-consciousness is indeed equal, if not superior in validity, to any arguments from uniformity in the universe of which the self regarded objectively forms a part. For this uniformity is a law of order assumed in the interests of that orderly world which is of value to the self. It can, however, be greatly strengthened by the argument from the view of the historic reality to which the self belongs, and starting from which the issue in the ordinary form is in fact superseded. For the self is in the deepest sense of the term a beginning (ἀρχή) of a new nature in the process of things, namely value, which is a quality that cannot be measured or weighed. The principal metaphysical difference between this interpretation and that of Kant, the greatest exponent of freedom from a metaphysical standpoint, is that it does not admit of Kant's hard division (above referred to) between the noumenal self and the empirical, and depreciation of the world of experience as phenomenal. There is a noumenal element in every self, but instead of acting in a phenomenal world, in a way which remains mysterious, and even undiscoverable, it gives to the process of experience its significance and actuality. Our experience is experience in a real world, in so far as it has meaning and value for us. But this value depends on the creative energy conveyed through personality.

Professor Nicolai Hartmann would get rid of Kant's

"methodological drapery", the two worlds, the intelligible and the phenomenal, whilst following Kant in the doctrine that there can be in the causal nexus "a unique determination which is not causal in its origin".[1] For the Kantian dualism he substitutes "the double stratification of the world". There is another order besides the causal which we meet with in the will of man. Behind the causally determined stratum there exists a second—in man the two are connected, and "the order of the second strikes into that of the first". This conception of the double stratification does not appear to avoid the *ethical* crux of the Kantian doctrine.[2] It seems on Kant's premises that wrong action cannot proceed from the will. When the will is active, the act belongs to the intelligible realm, the freedom of man, and evil has here no place. Its reality then is very dubious, and the responsibility of man for wrong acts at the least uncertain. To escape this pitfall into which other important doctrines of freedom have fallen, the duality must be carried back into Professor Hartmann's second order. It is liable to appear within the will or to avoid abstractions within the personality.[3] As I have already urged, the seeming paradox that evil proceeds from the same principle in the nature of the self as good must be admitted (and it is in fact recognized by Hartmann). The problem of freedom as ordinarily understood does not appear serious to Hartmann. All the usual difficulties would be swept aside by his argument that "it is only in principle that moral value is connected with freedom. The person must in general have the possibility of behaving in either way. The amount of his conflict, the strength of the opposing motives are irrelevant. If one traces back the chain of actions in which the disposition has evolved, one comes somewhere unconditionally upon a primal attitude".[4] The ethical problem of freedom he regards as entirely unpsychological, and the error is great of seeking "in the domain of psychic events for a point of contact with it". With this as

[1] Op cit., Vol. III, *The Problem of Freedom of the Will.*
[2] But see Note at close of chapter.   [3] Ibid.   [4] Ibid.

far as it goes I am in accord. But by setting the problem in the widest perspective, we shall be better able to realize the strength of the position, which follows from the real nature of the self, whilst the subjection of the will to causal determination holds good only on a hypothesis useful for scientific purposes. In this I think I am in agreement with M. Bergson's treatment of the ethical issue:[1] The creative principle in personality is then manifested in all the fields of value experience. Freedom in the widest sense is the consciousness of capacity to contribute, in some degree, new meaning to the process in virtue of the uniqueness of the self. In practical freedom the addition of meaning involves the bringing about of alterations in the forms of change. This takes place in all creative work because of the duality in the cosmic order. It is not enough that the genius in art perceives in the universe forms of sublimity and beauty, splendour and tragedy hitherto unapparent. He must so modify the data before him, e.g. in his own materials for art, as to enable others to have similar experiences. The "ought" is present in the inspiration and the law of his activity because a higher value presents itself as something that ought to be. This is another form of the principle which drives the self to transcend or extend the boundaries of value in his experience. The peculiar force of the "ought" where the activity is concerned with human relations, or the worth of its effects for other selves, is the distinction of the moral obligation, and hence the emphasis on ethical freedom as freedom in the most essential sense. Professor Hartmann's interpretation, in which a conflict is introduced between this ought and freedom,[2] appears to me unreal, and here Kant's insistence that the ought is implied in freedom, and is its other aspect, seems to have greater truth.

With the deepening of the obligation goes the intensification of the need for freedom. There is neither obligation nor

[1] *Essai sur les données immédiates de la conscience.* Translated as *Time and Freewill* by F. L. Pagson.
[2] *Ethics*, Vols. III, XVI, and XVIII.

freedom, unless I am responsible, i.e. unless the act proceeds from the reality of the self. Now the act in which the reality of other selves, their indefeasible right as selves freely to work for that value they are capable of developing is denied, i.e. the act we call evil must also be conceived as free and proceeding from the real self.[1] We have then to admit that the erring self is responsible, and is possessed by that craving to increase the value he feels in his own being by making that of others instrumental to this, which characterizes selfhood when the individual is blind to the reality of other selves. The fact indeed that all men feel the need of freedom, however constantly they mistake its nature, the tremendous consciousness of power in the belief that freedom has been achieved, even the sense which may be quite illusory that a higher type of existence has been attained, seem to be the cause of the unbridled and reckless struggle of many men of great natural gifts to seize by force the conditions which they suppose necessary to the freedom of their powerful individuality. The saying that in gaining the whole world they lose their own soul is strictly applicable. It was suggested earlier that with consciousness of the reality of other selves both ethical and cognitive development begins. In extraordinary examples of blindness to the reality of others attendant on the passion for power, there seems to occur a gradual loss of the sense of reality in general. Thus, before Napoleon started on his Moscow expedition in which his total disregard of other men's opportunities of life and happiness was shown in its most appalling form, Dr. Eugen Stschepkin observes, "Having hitherto succeeded in all his enterprises, he had lost all sense of the attainable."[2] And Dr. Julius von Pflugl-Harttung, that during the campaign of 1814 Napoleon "had lost all sense of reality. Like a desperate gamester he tried to win back what had long been lost".[3]

A similar obsession appears in the case of a man who, in a

[1] This position is further developed in Chapter IX.
[2] *Cambridge Modern History*, Vol. IV. *Napoleon*, Chap. XVI.
[3] Ibid., Chapter XVII.

strangely different environment of action, a very different type lacking the romance of the soldier's pageantry, appears to have had a like absorbing passion for power. The biographer[1] of Ivar Kreuger observes that "Kreuger's chief incentive was to become one of the mighty ones of the earth". This greatest of fraudulent financiers said, "I can only work with people whose backbones I have broken." "As consciousness of power rose, he became delirious with power—completely blinded by lust for power and contempt for humanity." His interests (very narrow on the whole) included interest in the history of great conquerors. "He thought himself related to them, especially Charles XII, Napoleon, Bismarck."

Moral freedom is then derived from the essential nature of personality. It *is* this nature if we widen our conception of freedom beyond the somewhat narrow Kantian doctrine to embrace the creative principle in the self in all its aspects. The chief distinction of this view from that of Kant is its insistence on the fact that reality is experienced by the self as a unity in its emotional-cognitive experience, not in the intellectual nature alone, and its free activity is an expression and result of this consciousness. Also the source of disvalue as well as of good is here found when we interpret history from this standpoint, enquiring to what extent we can trace in it the signs and results of human freedom. The chief problem lies in the discovery in what degree the potentialities of personality have been at any time realized in the determination of the main streams of the process. In the strict sense, as earlier indicated, what we call history is misnamed unless the free energy of human selves informing the process is present. We should have simply a portion of the process of nature of which beings in some respects like ourselves form part. It is history, however, for the historian and for posterity in so far as they contemplate the record and find significance in it as a phase of the ages in which the rudiments of freedom might have been

[1] Manfred Georg: *The Case of Ivar Kreuger*, translated by L. M. Sieveking and Ian F. D. Morrow.

already traceable and of personality unconsciously imputing value. Sir James Frazer speaks of the tremendous debt we owe to those men of the primaeval cultures who first strove through "magic" to find some order in the world.[1] And Professor Myres of the first men who when the Ice Age came "made fires and clothes rather than follow the sunshine, and vindicated the reasonableness of a world that seemed so reasonless".[2] Could these gallant flights from slavery to natural forces have been made without any stirring in their hearts of the free energy of the self?

Max Scheler, however, appears to hold that what he regards as the over-human principle which is the bearer of the values, has appeared in humanity at a certain stage of its development, bringing to manifestation a wholly new type of values and acts.[3] As I have argued, the personal type must be conceived as always potential in the human being. And here to other grounds for this position I would add the fitness, one might almost term it perfectness in some respects, of the psycho-physical constitution of man to be what Scheler and others call bearer (carrier, *träger*) of the higher values. To assume that there may have been long ages in which this instrument existed without any possibility of experience of these values seems inconsistent with rational inference, from the gradual development, in general, of higher order powers. There seems also to be, as the study of anthropological works suggests, sufficient evidence in experience to disprove the position. Scheler himself in his analysis of the different kinds and orders of value really provides evidence of the arbitrariness of a distinction which would sever to the degree of metaphysical separation the values of life from the higher spiritual values. That a value is higher, he holds, is grasped by a special act of the knowledge of values, viz. preference (*vorziehen*). Preference

[1] *Golden Bough*, Part II, "Royal and Priestly Taboos and the Perils of the Soul."
[2] *Who were the Greeks?*
[3] *Der Formalismus in der Ethik*, p. 283.

is not equivalent to choice or an act of striving. He perhaps implies a rejection of Spinoza's dictum, "In no case do we desire anything because we deem it to be good. But we deem a thing to be good because we desire it."[1] A closely similar view is expressed by Ehrenfels.[2] The act of striving according to Scheler must be based on knowledge of the higher nature of the value. This preference is *a priori* and holds good between the values themselves, independently of the goods which are determined by them. Where we choose the aim which is founded on the lower value an illusion of preference must lie at the basis. This would, I think, support the position that evil as well as good has its source in the personal principle. The order of rank of the values is itself absolutely invariable, whilst the rules of choice in history are essentially variable. The feeling or emotion of values he holds to be necessarily founded on a priority and posteriority in this absolute order. The act of preference is an intuitive evidence of superiority which cannot be supplanted by any logical deduction. The value of life, "pure vital subjective", he considers independent of all spiritual values, having its own series of values. Yet this series is ultimately founded on that of the spiritual values. For "the order of values is only to be comprehended through spiritual acts which are not themselves vitally conditioned. That man is the most valuable of the animals, for instance, would only be an anthropomorphic conception if the value of this knowledge of value was only relative to men. If the values were merely relative to life, life itself would have no value".[3] This reference to Scheler's position is given because it represents an important and interesting attempt to meet the problem of a personalistic ethics in face of the facts of man's position in nature and his racial history. There is much in it with which I am in accord, allowing for Scheler's more

[1] *Ethics*, Part III, Proposition IX, Note. Translated by R. H. M. Elwes.

[2] *System der Wert-Theorie*, Band I, Erster Teil. This gives the psychological interpretation.

[3] *Der Formalismus in der Ethik*, I, Teil II, 4.

objective view of values, but not the conception of the sudden emergence of personality with the higher values of which the person alone is the bearer.[1] Scheler's own doctrine of "acts" and "functions" as bearers of value, hearing, seeing, and feeling being functions, appears to make any such sharply defined separation between the order of human existence in which the higher values are experienced and the order below this untenable. Is pure aesthetic feeling conceivable in abstraction from hearing and seeing which depend on the sense-organism? If life is the bearer of values the order of which is comprehended by spiritual acts, the barrier seems to break down. But it breaks down not because there could be value without personality, but because the beginnings or rudiments of personality are everywhere where there is humanity. That the inner being of the person, the subject which cannot be fully known, is unable to manifest itself in knowledge, feeling, and action, apart from those conditions necessary to freedom, which have been more absent than present in history, has been earlier argued. Nevertheless, the power and independence of personality in the world is so great that there are individuals lacking from birth the senses of sight and hearing, in whose lives the values for which these organs might seem essential are present, or at least some spiritual experience which conveys to them the essence of aesthetic experience and makes possible the perfection of human relationship.[2] It may, however, be pointed out that these experiences seem to depend on the existence of other selves possessing sight and hearing, and also love for the person thus scourged by nature.

At this point a further explanation seems demanded of that perception of the reality of another self which, as has been argued, makes possible the transcending of the limits of finite selfhood, and entrance into the knowledge of value as it is for other minds. This problem is closely connected with

---

[1] *Der Formalismus in der Ethik*, I, Teil II, 4.
[2] Cf. Helen Keller: *The Story of My Life*, "The World I Live In."

that of the presence of personality and whether it "emerges" in Professor Alexander's sense of emergence.[1] Whilst aware in some degree of the existence of other selves, as of our own, we do not normally know the values they experience from the inner side. Their values then are not altogether real to us in the sense in which another self becomes real or actual, when from a mere X, as it were a number, he becomes an object of sympathy or of love. This experience may relate to a single individual, or to a large number who through a profound emotion of sympathy are realized all as persons—as in the example of Wilberforce, aroused to the resolve to dedicate his life to the emancipation of the slaves. We may use the analogy of a passage from solipsism to belief in the existence of other selves even though genuine solipsism be inconceivable. For many men large numbers of their fellows are not essentially selves, but are as figures on the stage of their lives. The belief that they have like emotions and purposes with ourselves is then a general belief in regard to the class man rather than a living conviction in regard to each individual.

Now when the experience occurs (whether gradually or suddenly) in which an individual feels himself to have direct knowledge by insight of those selves in whom his interest is deeply aroused, it is probable that this is in general illusion, but it is *as if* such knowledge was possessed, and in certain cases as I believe it is not illusion. The activities which make the experience possible are especially associated with personality, but their high development in human nature does not conceal the truth that their foundation partly lies in vital qualities which man shares with the higher animals. Kant's eloquent apotheosis of personality then, whilst appropriate to its supremacy over all else in human nature, seems to create too great a gulf between the noumenal self and every other form of living experience, including that of man himself, as a member of nature.[2]

[1] *Space, Time and Deity.*
[2] *Critique of Practical Reason*, "Analytic", Chapter III.

We may now notice the part played by imagination in the moral life.

"Life at sea", writes Sir Wilfred Grenfell, "breaks down conventional barriers, and almost compels fellowship, and an intelligent understanding of the difficulties and tragedies of the soul of one's neighbour. That rare faculty of imagination which is the inspiration of all great lovers of men was unnecessary here."[1] To ordinary reflection, using the methods of introspection related to observation and confirmed by intercourse with those who vividly conceive the feelings and needs of their fellows, also through the impression conveyed by the "literature of imagination", depicting inner experiences of many types of men, imagination appears to be the "open sesame". The point I am concerned to emphasize is that whilst in this activity we find creative personality in its most generally characteristic form in which self-transcendence is the essence of the experience, we may trace here one of the most remarkable illustrations of the fitness of the psychophysical nature for the creative activity of the person. This seems to be almost entirely ignored by Kant. Whether we examine the psychological elements of imagination, or the evidence of anthropology, this impression is equally conveyed. With regard to anthropology references that have earlier been made afforded illustrations of this truth. Throughout the stages of man's advance from the discovery of the production of fire, throughout the use of cave or lake-dwelling, for a life that was not merely animal and the first erection of huts rooting him as it were in mother earth,[2] the play of man's imagination in its early movements finds appropriate tools. There begins the activity of that power which in later days produced the tremendous myth and drama of Prometheus, stealing from the gods themselves the fire necessary to man's culture, the many-coloured visions and resounding voices of

[1] *Forty Years for Labrador*, p. 66.
[2] *The Downfall of the West*. Oswald Spengler's suggestion of the significance of the change from a nomad to a pastoral form of existence.

the poetry and art of home life, the awakening from the animal dream to the spiritual consciousness of other selves, whose emotions are imagined. The psychical nature supplies the basis. Attempts are made by certain thinkers to explain the great development (as though they were ends in themselves) of activities and forms of life originally instrumental to needs of life and self-defence, later the vehicle of beauty, love, loyalty, etc., as evidence of superabundance of vital force, or a natural tendency of the instrument to go beyond its instrumental purpose. Such are Ehrenfel's illustration of the antlers of the stag grown to a useless though graceful burden, and Wundt's principle of heterogony of ends. But the underlying principle of the development of the instrument to an end valuable in itself is the creative energy working through the subsidiary conditions. As regards the fitness of the psychical conditions we need only study the analysis of imagination in such work as that of Ward and other modern psychologists to be reminded of the many and subtle elements and processes, conscious and barely conscious, which go to the preparation of that instrument which at the call of poetic feeling may range through the universe of experience to bring together pictures and ideas never previously contiguous. Or it produces that constructive harmony of thought and emotion attending to which we pass for a brief moment into an existence that is not normally ours. The psychologist can show us all the marks that distinguish the imaged from the presented, the new kind of effort required of "constructive imagination" to dissociate these representational complexes, as a preliminary to new combinations, the relation to memory-images, the function of association, the effect of trains of ideas, time-factors and so on.[1] But it is not strictly his province to ask how all these factors minister to creative activity. The significance of imagination in other fields than that of practice ought here to be considered. It may be expected that in the

---

[1] Cf. Ward: article on "Psychology," *Encyclopaedia Britannica*, ninth edition.

M

sphere of art where the creative activity would appear to be least tied and bound by the conditions which hinder the introduction into life of the ideal values, since freedom from these limits is essential to it and they are always extrinsic, we should perceive truths in regard to the nature of the self not discoverable elsewhere. Without attempting to pronounce upon the nature of genius in art, which involves problems hitherto insoluble, we may refer to one or two relevant questions whose consideration bears closely upon the problem of the self in history. It has been asserted that in all the great experiences of value there occurs a striving for self-transcendence, and this is obviously at its highest in the experience of the creative worker whether in practical effort or in aesthetic construction. The bringing together of these two forms of activity so far apart in their expression may be criticized, but my position is that as creative and as forms of freedom they are near in the reality of the self. The word creative may, I think, be used in the same sense in so far as something new is introduced into experience proceeding from the subject's individuality. Let us refer to one important issue as conceived by Gabriel Séailles. In his view the genius differs from the ordinary man, not in the kind of his power, but in the degree.

"Le génie n'est pas un monstre. Si nous le comprenons c'est qu'il a quelque chose de commun avec nous, s'il nous charme, c'est que ses créations répondent aux lois de notre esprit."[1] He conceives a creative power in the mind, beginning with sensible intuition or perception, continuing in scientific method, induction, hypothesis, etc. The constant effort of the mind to constitute itself, to form its ideas entirely in harmony with itself—all this indicates the quality which reaches the highest stage in genius. But in order that the genius should be able to manifest himself freely, he would require a material which is no longer distinguished from the mind (*l'esprit*). This is effected in the interior life of images. Séailles holds

[1] *Essai sur le génie dans l'art*, Introduction.

that there is a fundamental law which attaches thought to life, namely, the tendency to bring the diverse into a unity, and to ensure variety by grouping round the unity the elements to which it can give order. "L'art est la conséquence nécessaire de la vie des images dans l'esprit." This is an interesting indication of the process by which the mind as aesthetically creative brings its values into life and to this analogies could be found in the introduction into practice of the ethical ideal. Inspiration, Séailles declares, is the natural and normal state of the mind, the virtue itself of thought. The mind working for harmony, "works for beauty in the act of struggling for life. Art and science have one origin in the spontaneous tendencies of the spirit".[1] The view that experience of value is necessary to the life of personality is very near to this. Yet there is a truth also which cannot be denied in Professor Max Dessoir's view of the chasm which divides the men who feel themselves to be dedicated to an extraordinary life from the average mediocre folk who live and propagate their kind.[2] It is perhaps in the forms of their life and work that the gulf seems so profound, rather than between the ordinary and the extraordinary individuals as persons. The seed of the creative spirit is present in all men. It may be all but impossible to detect where the conditions for freedom in the sense in which it has been maintained in this work are absent. It may be transformed and used for destructive purposes rather than creative where the instinct to self-transcendence has degenerated into the desire for self enlargement and magnification through power. An experience of Dr. Albert Schweitzer may here be recorded. On first meeting with the Africans to whom he had gone out as mission doctor he put to himself the much debated question, whether they were prisoners of tradition, or beings capable of really independent thought. "He found that they were far more interested in the elementary questions about the meaning of

[1] Op. cit.
[2] *Ästhetik und Allgemeine Kunstwissenschaft*, Zweiter Haupttheil I, 4.

life and the nature of good and evil"[1] than he had supposed. Once the man's life has been dedicated to art or to a special realization of the moral ideal, liberated through all the discipline demanded the deepest element in his nature is released and orientates itself towards the objects of its spiritual experience. It does then become—though for few continuously—different in kind from the average life. Yet it seems impossible to assert that any self is incapable of moments of experience like in quality to those of Dessoir's dedicated men. And in the practical sphere a thousand daily acts of heroism, in which the agent's nature seems flooded by a new force, unsuspected in himself, would appear to refute such a denial. The view which does not regard the genius as a being belonging to a different order from that of the ordinary individual seems more in harmony with the concept of personality as intrinsically an originative principle. Although by no means predominantly pervasive in history, its potentialities may be much greater than have hitherto been realized under the conditions of our experience. As regards the possibility of the transformation of experience by realization of these potentialities in a much higher degree, this implies the overcoming in some measure of the dualistic character, which we have examined as inseparable from history. For this seems to make inconceivable any permanent advance in the spiritual quality of experience. This problem will be considered in the chapter on "History and the Future". Here we may point to the following significant fact. Occasionally in biography or autobiography we meet with pictures which revive the hope of discovering in conditions that have actually existed the clue to more ideal forms of human relations and the achievement of value. Such a picture, for instance, is given in Max Müller's account of his childhood in the quiet and simple little town of Anhalt, the association of simple living with vivid activity of artistic life.[2] Some features of the "city-

[1] *My Life and Thought*, Chapter XIII.
[2] *Auld Lang Syne*.

state" type of community appear in this picture devoid of the influences of pride of Empire, or embittered rivalry with other communities. An intense enthusiasm for music was shared by all who met in simple social gatherings, the guests as well as hosts providing the entertainment, which was thus a creative experience. Mendelssohn and other men of genius were frequent visitors. Scenes similar to this, in which the problem of winning from existence the value which is necessary to personality without alien admixture seems almost solved, flit now and then across the stage of history. Or they hardly drift over the stage, but can be dimly seen in the far distance, as in those glimpses we get in the background of some pictures of Titian, Memling and other old masters, where a little window, arch or other opening allows a view of distant hills in the sunshine, a dreaming church spire, winding paths and peaceful wanderers. In general these openings are made for us by the biographer and author of memoirs, rather than the historian, who is occupied with the centre in which all the movements of history at a certain epoch seem drawn together in their most massive aspects, pageants of state, revolutions, military or industrial, behind which we may feel the crucifixion of the true spirit of man. These ideal pictures, which recede further and further away as we strive to analyse their elements and single out their causes, represent perhaps those pools sheltered from the torrent of the historic process in the simile earlier suggested.

A few more illustrations of the attitude to experience conscious or unconscious of the creative mind in art and in practice will help to bring out the main position of this chapter concerning freedom as the energy of the real personality in the process of events. Michael Angelo thought of his art as the only one, "For if we justly estimate what we do in this life, we shall find that everyone unconsciously is painting the world—by creating new forms, or by his way of dressing himself, by buildings and houses, by seafaring with the help of sails, by drilling armies, even by dying and

being buried—in short by every action of humanity."[1] Everyone, then, is painting the world, the sailor as well as the artist
of the Sistine Chapel, the man who seems to do nothing but
live and die, as well as the sculptor of the Medici Tombs.
Romain Rolland thinks that "Beethoven is incapable of seeing
the life of other beings as it is; his own is too vast, for him it
is the measure of everything; he projects it into everything."—
"In a mind like that of Beethoven . . . the external world
counts merely as a reflection, an echo, a symbol of the interior
drama."—"Beethoven scarcely ever emerged from himself,
but this self is a universe."[2] These words may seem to suggest
a kind of inverted Pantheism, which would not be true of
Beethoven. What they signify, however, does contain truth.
The greatness of Beethoven's personality seems in his greatest
works to flood the world with value, and in transcending
himself, as in passages of the *Eroica*, the fifth and the Choral
Symphonies, he transcends the cosmos which is filled with
the conflicts of his soul in music. His attitude to Napoleon
gives a remarkable illustration of the idea that creative genius
in action is comparable to that of the artist. "Beethoven saw
in Bonaparte a fellow-artist, a creator in another sphere of
action, the creator of a good world, 'good' because more
free, richer in individuality, and yet more harmonious in
structure."[3] He thought of politics as the art of "creating a
society that will express a richer and fuller life". Napoleon's
passion to impress his own individual self upon the world,
humanity, posterity, history (the distortion of the personal
principle), was, however, wholly alien to Beethoven's creative
"genius". When he realized the character of Napoleon's
activity he tore up the title-page dedicating to him the Symphony Eroica, and said, "I see he is just an ordinary man".
Moral genius in action as Beethoven conceived it is a true form
of genius, that is of creativity, freedom in the highest sense.

[1] Quoted by Emil Ludwig, *Three Titans*.
[2] On Beethoven's Symphony, *Eroica*.
[3] W. J. Turner: *Beethoven*, Book II, xiv.

Let us now turn to striking forms of free activity in the practical sphere. But before adducing further examples, in order that we may bear in mind the relation of this activity to the activity of animal life, which seems, as earlier argued, to foreshadow it, I would refer to a view maintained by the late Herbert Wildon Carr. He held that the specific difference in human action was sufficiently explained by the possession of intellect. In a description of the behaviour of the worker-bee, he argues that the materialistic and mechanical principles are here completely bankrupt in means of explanation. It is "life" which "endows individuals with positive freedom, but makes that freedom subserve a specific end—the common life".[1] Thus he conceives freedom to be characteristic of all the living phenomena of nature, and in this light explains the basis of ethical freedom; whilst in the human individual invariability disappears, the act of choice may intervene, because of intelligence. It is in this way that man can pass beyond the natural life to a realm of spiritual values. It will be noticed that in this view the important point is that the individual end has already been transcended for the sake of the common interest in animal life below man. On these lines, it may be argued, the principle of a natural and inevitable advance to a high form of self-transcendence is established, and no metaphysical gap intervenes between animal and human life. The complex evolution of the brain is all that need be added to account for peculiarities in man's behaviour. In my view, as earlier stated, the possibility is not to be excluded that wherever there is life there is the potentiality of the attainment of personality. But this must remain speculative though belief in it might relieve some of the hardest enigmas of animal existence. At the point reached by the present discussion, however, in connection with the problem of the relation of man's status as member of the living world to his status as endowed with creative personality, the truth on which I would insist is that throughout history human

[1] *The Unique Status of Man*, Chapter VI.

nature provides the conditions in which the personal principle
with its striving for value can be realized. This is not discernible elsewhere. The fact that in animal life, and pre-
eminently in reproduction, the individual end is subordinated
to that of the species, and that there is much in the conditions
of human life which seems to suggest man's kinship in this
respect with his "cousins in feather and fur"[1] does not disprove
the hypothesis that in human experience self-transcendence
is of a generically different kind. It is not only that greater
and greater wholes arise for the contemplation or imagination
of the intellectual being, from the community or nation to
humanity, from humanity to an intelligible or spiritual cosmos.
Nor is it merely that with these larger visions the emotion
and striving through sacrifice towards such ends deepen to a
change in kind of value. It appears that expansion of the
object to greater universality follows as a result of experience
in the subject, which is the fundamental source of the differentiae
of human activity. The essence of self-transcendence for ideal
ends belongs to the nature of personality. There are experiences
which are very ordinary, the natural delight in exercise of
initiative, the new life or "conversion" (as it is sometimes
called) which begins when the individual finds the way open
to freedom in work and service, or the "responsibility" which
demands independent exercise of judgment. All who have
had practical opportunities in throwing open such possibilities or have heard first-hand intimate accounts of it, will
surely agree that we are here in contact with a real principle
in the nature of man. It is most striking where human relations
offer opportunities for self-transcendence.

"To love one's neighbour as oneself is not a mere pious
statement. It is every whit as much a law of life as fresh air
is to the body. To live to oneself only is never to live at all."[2]
This law of life I take to be primarily the law of personal life.

These truths are inscribed in the lives of men who have

[1] Dean Inge: *Christian Ethics*, V, p. 280.
[2] Wilfred Grenfell: *Forty Years for Labrador*, p. 347.

served their fellows in an eminent degree. I would refer to the autobiographical writings of three men who have all made use of a medical career for creative activities which have had extraordinary effects in human good—Sir Ronald Ross, Dr. Albert Schweitzer, Sir Wilfred Grenfell. The facts in regard to the standpoints of these men, their methods of thought and work which are especially significant in relation to the present argument, are as follows. The characteristics common to all, their choice of the medical profession, their devotion to human welfare and love of men are exhibited in forms so wholly individual that it seems to be only a rough classification which brings them together determined by the immense importance of their beneficial work, and the fact that the cure of sickness is in a sense in all three the primary practical aim. The uniqueness of the personal springs of action, its unfathomable subjective sources could hardly be given more vivid illustration in any grouping based on an important similarity. Sir Ronald Ross tells us that he had no strong sense of vocation in early life, his chief preoccupation and pleasure was in his world of imagination.[1] He approached his life task with unconscious steps. He was not ambitious; the medical profession was not his own choice, and at first little to his taste. The most astounding quality in his earlier career was its versatility; perhaps we may see in this the ceaseless unconscious quest for the direction in which he could overpass the limiting conditions of existence. After many experiences we find this lover of beauty who delighted in gorgeous dreams, highly coloured romances, poetic cadences, breaking out into lyrical paeans over sanitation. For he had seen

> "The pitiful faces ask, Can ye not cure?
> We answer, No, not yet—we seek the laws."[2]

Love of men as individuals had drawn to itself all the other impulses of a nature rich both in artistic and scientific tendencies. "Here is a city seething with filth and disease. Your

---

[1] *Memoirs.*   [2] Ronald Ross: *Philosophies.*

job, Samaritan, is plain. You must wipe away those slums, that filth, these diseases."[1] There is only one way for each self, though the majority may not find it, and spend their lives labouring to walk along the rails laid down for all persons of such and such classes or professions. But this common way, too, is necessary to history, which treats of the community, the general movement; and into which the individual himself enters as a category. Also this has truth as a highway of life. It represents truly the planes of experience on which not only the majority, but all men and women must move as to a great part of their existence. For the types of civilization we have been able to evolve require these forms of order and system, and they are necessitated by something which seems inseparable from our historical being.

Sir Wilfred Grenfell tells us that he discovered his vocation after one conversation on the subject of careers with the old family doctor, who showed him a brain in a jar. "I was thrilled with entirely new emotions. I had never thought of man's body as a machine."[2] There stands out in his experience a combination of unusual daring and even recklessness in physical difficulties and dangers with intense belief in the sole efficacy of love. "I have always felt that reliance on physical strength alone is only like war—an insurance against failure. Only unselfish love can win in the end."[3] Love is no doubt the ultimate power in the lives of all these men, driving Ronald Ross to the discovery of the secret of malaria, Sir Wilfred Grenfell to forty years' work in giving new life, hope and happiness to the lonely and suffering fisher-folk of Labrador, Dr. Albert Schweitzer to the relief of the miseries of African negroes. But even love is a power unique in its deepest quality for each, using the poetic imagination and scientific zeal of Ross, the delight of Sir Wilfred Grenfell in physical adventure in Labrador sea and ice, and his native passion for medicine, the music, philosophy, theological fervour and interest of the

[1] *Memoirs.*
[2] *Forty Years for Labrador*, p. 29.   [3] Ibid.

scholar Dr. Schweitzer. The latter writes, "Enormous values come to nothing every moment through the missing of opportunities, but the values which get turned into will and deed mean wealth which must not be under-valued. Our humanity is by no means so materialistic as foolish talk is continually asserting it to be. Judging from what I have seen of men and women, I am convinced that there is far more in them of idealist will-power than ever comes to the surface of the world. Just as the water of the streams we see is small compared to that which flows underground, so the ideal which becomes visible is small in amount compared with what men and women bear locked in their hearts, unreleased or scarcely released. To unbind what is bound, to bring the underground waters to the surface, mankind is waiting and longing for such as can do that."[1]

He speaks out of an extraordinarily rich experience—labour in the service of art and science, search for the historical understanding of the life of Christ, philosophy, music, medicine, work in an African medical mission, friendship in all these spheres with thinkers, teachers, students, musicians, suffering negroes. The truth he finds throughout is that which I have attempted to express in a more abstract way—"far more idealist will-power than comes to the surface", "the idealism which becomes visible, *small in amount compared with what men and women bear locked in their hearts*" (italics mine). This is the deepest quality in the subject, which can never be completely known. Also, as Dr. Schweitzer has pointed out, it is never fully conveyed into deeds. In my view it is not possible under the conditions of our experience that all that is locked in the heart should be released. Yet we cannot define the bounds which the free individual may reach in his creative effort. Before I had come across the passage quoted, I had written down (in poorer language) almost the same thought suggested by the impression of Dr. Schweitzer's own life, as typical of the conception of the personal principle developed

[1] *My Life and Thought*, Chapter IX.

in this book. The essential self enters this experience and contributes to it all the value of his own being. This means from the other side that he draws out of each field of activity a meaning wholly individual. The truth of the event is not that vocations usually distinct are combined in one life—they *are* the life of this person. He must enter upon this kind of practical service because he is theologian, philosopher, musician, or rather because he is something which could only find the highest value by taking up these types of activity successively. There is always more in the creative subject than can be brought into experience. The longing to find out the truth about the Life of Jesus, the joy in a new understanding of Bach, the wrestle with Kant's religious metaphysic, even the mission to save the glorious old organs from the tyranny of modern mechanism, all contribute to the genius of Dr. Schweitzer's service of love amongst some of his fellows who lacked any contact with these things. Perhaps it will be said that these unusual individuals must not be taken as typical. To this I should reply that the conception of personality is not built up on the rare evidence of lives of exceptional men. But we find in such lives illustrations beyond anything that could have been looked for of the view to which I think we are brought, both by enquiry into the nature of the self and by experience of more ordinary men and women. Sometimes it seems to happen that the individual who might well have led an average life has been turned to a course in which he becomes a person outstanding whether in general estimation or in the thoughts of the few who really know, because a moment of realization of creative will or Dr. Schweitzer's "idealist will-power" coincides with a direct view of the field within which it can work. This is perhaps not unlike Plato's turning of the eye of the soul to the light.

It is here important to note that the total inadequacy and barrenness of the timeless theory of selves appears evident from close study of individual histories. Will it be argued that the greater the timeless reality, the more profound and varied will appear the life-interests of the individual, his experiences, the radiance of his character shining in success and failure, the virtue and strength of intellect expressed through the form of the temporal process? The general answer to this type of interpretation was given in the earlier examination of the nature of the self,[1] and the argument that it is impossible to define this in abstraction from history. History, indeed, in this aspect (though it is only one) might be likened to the coral reef, of which memories are the omnipresent multitude of ever busy builders. There is no self without memory, no self without history. It has been maintained that experience provides overwhelming testimony to this fact. Is it conceivable that the content and essence of such lives as those to which reference has been made could be transformed so as to dispense with the temporal vehicle and yet reveal the value which distinguishes the self from all others? Must not all the significance vanish which is dependent on development, the travail of the deepening of feeling and thought, when we think of the self as a timeless being? McTaggart in fact, the most distinguished representative of this view in recent philosophy, admits that the self in reality becomes a principle of intelligence alone, for in the non-temporal reality volitions and emotions must be shown to be in truth cogitations. Volition then is understood as acquiescence in what is.[2] McTaggart's position may be described as resulting from a brilliantly sustained effort to demonstrate that the highest value of personal experience does characterize a universe of timeless reality. The temporal process must be unreal in his view, because irrational. The reference is introduced here not as a criticism of McTaggart's whole position, whose finely knit argument would require an elaborate examination, but to draw attention to the difficulty of conceiving our highest values as present in a timeless experience. And this by implication he appears himself to recognize.

[1] Chapter III.
[2] *The Nature of Existence*, Vol. II.

NOTE TO CHAPTER VII

As Professor Hartmann's treatment of the problem of freedom appears to be the most striking and original in recent moral philosophy, some supplement seems necessary to what was said in the text, in order to make clear the relation of the position taken in this work to his view. In important respects there is agreement, especially in the doctrine that freedom proceeds from the principle of the person, which, "in so far as it throws its own determination into the scale, we do not know".[1] I am also in entire accord with the position that "the will must be just as free in its badness and degradation as in its goodness".[2] Hartmann's abstraction of the self-determination of the will from the moral principle, so that there are three orders or kinds of determination, the law of nature, the law of the ought, and the principle of the person, involves, however, a very different conception of personal creativity from that which I have presented. He breaks up what, in my view, is a single process of moral experience, when he conceives the moral principle with its ought over against the person, who may or may not throw his own determination into the scale. Values or principles of the ought, as for instance the finalistic, do not determine the will coercively. "The value determines if at all with the help of the autonomy of the person." The problem does not arise in this form in my interpretation, because this autonomy of the person appears to be no other than the principle individual in each, impelling him to create such value in experience as he can conceive. It is the confusion in the individual's feeling and discernment of value which is the cause of his rejection of a higher. Professor Hartmann's scheme certainly has the merit of bringing into full daylight the fact of freedom, neither compelled as an intelligible principle to obey the categorical imperative, nor as a member or link in the sensible world to follow the sequence of

[1] *Ethics*, Vol. III, Chapter XVII (*b*), translated by Stanton Coit.
[2] Ibid., Appendix.

natural or "anthropological" causation. The ought, however, does not appear to be a distinct principle, but to be the moral and spiritual necessity of realizing the value present to our minds if we are to remain true to type, not to fall below the personal order of being. "We are seeking", says Hartmann, "for the principle of self-determination as such, the mysterious potency which is given to persons in preference to all real entities." But though mysterious and baffling to our insight, we make it more mysterious if we abstract it from the value which it requires us to realize. This is not an external principle imposing a law to be accepted or rejected by the person, but the ideal of his own highest experience, and therefore both freely and necessarily accepted, as something in which he finds himself transcended. The chief difficulty which I find in Professor Hartmann's view is that in rejecting every principle strong enough to show reason for the act—except autonomy itself—lest the reason shown should take on the character of a cause necessarily determining, he leaves us with a bare X, the self-determination of the will. Either this approaches dangerously near the freedom of indifference, or, as "an irrational type which cannot be pursued further", it is wholly unknown. It is the latter alternative which is accepted in Professor Hartmann's philosophy. We must agree that there is mystery or a factor not wholly intelligible, but the analysis of the concrete spiritual process into abstract and independent elements or entities seems to add to the obscurity in the *idea* of freedom, though as to the *fact* it is set in a strong light by his impressive argument.

CHAPTER VIII

HISTORY AND ETHICS

ETHICAL SYSTEMS AND THE SOURCES OF VALUE

"There is surely nothing that a man possesses more fitted than the soul for the avoidance of evil, the discernment and choice of the supremely best, and having made the choice to dwell together with it for the rest of life. Therefore the second place was assigned to it in the order of value."

PLATO, *Laws*, 728. Jowett's translation

IN the preceding chapter it was argued that the nature of human freedom can best be understood if we approach the problem from the standpoint of history. The position may seem paradoxical in view of the fact that it is the study of history which furnishes the greatest sources of scepticism as to the possibilities of freedom. If we concentrate on the problem in the individual life, we find important grounds for belief in the liberty of the essential self. There is the inextinguishable verdict of self-consciousness, the immense weight of the ethical argument that freedom is essential to moral responsibility and we are under the moral law. Also we have much experience of the original energy of individuals overcoming gigantic obstacles and acting in ways that could not have been predicted and seem beyond their natural capacity, in response to ideals, the claims of love and loyalty, the passion for adventure. We may be half-convinced in the study and the laboratory by a deterministic theory of all processes including the human. But in the practical sphere we are not conscious of its force, and we continue to act on the assumption that something at least, if not everything, depends upon the self. When we turn to history, we find indeed that its course presents a degree of irregularity which precludes the bringing of the events under the type of uniform laws such as prevail for our categorial knowledge in other departments. We notice also that, as the historian points out,[1] the individual is the disturbing factor. The great man is apt to upset all our calculations. Even little men will not perform their parts as pawns on the chessboard. To quote Troeltsch, "History is an immeasurable, incomparable profusion of always new, unique, and hence individual tendencies, welling up from undiscoverable depths."[2] But are we able to set down this profusion of the unique and individual to the credit of freedom? Freedom is something positive. No modern defendant of freedom is content with the liberty of indifference. From the standpoint of this treatise, the originative principle proceeds from the core of personality, and since through personality value is found in the process and added to its course, history, it seems, ought to exhibit a continuous increase in the efficacy of human ideals. As the argument of the chapters on the factors of history has reminded us, no such universal tendencies can be found in history in so far as known. Even partial exhibitions of such phases of advance in distinct civilizations are incomplete, and as we attempt to grasp the results for human happiness of the Roman peace, or for spiritual harmony of the Christian charity, they wither under our observation. The conclusions in this respect of earlier sections are here only recalled, as a preface to the explanation of the approach to ethics and primarily to freedom, from history. In the first place, if history cannot reveal freedom, the liberty of the individual in the sheltered environment in which he may be set by ethical theory is of no avail. This fact is indeed recognized by the greatest philosophers and prophets of practice, though the philosophers do not always seem to perceive its implications. The prophets and reformers are continually occupied in the quest for principles which will overpass the relativity of epochs, generations, even civilizations, reveal that value cannot perish out of the world, and that transvaluation has some absolute limit. The prophet, however (and obviously the

[1] Cf. Bury, referred to in Chapter VI.
[2] *Christian Thought*, see heading to Chapter VI.

reformer), does not appear to recognize the necessity of showing that these principles must be such as have always been accessible to man,[1] and that if valid, their working in past history must be discoverable, though little may have been achieved. In the second place, as we have argued, freedom in its true form, as positive and creative, can be shown to have been the source of everything in the character of the human process which constitutes it as history. The fact in regard to the absence of continuous progress in the process of history cannot undermine the belief in freedom, since history even without progress is only possible on the condition of the creative energy of selves. Only thus is man able to keep his head above the waters of the eternally meaningless. It is the approach to history from ethics with its postulate of the necessity of freedom to moral action, history being conceived as the drama of combined human activities, which gives birth to the tremendous claims of progress in a world of persons, which have never yet been fulfilled. In order to emphasize the exact nature of the problem which thus arises, it is necessary at this point to refer to the standpoints of some of the great ethical systems and consider the relation of their methods and ideals to the sources of value, in the creativity of the personal principle as we have conceived it. Reflection on these systems in the contrasts they suggest with the historic world leads, I think, to the impression that they imply a greater optimism than is justified as to the possibilities in attainment of a valuable existence, and unconsciously, perhaps, a greater pessimism as to the interpretation of the past and hope of the future than is consistent with their character. It should be added that in the view of the self developed in this treatise the distinctive character of the ethical problem for man is engendered by history. As previously noted, the irreversibility of the temporal process is all-important for ethics. If indeed the task of man as "bearer" of the moral value were exhausted in his function of contributing to the realization of "Good" as

[1] See Chapter VII.

an added perfection of nature, it might be otherwise. It would be for him to erect beyond the natural order the order in which the moral perfection would be expressed in human relations, an added glory of nature, through which the waste of the over-lavish production of life and the harvest of competition and internecine conflict of living things might be atoned for, and the stature of man as nature's greatest achievement raised. We can suppose the passage of unlimited ages for the con-summation of this task, unattended by agonizing regret for the slowness of the advance. Successive races would take up the problem, experimenting in forms of the control of nature by intelligence. The irretrievable loss of splendid civilizations and irreplaceable personalities need not be felt as a stain on human progress. Irretrievability, in fact, would not have its ethical sting. Man starts afresh as an artist throwing away his spoilt or imperfect pictures. History need not burden the new race with grief that the sun has set on Crete and Babylon, Athens and Rome, nor the sons be tortured with regret, that they suffered their fathers to pass away without the vision of the new dawn. Man's work would lie only in the direction of his future and the dateless architecture of the good. His moral teachers would not be required with Professor Hartmann to hurl defiance, as it were, at historical experience, declaring that it cannot be decisive, and "the creative element in man is necessarily in opposition to it".[1] The very terms, indeed, of Hartmann's noble protest involve recognition that ethics demands at some time, though far off, a change in the character of history. As history and the greatest moral philosophy have shown, the moral consciousness of the individual is under no illusion, the result of long-established custom, law, public opinion, religious "sanctions". Since the problem of ethics is bound up with the nature of selfhood, as belonging to past and future, the irreversibility of the past is a main source of moral experience, involving that in certain respects what has been done *is* irremediable. Hence the ethical emotion of remorse,

[1] See Chapter VII.

which need not trouble the unhistoric ethic. On these facts depends the full force of the moral ought. The abstraction suggested above of an ethics of the Good as an ideal state of existence to be brought about sooner or later, after many trials and errors, and once achieved indifferent to the past, is a false one, and the idea only thrown out in order to make clearer the centre of ethics in personality. The abstract treatment is, however, approached both in some ethical theories of the Good, not excepting that of Aristotle, and in the exaggeration of creative personality, by some philosophies which would release personality from any limitation of its activity resulting from past action.

In the Platonic philosophy we have the fountain-head of objective systems of ethics, in which moral values are conceived as having a type of being in independence of the selves who experience and endeavour to realize them. We naturally turn to this as the greatest example of an ethic which seems to present absolute principles in complete detachment from history. Plato himself was indeed as a teacher a great realist who showed a profound consciousness of the difficulties of bringing the ideal to life in human society, whether in the almost impossible practical task he set himself in Sicily or in the severe discipline prescribed in the *Republic* for bringing to birth and full growth in passionate and gifted youth the one desire for absolute good. He was intensely aware of the colossal difficulties of fashioning a state to reflect the cosmic good. In the *Republic* and still more in the *Laws* there is abundant evidence of the difficulty of his faith in human nature. We must notice how little if any scope is allowed for moral creativeness in the philosopher, the discovery of an ideal diverging by a hair's breadth from that laid down in the code for the state. The philosophic guardian has indeed an insight into the good, but it does not appear that this priceless gift is his for the discernment of an ever higher goal for his people and finer means of attaining it. He will excel in devotion to the state, but it seems doubtful whether extraordinary aspira-

tion is to play a part in his well-ordered life, or a new illumination to be brought back from his moments of higher contemplation for the experience of the citizen's common day. It is
not suggested that the gifts which in the ordinary state would
have attracted to him the fickle enthusiasm of the mob are
to be sublimated into a divine force of personality which
would enchant into nobler impulses and modes of life the
workers of the third class. There is sufficient evidence in the
Dialogues that Plato had been impressed by the genius of
individual men, and in the enigma of the identity of the
philosopher, who speaks as Socrates in the majority of the
Dialogues, he left a memorial to the greatness of a single personality in the form of an enduring problem for philosophy.
But he believed average human beings to be incapable of
living together according to justice and harmony without
much restriction of their native tendencies. It is of great
significance, however, that in the *Laws*, his final work in
which, though private life is permitted, the régime of its
regulation is most elaborately worked out, there are signs of a
development of his conception of the soul, the person, the
principle which knows good and evil.[1] Plato's conception of
the nature of the moral self, and of the hindrances to its
performance of its true work ($\tau\grave{o}$ $\tau\grave{a}$ $a\mathring{v}\tauo\mathring{v}$ $\pi\rho\acute{a}\tau\tau\epsilon\iota\nu$, *Republic*), is,
I think, nearer than may appear on a first consideration to that
of a philosophy which makes personality the central factor of
moral history, rather than the objective system of ideals or
eternal forms manifested in experience. I would refer in the
first place to his profoundly realistic statement of the conditions militating against the realization of valuable life in the
community. Foremost is the problem of the regulation of
numbers which he regards as of the first importance, expressing
this conviction under the symbolic form of an ideal number.
There are the twin dangers of over-population, on the one
hand, and under-population on the other, brought about by
"a deluge of disease or a plague of war". But "even God is

[1] Cf. A. E. Taylor: *Socrates*.

said not to be able to fight against necessity" (ἀνάγκη). Here he expresses in the Greek way the baffling fact of frequent destruction of the meaning and value of man's work by the operation of natural factors. For over the enigmatic relation between those almost or altogether uncontrollable events and the reasoned course of man's spiritual activity which they throw into confusion and disorder, mysterious powers conferring dignity upon our discomfiture are found to preside, necessity for Plato, chance at times from a different viewpoint for Aristotle. Over-population, the tendencies external and internal that generate war or disease—these things are not definitely to be charged to an evil principle in the soul. They belong to man's environmental situation, including his physical nature. It will be suggested in a later chapter that whilst we cannot (consistently with the standpoint of this work) appeal to a "Spirit of History" which can draw together all experience of human suffering into a knowledge which will enable final victory over these difficult factors, it is possible to conclude that history in the end does count towards a greater power of personality in relation to them. In the second place, Plato's recognition of the problem of unfavourable natural or necessary conditions is counterbalanced to some extent by the immense stress he lays in the *Laws* on the soul, as the principle of all moral regeneration, the imperative need of honouring the soul, and rejecting the false ways of such honour.[1] The spirit of his ethical analysis is more subjective here than in his other Dialogues. The subtleties and deceptions of egoism have seldom been exposed with equal penetration. We may perhaps interpret Plato's deep distrust of the admission of change into the spirit of the community, his harsh measures for the exclusion of its influence, as indication that he was here attempting to fight down almost a first principle of selfhood, to alter the perhaps unalterable vital force. For in man this force belongs to the historic order, where change means not only decay but also growth in value. It must be remembered

[1] *Laws*, Book IV.

how important for his philosophy was the truth that the soul is a principle of change. "All things which have a soul change, and possess in themselves a principle of change, and in changing move according to law, and to the order of destiny: natures which have undergone a lesser change move less, and on the earth's surface, but those which have suffered more change and have become more criminal sink into the abyss."[1] Now "Law is the mind of the State",[2] or distribution of mind therein. Thus the bureaucratic system is lent a sublimity which may give hope of successful control of those recalcitrant forces also ennobled as "necessity". If it is conceded that in this strain in Plato's moral philosophy we find implicit the germ of an Ethics from the standpoint of personality, with the corresponding admission of the dualistic factor in the social-historical process, a contrast must be allowed between this position and that which is regarded as more typically Platonic. In the *Philebus* human life is presented as the scene, so to speak, in which the cosmic good can be enacted, in the orders of beauty, measure, truth, knowledge, and the pure pleasures. This perhaps expresses only a partial point of view. It is ethics in relation to the perfection of individual life. The difficulties which enter in through the relations of individuals in the state need not cloud the picture. In the *Republic* or the *Gorgias* there is perhaps nothing that is inconsistent with the ethical teaching of the *Laws*, but the absence from the latter of the philosophy of the Form of good creates a different spiritual impression, even suggesting a different metaphysic of values.[3]

It is the objective idealism of value, almost universally regarded as the essential Platonism in ethics, with which any idealistic view that does not accept it in the strictly Platonic sense has chiefly to reckon. The fountain-head of all later theories of absolute value, this is indeed inseparable from

[1] *Laws*, X, 904. Jowett's translation. [2] Ibid., IV, 714.
[3] For the present purpose the problem of the development of Plato's philosophy and its relation to that of Socrates may be ignored.

Plato's doctrine of the soul, as is clearly brought out by Professor Taylor (who, however, ascribes the doctrine to Socrates).[1] Yet in this aspect of Platonism we find an interpretation of practical life which, if we follow out all its implications, might be sharply contrasted with the other aspect in which the overwhelming difficulties of the soul in the achievement of inner harmony are set forth. How is this consistent with the idea of experience as deriving such reality as it has from the realm of the unchanging patterns of the good in all its forms? The deepest contrasts of ethical interpretation within idealism are not then foreign to the mind of Plato. It belongs to the scale of his thinking that this is not obscured. In the light of the absolute theory of the good, the cares and vacillating interests of daily life might appear to be reduced to nothingness. Yet there is in the phenomenal world a being which, only trembling on the confines of existence,[2] is capable of knowing reality and the good, constantly overwhelmed, however, by a kind of blindness in which its divine gift cannot be used. No man does wrong voluntarily.[3] Yet the best state cannot be realized, and the second best depends on conditions which rob the individual of free choice of his form of life. Thus the great paradox of the practical life stands out unveiled in Plato. It is beyond the limits of our argument to examine the sources of the theory of forms, except only in respect to the interpretation of the moral values as having an objective unchanging type of being independent of the soul. Plato himself is of course aware of this difficulty, as is evident from the famous passage in the *Sophist* admitting the inconceivability of true Being as other than life and mind.[4] When indeed we attempt to conceive the significance of justice in itself, and the other virtues as changeless forms of which all the virtues in the selves and their interrelations are imitations

[1] A. E. Taylor: *Socrates*, Chapter IV.
[2] Cf. the origin of the individual soul in the *Timaeus*.
[3] *Timaeus*, 86 E. κακὸς μὲν γὰρ ἑκὼν οὐδείς. The position is of course fundamental in Plato.
[4] *Sophist*, 249.

or reflections, can we give meaning to this doctrine except by attributing to the forms themselves a kind of spiritual being? Otherwise their nature is unknowable. This is not to raise the question whether we can conceive any existence except that of a psychic type. The immediate question is whether there can be validity in the projection of qualities with which we are only acquainted as qualities of selves into a kind of objective existence abstracted from conscious being. This objection to Platonism, considered as the philosophy of moral ideas as forms, would hold even without the individualistic view of character and act, though it is enforced by this. Here I mean the position that justice or courage in A is not identical with justice or courage in B, but each man's virtues are what they are in the concrete whole of the self. It is the influence of our generalizing type of intelligence together with the convenience of language and exigencies of practical life which justify the general notions of the virtues. The conception of their existence then in any form, apart from persons, seems fallacious. But if it were possible to concede such existence (or subsistence) must not its forms be spiritual? Possibly this has been the nerve or significance of ethical Platonism and all kindred doctrines, as, for instance, that of Professor Nicolai Hartmann. Certainly, when the ordinary man speaks of the spirit of justice, he appears unconsciously to personify, and the mythologist or animist only half asleep in his soul awakens. Without the presence in some degree in our imagination of this higher animism, should we feel the same glow and exaltation in the confidence that we are following justice, faithful to truth? The historic experience, as I should argue, leads to the more subjective view. Those imperishable forms of virtue cannot be united with the soul except in so far as it is from the originative principle in the subject that they proceed. The virtues arise as aspects of the striving for a higher experience which it is possible to conceive and objectify as ideas or forms. On this view not less than on the other the soul is nearest to reality in the experience of value.

That the abstraction of a realm of moral ideas cannot be maintained receives, I think, a remarkable illustration if we turn from Plato to an important modern work in which a similar position is advanced with considerable force in connection with phenomenological philosophy. Professor Hartmann works out in his *Ethics* with trenchant logic all the implications of a doctrine which derives moral values from an order of being or of essences transcendent in relation to man. He applies the theory to a group of the finer qualities of spiritual life which he traces in the higher experience, and adds to the traditional Aristotelian and Christian virtues. Ethics must include in the values existing as "essences" not only those principles more or less recognized in all cultural ages and systems which many influences help us to treat as real beings, whether animistically or aesthetically viewed, but many subtler qualities of a noble life to the objectification of which we are not aided by familiar names and traditional canonization, education and literature. Professor Hartmann thus conceives a world of values, or value essences eternally existent or subsistent, and introduced into human experience in so far as amongst the beings therein active occur persons who are "bearers" of these values. He supposes a "hidden life of the idea" in the age which is lifted by some prophet into the light. At such a moment there takes place the Platonic anamnesis on a grand scale, everyone recognizing what in a sense he already knows. He points to the occurrence of situations in which everyone perceives the same value as evidence that values have an existence in themselves. It may be doubted, however, whether such situations do occur. Certainly there are times when a similar sense of need seems present throughout a community, and a similar idea or value to be discerned very widely, giving satisfaction to the need. Probably the greatest illustration of this is that which is given by Professor Hartmann. "One central value, or even a whole group of them, enters into the ethical consciousness, and radically transforms the view of the world and of life. Such a valuational discovery occurred in primitive Christianity, in regard to the peculiar moral significance of neighbour love." Other students of spiritual conditions in the Roman world at the beginning of the Christian era have conceived the Christian doctrine of immortality as the chief source of the transformation since it met the deepest need of that age. Even here, however, our interpretation would hold good. The need for the new view of the world and the value which meets it are both individual experiences. The individuality is greatest in proportion to the spiritual quality of the experience, and least distinguishable in proportion to the strength of those less human factors in man exhibited in the phenomena of "mass psychology". (This truth was illustrated in the discussion of the category of nation.[1]) Hartmann's "hidden life of the idea" in the age would on this view be a metaphorical account of the event, expressing the intellectual need of an objective interpretation and the emotional need for ascribing independent reality to a great experience. In other examples of this thinker's interpretation of the moral values, striking illustrations may be found of the method of unlimited objectification. He distinguishes the "ontological" and the "axiological" character of the relations between persons. The value, for instance, of trust, fidelity is an *ens sui generis*[2] added to the material by the act. With this I should agree, up to a point, but not that the meaning or value added has a being independently of the person who introduces it. When we consider how the situation comes about we perceive that there could not be a material structure of the relation of trust unless the persons concerned found value in the existence of this relation. Can therefore the abstraction of the value from the fact be treated as other than an intellectual subtlety or logical analysis of the whole situation into its elements, which can be conceived apart, but could not exist in separation? In my view, moreover, the virtue—fidelity in this case—is not identical in any two cases. The fidelity of Pylades to Orestes is not the fidelity of Horatio to

[1] Chapter VI.   [2] *Ethics*, Vol. II, Chapter XVI.

Hamlet, or of Mary Seton to Mary Queen of Scots. The stronger the love, the more unique in every instance. How inadequate the notion of "carrier" (*träger*) to convey this truth! The doctrine of the ideal world of values is tested or strained to the utmost in Hartmann's treatment of personality itself as an objective value, and here, I think, it breaks. His very consistency in this crucial case seems to reveal that in the analysis of moral experience we must begin at the other end, not with the objectified quality, but with the individual source of which the value experience or spiritual qualities are unique manifestations. These must, as we have all along recognized, be perceived and grouped together, or classified with experiences of other persons resembling them in important respects. To the value of personality, Hartmann attributes an ideal self-existence. Here the value is evidently the personality of the individual, i.e. not the universal quality of possession of individuality, but "what distinguishes the individuality of one from that of another", or "that which distinguishes personality qualitatively in idea". He appears in effect to give to the person himself the status of one of his own qualities, yet without the universality which attaches to qualities as such. But we have to do "not with a single quality but with an unlimited variety, with an entire perspective into which the table of values issues".[1] This unlimited variety would certainly distinguish the personal value from all other values, but is it not with the source of the unlimited variety that we are here concerned, something that cannot be objectified? It would appear that personality (like Plato's soul in the *Phaedo*) in entering the world of ideas would sacrifice its essence as individual. Hartmann, however, supposes his doctrine to be consistent with the individuality of persons. It is the ideal being, "the ought of only one special person. It is his moral ethos which he is responsible for fulfilling". If this be granted and personality belongs to the same realm as the other values, those ideas or essences of justice, wisdom and the rest, then

[1] *Ethics*, Vol. II, Chapter XVI.

its inclusion throws a searching light upon these. Must they not all logically share its nature? An ideal world of persons or souls is revealed. There seems to be involved an animistic root of this whole method of thought, though it is not of course the only root. Possibly it might be held that personality as essence can be regarded as a value summing up all the values of the person, the individuality consisting in the special form of the relationship of these, their balance or proportion. Yet in this form also, I think, the attempt to conceive person as idea or value essence must fail, because person is essentially subject, whilst the value essence or idea is contemplated as object. In truth these values of personality which "cannot coincide with the actual personality", which have "ideal self-existence", are inconceivable except as spiritual beings. Nor can we (as already indicated) remain at this point. The moral experiences, the love of the self, his joy in knowledge, have their true nature, not as real essences, but as his experiences, his ideal life, aspects of which he perceives in contemplation, objectively. Hartmann himself appears to be not far from this standpoint when he observes, "The sensing of the universal values is not purely an inward contemplation, but proceeds by way of observing an actual moral life."[1] But if it is in an actual life that we perceive the values, it is in that life that they are what they are, and not in a realm in which abstraction is made of the creative energy of the person. This position has been illustrated in the last chapter through reference to autobiographies. It is not to be questioned that any ethical interpretation which ignored the significance of that strain to the transcendent which is the primary fact in the moral life would fail. What then have we to put in the place of the Platonic forms and all kindred philosophies? Can there be a struggle to transcend without knowledge in some sense of the transcendent good? Further consideration of this problem must be postponed.

Returning to the consideration of Greek ethics from the

[1] *Ethics*, Vol. II, Part II, Section VII, Chapter XXXII (*k*), "The Values of Personality."

standpoint of the present chapter, we might expect to find that
Aristotle, who in his own view and that of probably the majority
of students treated this subject in a more practical way than
Plato, was nearer to the historical view in ethics. His attitude
to the problem of the moral life, however, can, I think, be
shown to be more remote. The following observation is made
by Professor Taylor: "The reading of the *Nicomachean Ethics*
has always left me with the suspicion that one of the differences
between Plato and his successor was that Plato went for his
knowledge of men and women to the book of life, Aristotle
to a collection of stage-plays."[1] It may at least be agreed
that Aristotle's *dramatis personae*, the high-souled man and
his lesser compeers, whom he treats with so meditated an
urbanity, have the guise of members of a world artistically
organized, living statues who have shaken off the dust and
débris of their environment. We are not in the world of historic
actuality. But perhaps this is the proper method of ethics
since it is concerned with the ideal? The answer to this—
already implied—is that whilst the existence of ethical systems
does depend on the possibility of a branch of investigation
concerning the ideal for individual life, the individual and the
society in which he has to live in accordance with the highest
that is in him must be the actual individual and society in the
historic world. We must not be presented with a state of
affairs in which we feel that there has been abstraction from the
actual. In perhaps the finest passage of the *Ethics* Aristotle
rejects the counsel that "being men we should think human
thoughts and mortals mortal, but rather in as far as in us lies
we must be immortal and do everything that we may to live
in accordance with the best that is in us".[2] He is however,
speaking of the contemplative life, in which in his view it is not
necessary to have society for the practice of justice, and even
friends are not indispensable. Self-sufficiency is here the ideal.
As regards the "practical" in Aristotle's sense it demands the

[1] Critical Notice, "Mure's Aristotle," *Mind*, October 1932.
[2] *Nicomachean Ethics*, X, 7.

rejection of any idea of an absolute good. It must state the good for man so that it will have a universal appeal to the rational nature which is his peculiar distinction. The good life then will consist in the highest expression or energy of this nature. The principle that the aim of ethics is to determine the nature of the Chief Good and the means of its attainment was arrived at by Aristotle by an extremely common-sense method together with logical control of the results. The practical form of means and end, each end itself becoming means, suggests a process to which some term must be fixed to avoid an *ad infinitum*. This term is straightway identified with the Chief Good. The apparent simplicity of the argument veils a profound obscurity. Aristotle is assuming that the gradation of increase in value is continuous from the first purposive activity instrumental to a useful piece of work to the conclusion which reason must assume. These assumptions have to be investigated in relation to the essential experience of value. If a work of art is being created, or men are labouring for the emancipation of the slaves, it is true that the nearer the workers are to the achievement of these things the better the state of the movement or the greater the value of the aesthetic or moral product. These are the objective results. The relation of means to end is not necessarily identical with the ethical relation of instrumental to intrinsic good. It cannot be assumed that the earlier stages in any life-task are therefore more elementary in value. In the progress of the most socially beneficial task it is impossible to say that spiritual energy was at its height at the moment of completion. It cannot at least be laid down as a universal principle that to the later stage the higher moral perfection will correspond. If, however, Aristotle means that the order is one of pure value throughout and the definition of the Chief Good as "the energy of the soul in accordance with virtue", reflected back upon his line of argument determines the temporal stages as degrees of value, then his famous introduction to *Ethics*, I, with its familiar examples might be taken as a parable. Yet the identification of the Chief Good with the

Final End would remain very ambiguous. The conception seems now nearer to the Platonic Form. It is the ideal of value manifested in a life that reflects it.

Aristotle's statement of ethical method has been of great importance in the history of the subject. We may ask, however, from another point of view, namely, that of individual interpretation of the purposive sequence, whether his view of method is true to the facts. It does indeed happen that a man may devote his life to the achievement of some supreme purpose, and attaining this feel that his active life is over. But even in such a case the sense of a conclusion seems due rather to conditions of human experience contingent and irrelevant, such as the decline of physical vigour. In respect to the satisfaction of the moral experience the personal ideal, there can be no finality, and it may be questioned whether this is ever felt in the consummation, though it is sometimes anticipated in the conception of a large task of strong appeal. When Cecil Rhodes wrote in 1877 on his plan of life: "It often strikes a man to enquire what is the chief good in life. To one the thought comes that it is a happy marriage, to another great wealth, to a third travel, and so on, and as each seizes the idea he more or less works for its attainment for the rest of his existence,"[1] there appears to underlie his words the fallacy ("naturalistic") to which Professor Moore draws attention in the identification of "Good", as value, with some particular good or goods.[2] John Stuart Mill's doctrine of "the greatest happiness of the greatest number" appeared to him to offer an ideal which could not be surpassed as the goal of human endeavour, satisfying "the imagination by its vastness".[3] He imputed to it all the value which could be added by conceiving the virtues as not separable from the end in the good life, though theoretically they constitute the means. One such vast object may seem to the individual to absorb all others as his goal when he reflects on his activities, objectifying them in causal sequences of means and ends. But the power which

[1] Sarah Millen: *Rhodes.*   [2] *Principia Ethica*, I, B.   [3] *Utilitarianism.*

impels him to form one purpose after another in this direction is the drive of his own inner being or personality towards the better realization of the values which are individual in his experience. Admitting then that the ideals of ethics are not invalidated by remoteness from the actual, they must nevertheless bear a true correspondence with the principle of action, namely, the self and the nature of its striving to bring value to experience.

The experience revealed in the *Memoirs* of Sir Ronald Ross, referred to in the last chapter, shows here again how rough and inadequate is the interpretation of the good life, even one dedicated to a high achievement in human welfare, under the category of "Summum Bonum". His life-purpose dawned for him as his joy in splendid visions of imagination became a passionate imagination of the piteous and unlovely sufferings of men. We feel through these memoirs a spirit ready to fling itself with astonishing and invincible ardour into a problem the exceedingly baffling nature of which was coupled with the enormous value of its solution to myriads of human beings. The discovery of the secret of malaria as object attained would have been the same in its effects if achieved by another. As a spiritual event it was what it was as the outcome of Ross's personality alone. Every event of his life had contributed to this—the poet's dreams, scientific ardour, happy friendships, exaltation in natural beauty.

Ethical systems which issue from a metaphysical background of the unity of Mind or Spirit superior in reality to the finite selves, appear to be still more remote from the historic view than those already considered. A remarkable example is the system of T. H. Green, in spite of his recognition of the "Personal Character of the Moral Ideal", and the importance of the question of Moral Progress. For Green, the moral self is what it is as proceeding from the "Eternal Self-consciousness", which becomes in man organic to an animal being in time.[1] It appears that the essential nature of the human self cannot logically be conditioned by its experience

[1] *Prolegomena to Ethics*, Book I, Chapters I–III.

in the temporal process, the value of which must be subordinate. The problem of the endless diversity of human conduct, or how it comes to be that there are selves who do not exercise the prerogative of self-consciousness, namely, the striving for satisfaction of the true self identified with the higher objects of striving, receives no solution. Green's philosophy of progress shows recognition of the need for an interpretation of the profound differences of moral ideas and standards in history, though these facts are difficult to reconcile with the underlying metaphysic. According to his postulates the temporal development can only be that of the animal nature, since the spiritual principle is derived from the timeless being. But it is the latter which is the source of the moral life. Green's system seems to have been formulated as a refutation of the evolutionary ethics of Spencer, with its theory of the origin of the moral ideal from a stage of human development in which it had not dawned. The essence of his answer is that no consciousness of the moral ideal could have been generated out of a state devoid of all implications of it, and that some notion of common good was present in the simplest social forms. Thus he attributes in a large and general sense reality to the historic process. But this general and vague recognition of the process seems in the end to lead to the unhistoric method of dealing with that which is the chief source and essence of history, the self. As the selves of his underlying metaphysic seem (as real beings) to lack that individuality which history alone can give, since they are all individualizations of the eternal self-consciousness, so the selves of his historic process lack the individuality of unique personal activities, for they are but instances of humanity, whose significance is derived from the general idea of human progress. The personal character of the ideal, or the need for satisfaction of the true self, does not provide a ground for differentiation, since it proceeds from that timeless source which is One in all.[1] Moral progress is

[1] Green insists that the divine principle can only realize itself in persons, the idea of spirit in spirits, but this is difficult to reconcile with his metaphysic.

characterized by the co-working of two principles, the deepening of the concept of moral good, and the extension of its area or the range of persons for whom the good is desired. These principles are to supply a key especially to the advance from the Greek to the Christian ideal. A comparatively limited era then would be illuminated, and from a standpoint which is abstract in relation to the enormous complexity of history, the advances and retreats, varieties of experience, streams wandering from any current selected as central. This is not to question the value of Green's analyses of virtues Greek and Christian and penetrating treatment of the deepening of their meaning. But the root cause of the unhistoric character of the method is the impossibility of interpreting from the fundamental metaphysic the individuality of selves and their visions of value on which actual history depends. The method which does not start from the unique selves cannot reach the selves that make history. The whole work of the interpretation of history has to be undertaken afresh without aid from the metaphysic which should be its source.

A comparison of this system with McTaggart's philosophy of timeless selves[1] reveals that with all the contrasts of metaphysical background the two positions approximate in the results for the individuality of selves. The reason for this is that although the temporal process seems undoubtedly more than appearance for Green, whilst the individuality of the selves is of the first importance for McTaggart, the truths that individuality is ultimate, and that since it is creative it necessitates the temporal process, are inseparable. But individuality does not appear to be ultimate in Green's theory, whilst time is unreal in that of McTaggart. Reference was made to the effects of this position on the import of the value experience at the close of the last chapter. Spirituality is "the quality of having content, all of which is content of one or more selves". The logical argument which forces upon McTaggart the conclusion that substance is only found in spiritual existents,

[1] *The Nature of Existence*, Vol. II.

since these alone exhibit the principle of having "parts within parts without end, determined by determining correspondence",[1] need not detain us. It has been admitted that logical rationality cannot be found in historic experience, and a metaphysic logically consistent, since it excludes the reality of time, cannot give validity to our highest values. The highest value in McTaggart's view is love, and in this we need not dissent from him. But since emotion in his system can only be a form of cogitation, the philosophy of love is in an ambiguous position, if indeed the logical basis does not here break down. With characteristic consistency McTaggart does not in any way conceal the impoverishment of value which follows upon the unreality of time. The experience of increasing knowledge, with wonder and curiosity, and that of aesthetic appreciation must be sacrificed. (The latter rather curiously is supposed inseparable from spatial experience.) It seems doubtful also whether moral experience belongs to reality. "It is not certain that there is really any disapproval of crimes, or any approval of or acquiescence in acts of virtue; but the fact that there are apparent approvals, disapprovals and acquiescences, is sufficient for morality."[2] It appears then that with the unreality of time, the experience of truth, beauty, good, is profoundly modified. The experience of love remains, but is it not rarefied almost to a change in quality? (not, of course, in McTaggart's view). If so, the ground lies in the fact that McTaggart's principle of individuality cannot maintain itself without the reality of the temporal process. The crux is in his purely intelligible conception of the selves, whose whole content consists in perceptions, the objects of these perceptions being selves having a content of perception, and the perceptions of these selves. There is no sufficient source of differentiation and uniqueness in this characterization.[3] The *Thou* is hardly other

---

[1] *The Nature of Existence*, Vol. I, Book I, Chapter XXIV.

[2] Ibid., Vol. II, Book VI, Chapter LVII, "Emotion and Volition".

[3] Cf. article by the writer, "Time and the Self in McTaggart's System", *Mind*, Vol. XXXIX, N.S., No. 154.

in nature than the *I*. Conversely, Green's idea of historic development loses its concrete significance, since the indefinite individuality of selves is limited by their origin in the one eternal self-consciousness.

The postulate that creative experience is essential to personality is not necessarily implied by this criticism, but if it is granted, it throws much light on the unreality attendant upon these two systems in respect to principles which are vital to them, to McTaggart's system the individuality of selves, to that of Green the interpretation of the historic process. The individuality of McTaggart's selves fades away because they have no history. The significance of Green's historic process is dimmed, because the selves are overshadowed by that Self-consciousness of whose eternal Being they can in the end be but Spinozistic modes. Is there any metaphysical alternative?

We must return to the problem left over from the consideration of the contribution of Platonic idealism to ethics, and of Hartmann's doctrine of values as essences, with its Platonic affinities. To what principles can we point as satisfying the demands of an idealistic ethics, if the ethical Forms, or Essences, are rejected? Only a partial indication can be given at this point of the answer which seems possible from the standpoint of this work. What is the real source of the strain to transcend actual forms of experience by means of the increase of value, and in particular to transform these by the enhancement of good in human relations? The fact that our activity is made possible by the clear idea of the future, apart from which the passage from change to change gives the living being no superiority of value over the things of the inanimate world, may be taken as a starting-point. It appears to be man's consciousness of a future, perhaps illimitable, which is the origin of his awakening to the possibilities of creating a different type of existence. But this is an awakening rather than an "emergence", for the potentialities of the life of value are, as I have argued, universally present in the human type. The idea of creation is obviously impossible without the thought of a future. The two ideas arise together, as dawning intelligence makes the latter possible, and the first freedom from all-controlling necessity the former. Prior to the clear thought of a not wholly determined succession of events to come there can only be the morals of custom, continuance as hitherto ordained, resistance to any novelty. The historical view of the self involves the idea of the self in the yet unknown sphere of possible action, as well as the past experience, which is a great part of self-consciousness. The forward as well as the backward-looking seems essential to the being of a self. From this clue it may at first appear that the transcendent principle we seek is to be found in the idea of the future united with that of the creativity of selves which lends it its value. As transcending object this future tends to exceed all limits, to become the future of all existence, the endless duration of spiritual being. Now the distinctive characteristic of man's activity is the desire that experience shall be in some respect other than it has been. At least from the beginning of reflection upon human life dissatisfaction with the past and longing for change have been leading themes. The past had not the value or worth, which can be the object of imagination or thought, and therefore of desire. In the idea of change from the imperfect conditions of the past into the desired form having more value, change to be effected by the work of selves, there is involved a certain standard of deed, the doing or free activity of the self. This certainly implies a vision of good. But the transcending principle must be defined, I think, as the principle of action. This is not to be identified with the will, since the will or conative function, as usually conceived in ethical theory, is an abstraction of psychological analysis. It is rather the principle prior to abstraction, of the self or personality, the law of whose being is to bring value into experience. As the ideal it is conceived to work with such creative strength as to meet with no hindrance, but in all situations and relations of life add the highest value they can admit. Vision, feeling, volition, are

aspects of the activity of personality which at its height is
present to our consciousness as the ideal activity transcending
our own. This is not akin to Hartmann's ideal essence of the
individual person, the "ideal being", the ought of only one
specific person. For he attributes to this a place amongst the
essences or ideas, whereas the principle to which I would
point is that of the highest in each self as subject. To the
difficulty of this concept it is perhaps due that some "personalists" resort to the assumption of the Absolute Person
underlying or immanent in all others. The grounds why I
cannot follow them are perhaps evident, but will be more fully
stated later. The interpretation of the transcendent principle in
ethics which I am suggesting may appear in some respects to
approach the noumenal self of Kant. The identification of this
self with the rational function as practical reason is, however,
wholly foreign to the present view, since I hold the self to be
not less near to reality in emotional experience than in rational
activity, and history seems to show that the greatest moral
effort and the most intense pursuit of knowledge are constantly
motived and sustained by such experience. As Professor Whitehead observes, "The notion of mere knowledge is a high
abstraction which we should dismiss from our minds."[1] I am
in agreement with Max Scheler that Kant is right in the
insistance on the *a priori* principle in ethics, but not in the
formalism which only admits to the *a priori* pure practical
reason, or the logical reason in practice.

[1] *Adventures of Ideas*, Introduction.

CHAPTER IX

HISTORY AND THE FUTURE

A

"Why do these lucent palms
Shew thy feet's failing thicklier than their might,
Who dost but hood thy glorious eyes with night
And vex the heels of all the yesterdays?"
FRANCIS THOMPSON: *Ode to the Setting Sun*

FROM the standpoint of knowledge there is necessarily an unceasing endeavour to bring the conceived future into line with the remembered and recorded past, by assuming principles regarded as prevailing in the past to prevail in all the succession of events to come. Together with and resulting from this assumption there is the tendency to conceive the future events as having sufficient similarity with those of the past to fall into such forms of order. The inconceivable variety of facts within recorded history has not prevented the scientific historian from tracing certain great uniformities in the relations of men to their environment, geographic, climatic, etc., and in the motive forces that determine human activities, from the needs of life and propagation of the species to the ambitions of the desire for power and wealth, the various emotions and social influences. The assumption that human nature within historic times does not essentially change, and that the immense diversity of activities defying particular predictions can all be interpreted from incalculably various conditions of relation to environment, together with psychical differences within the definite limits of the psychological nature of man, has appeared to have a high degree of probability. Thus, though from the beginning of reflection on these questions men have constantly found their expectations thwarted by the unexpected, the wholly unlooked for development of events, and even the reduction of the process of past history to schemes and systems of connected facts, to be baffled by the "contingent" or the irreducible individuality of the prime factors, the postulate of the existence of some kind of uniformity is not thereby inevitably removed. The standpoint from which the problem of order in history is regarded in this treatise has already been to some extent indicated, and will receive further reference in the following chapter, in relation to the outlook towards the future.

In the present chapter we are to examine the question whether any considerable change in the course of history, especially in relation to its value essence and principles, is conceivable by means of change in the fundamental historic factors. This subject was touched upon mainly in its ethical aspect in the chapter on freedom. Whilst recognizing amongst the forces that make history the blind factors to the meaning of which our reason cannot pierce, we have seen that the primary agency in events must be the activity of persons, if the term event is to have any human significance. It is the disorder within the personal principle itself which is the most crucial nerve of the problem. None of the interpretations which would transform the dualism here into that of the real and the unreal (or the phenomenal) seem adequate. Neither the noumenal self of Kant, nor Green's finite self as organ of the eternal self-consciousness as we have seen, provides an explanation of the action of the empirical self (Kant), or of the self which does not seek its own true satisfaction (Green). The profound emphasis of both these thinkers on personality does nothing then to solve the problem of the ill-regulated self. Nor does Scheler's doctrine of the person who is the correlate of his world and of value appear to do more in this respect. The indefinite concourse of activities which undeniably claim to be human and play perhaps for considerable periods the larger part in the making of history, at least as generally conceived, would seem, on his conception of the stage of existence at which personality emerges, difficult to classify, except under categories not distinctively human. The question then becomes urgent whether we can analyse in some degree the nature of the personal principle, which with Scheler we admit to be transcendent to the principles ordinarily regarded as "natural" if this distinction is valid, though potentially present at least in all human existents. It is from the standpoint of moral value that this investigation must proceed. From the beginning of considerations of the "soul" in philosophy, it seems to have been assumed that here we have essentially the principle that knows the good in Greek phrase. Professor Taylor, as we have noticed, has underlined this property of the soul, the conception of which Socrates (in his view) introduced into European philosophy. The soul is that which knows reality and good. But in the Socratic-Platonic dialogues the nature of the corrupt soul is not treated as something that is unreal in part, it is not distinguished as possessing a lower degree of reality to that of the good soul. Cf. *Gorgias*, 477 C. "It was agreed by us just now that injustice and the evil of the soul in general is the most shameful."[1] The source of the evil in Plato's view lies in the fact that the soul desiring necessarily the good, actually pursues the seeming good. The obscurity of the problem is not relieved by the more objective treatment of the Greek thinkers, projecting the principle of disorder into the object of the soul's vision. Nor does the contrast between the real and the apparent provide a more intelligible interpretation here than in its more subjective application within the nature of the self by Kant or Green. We are driven to seek a different type of solution. It should perhaps first be pointed out that from the standpoint of this treatise no explanation by means of psychological or physiological analysis of the abnormal or anti-social types of human being will be by itself sufficient, though it may be argued that these explanations themselves are not intelligible unless brought into relation with the real

----

[1] Σω· αἴσχιστον δὲ ἀδικία καὶ σύμπασα ψυχῆς πονηρία νυνδή ὡμολόγηται ἡμῖν;

sources of evil.[1] The explanation required must throw light on
the enigma of the frequent or constant failure of the essential
principle of personality to be true to type. Because, as has
been throughout argued, it is through the agency of this
principle that the temporal process acquires meaning and value,
and history is thus constituted. The first questions which
arise are such as the following: Are there distinct potentialities
for evil, as well as for good, so that, together with the realization
of the personal principle in history, its disorderly as well as
orderly manifestations must increase? Is there a principle
prior to good and evil alike in the nature of the person? On
this latter supposition good and evil, or moral value and disvalue, would be ultimate as principles in our experience, but
they would arise only out of the relations of persons in a
historic process. As already suggested, the failure to perceive
the real existence of other selves as selves is at least one main
source of activities which bring about what we term evil. But
this demands some more ultimate ground. The ground must
be discovered in the primary principle of personality if the
reality of evil at least throughout personal experience cannot
be denied. This principle, it has been suggested, may be
described as the necessary striving in the finite being to
transcend the limits of its experience. In some way it comes
about that this is corrupted, distorted. The desire to break
down our narrow limitations not being otherwise attainable
takes the form of the passion to dominate other selves, and
thus transcend the boundaries of individual selfhood by
subordinating and controlling their points of view and activities.
Yet the explanation is not completed, and perhaps an unknowable factor must be left over. We can but describe sources
of the phenomenon which can be postulated from our standpoint. It results on this view that good and evil are in our
present experience complementary. "Evils", says Socrates in
the *Theaetetus*, "can never pass away, for there must always
remain something which is antagonistic to good."[2] In general,

[1] See p. 225. [2] 176, A. Jowett's translation.

I can assent to this. Yet I can also understand the reason for
the continual recurrence in the history of philosophical ethics
even in Plato of the conception in various forms that only
good is ultimately real. For the striving to transcend our
limits is the striving towards an order of being in which we
win supremacy over the alien factors of otherness. And this is
the order of pure value, for disvalue brings with it the "other"
in manifold forms, even though it arise out of the personal
principle. This seems evident at least when we turn to
empirical illustrations. In a somewhat different aspect we
may see that the presence of evil is due in part to the extraordinary fact of the appearance of selfhood in a world. Here
is an atomic fragment of the universe in which arises a form of
consciousness which inherently implies the need to reflect all,
to find all things transparent to it, and the desire to act throughout, to transform the process of things into the likeness of its
vision. It seems hardly a transformation of this principle
which leads it to claim that it is equal to the All, and through
that claim to become in the moral order a great worker of evil.
It is the recognition of this almost intolerable anomaly which
has brought about the return of philosophy again and again
to the idea of the whole to which there is no rival, the only
individual, the rejection of the significance of separate selves.
Correspondingly arises the ethical ideal of the sacrifice and
sinking of selfhood, the merging of the self in the One. The
inconsistency of the existence of the self in the universe may
be seen in its nature as essentially subject. In the world of
objects it cannot be completely known. In that world it must
strive to act for the most part in accordance with universal
law, i.e. in the general system of events viewed with more or
less abstraction. Thus comes about the constitution of a second
self. But the subject self is in close relation to this secondary
self, which plays more or less the part assigned to it in the
general order, and from time to time this subject irrupts in
free activity into the process of events.[1] The self whose

[1] As pointed out in Chapter VII, this type of view has affinities
with that of Bergson.

activities are such as we define as evil is in its essential nature not rightly adjusted to a world in which other selves exist. It feels itself as the only subject, although intellectually it recognizes the being of other selves. Can freedom be attributed to it? In my answer to this question I should again differ from those thinkers who accept in any form the contrast between a real self whose act of will belongs to the intelligible realm, and an empirical or phenomenal self whose desires and activities are devoid of moral worth. In this view the acts of the latter self cannot be free, though this is not clearly recognized by all moralists of this type. Such actions are lacking in that principle which is the differentia of freedom. In order to make clear the grounds which determine me to the view that freedom must be ascribed (under a certain qualification to be specified later) to the acts of the bad as of the good self, I must refer to the position stated in regard to historic freedom, and the approach from this to the ethical problem. It was argued that in spite of the first impression derived from the course of history that it is here where we survey the human process on a large scale and in the mass, that the grounds for a deter-ministic theory seem strongest, whereas the hope of dis-covering freedom lies in the close scrutiny of individual conduct proper to ethics, the truth is more complex than this suggests. In the first place the very existence of history depends upon mind in selves giving and finding meaning in the process. Here is the basis of creative freedom. In the second place, those great events, series and groups of events which are regarded as historical in the highest sense, supreme in their human significance, and repercussions on the course of change, are found to be impossible without the creative energy of individuals. The relation of this fact to the problem of ethical freedom has been in part considered. It does not necessarily follow that where there is manifestation of creative energy there is always moral freedom. But this freedom is incon-ceivable in a world from which creative energy is absent. Now it is impossible to deny that many of the historic processes or movements which depend on the creative energy of men include evil tendencies, whether or not the sum-total of their effects is for human good. They include, namely, tendencies which are hostile to the expansion of personality. This may be due in some cases or in part to factors which have been examined under the conception of the "other" or blind conditions in the process. But they are also undoubtedly due at times and at least in part to those factors in which the corruption or degenerate form of the personal principle is manifested. It does not appear true to the facts to deny freedom to the original energy which is not aimed at realization of value—not thus aimed unless that is to be termed value in which any individual feels his being to be enhanced. It is value for him, and here the view maintained is in its ethical effect, though not in its metaphysical basis, not far from Plato's doctrine of the vision of the seeming but falsely seeming good. The spectacle or record of the activities of a Napoleon inspires in the student, together with consciousness of their effects on humanity, as evil rather than good, a belief in the immense creative energy of their author. The fact that from another point of view the apparent inevitability of his successive attempts to dominate mankind in the present and in posterity, makes his life suggest the irresistible progress of a natural force, does not prove his acts to be necessitated. The seeming inevitability characterizes a career in which the effort to overpass finite limits takes the form of the passion for power over other men whose being as selves is not realized, who are conceived but as innumerable hands and feet for the use of a greater being.[1] Such a self and its acts acquire an impersonality, the contrary of the impersonality which is superior to ordinary selfhood being inferior to this. There is no true self where there is no true recognition of other selves. Yet we are not entitled to deny freedom ethically understood to the actions of Napoleon. All the external conditions of freedom (i.e. for the release of personality) were present in his circum-

[1] See Chapter VI.

stances. As an intellectual being he possessed more than the average genius for conceiving forms of value, and in a high degree the capacity not always found with this, for inspiring men and organizing instruments for his ends. The potentialities of personality which, as earlier argued, essentially imply freedom had very favourable conditions for realization. The passion for power as above interpreted, which dulled and blinded him to the perception of other selves, ought not to be taken as a ground for a deterministic view of his activities. For it derives, as I have argued, from the personal principle, deflected. The simple observation of Aristotle may be not the less appropriate. "If any one with full knowledge so acts as to become unjust, voluntarily he is unjust. He cannot, however, merely by desiring it cease to be unjust, any more than the sick can become healthy.[1]

Ivar Kreuger, according to his biographer (Manfred Georg), was "delirious with power, completely blinded by the lust for power". But are we to deny freedom to this self, who cast the spectre of his corroding genius over the whole process of events in which he moved? He identified riches with power. This was natural, since his incalculable wealth or reputed wealth enabled him to act as though he were an independent government, making loans to governments as their equal. The method which he was able to work out was made possible by the conditions of his time, the state of international finance, his own special gifts. Here was a very different form of lust for power from that of Napoleon. But there was a similarity in the passions which urged them respectively to more and more impossible ventures. Also they resembled each other in their real ignorance of other selves and in their solitariness, though even Kreuger seems to have inspired devotion and unlimited confidence, whilst Napoleon fascinated millions of his fellow-men. Of Napoleon it is said, "As his creative genius became exhausted, his vast schemes only grew vaster still."[2] According

[1] *Nicomachean Ethics*, Book III, Chapter V.
[2] Emil Ludwig: *Napoleon*.

to my interpretation, this signifies that the mechanism of the
psycho-biological nature, which had been perfectly adapted
through many years' habitude to working out the ideas and
schemes of his original genius, continued to function when the
genius was beginning to fail. The complete harmony between
the personal environment as physical nature and the real
self, without which Bonaparte's extraordinary achievements
would not have been possible, did not involve that the change
which was destroying the power of the one must at once
transform the other. Vast dreams still haunted the psychical
being, and immense reserves of physical energy existed as
instruments for their attempted realization. But lacking the
clear vision of his essential genius, the resulting efforts met
with failure.

Is it a fantastic view which finds the ultimate source of the
principles animating such careers as those of Napoleon or
Kreuger, on the one hand, and Shaftesbury or Ronald Ross on
the other, or again—to take a life which seems to belong to a
wholly different category—of J. H. Newman as in reality or
ultimate origin one and the same? The main ground of that
which explodes, so to speak, as evil, in the soil of human
experience and history, is the misuse of a spiritual principle.
Nothing less would be powerful enough to bring about the
greatest destructions of value. Philosophically interpreted, the
intense striving of a Newman to enter a sphere of perfect
accord between vision of truth and form of life, his exquisitely
fine efforts to bring about this perfection for a community of
friends, to be gradually extended to a whole Church organization, express the strain to transcend human limits and live in a
sphere of unfading and absolute value in the form required
by his unique individuality. I refer to the period before he
was preparing to submit his mind in a considerable degree to
authority.[1] The strength of Kreuger's will, we are told, was
"increased by the fact that he had only a single aim", namely,

[1] Cf. *Apologia pro Vita Sua*. "History of My Religious Opinions
up to Part VI" (1841).

power through riches. If we can abstract from this violent moral contrast expressed in the lives of these two men when contemplated side by side, the saintly student for whom the only object worth striving for was religious truth and the fraudulent financier who only desired power, we may recognize that the yawning gulf is made by the different use of the pearl of great price, the freedom of personality to create its experience. Psychological study, including the study of abnormal psychology and "criminology", throws, I believe (without first-hand knowledge), much light on the mental conditions of anti-social selves. I do not think that its results are inconsistent with the philosophical view I am maintaining. In accordance with this view it would result that the conditions and states of mind analysed by the psychologist characterize that secondary self referred to above, which has been formed beyond the true subject-self, and which in such cases by long habit may all but completely bring about the submergence of the latter. The secondary self studied by abnormal psychology is of course constituted by the practice of constant activity in a scheme of means and ends alien to the systems whose value is more fundamental in the experience of any personality. To the degree in which the true self is incapable of breaking through the long-established system of life, freedom can no longer be attributed to such a self in its separate acts. But it must be regarded as free in the constitution of its form of life as a whole. This is the qualification referred to above in the ascription of freedom in the performance of evil activities as of good. The word "system" is employed in relation to a course of life which may appear lacking altogether in order and regularity, only in the sense that there is a certain definite form or method of disvalue pervading its means and ends. It will perhaps be said that the illustrations taken from the lives of extraordinary men do not throw light on the cases of the average social offender. In some aspects this is no doubt true. Especially it seems that the man of brilliant capacities must in general experience greater freedom from the hampering influences of

P

those alien factors which have been discussed under the category of the "other", than the ordinary individual. But in respect to the manner in which the original force of personality is turned into a channel in which its value is transformed, whilst its essential freedom cannot be lost or never completely, the extraordinary examples are not different in kind, and afford striking illumination. There remain the cases of selves in whose lives, from birth onwards, factors alien to freedom have been so all-pervasive that the essential personality has barely if at all been realized. The very difficult problem which arises in relation to these beings who in the past ages at least must have formed a large proportion of humanity is similar to the problem of the most primitive races and of the "higher animals". Beyond what has already been said in regard to the potential existence of personality, it cannot be considered here. But that the greatest source of evil in human history has proceeded from the deformation of the personal principle fully possessed of freedom, is a truth which remains unaffected. Here again, as against traditional views, I must state that the recognition of this truth does not in my view afford a *solution* of the "problem of evil". The view I have expressed in regard to the most potent cause of evil appears to be in harmony with the observation of the Platonic Socrates, concerning the chief source of evil in states, the *corruptio optimi pessima* (as Jowett condenses it). It is not necessarily, however, the individual genius, but rather the free personality as such, to which my view applies.

From these reflections on the personality which is productive of evil we must return to the question of the conceivability of change in the essential factors of history. The position which has been taken in respect to the impossibility of knowledge of the inner nature of selves as subjects may appear to preclude any conclusions on this question. What seems demanded in connection with the problem of the future seems to be a study which would on the one hand investigate far more extensively than is possible within the limits of this work all those conditions of history which have been here conceived as factors irreducible to any type of order in complete harmony with the personal, on the other make the difficult attempt of a deeper investigation into the roots of the self as subject, by means of what may be termed the more philosophical psychology,[1] and by reference to experience in actual life and in biography and autobiography. Only the slightest indication of these methods can be given. This may be sufficient to suggest the outlook from an empirical basis. In the following chapter a possible approach to a more definite position will be made from a more general standpoint. We may take up here again the question of the contribution of the lives of men and women described by themselves and by others. It appears that what I have termed original history cannot be revealed by biography, though genius in presenting the life, especially of one whom the writer has loved and honoured, may produce the impression that he has been able to live again this life *nacherleben* (in Rickert's sense). In autobiography we approach as nearly as possible the original experience, because here we almost meet the subject in the original act of self-objectification. Yet in that act, since the author usually writes for the eyes of others, he can scarcely avoid perceiving himself as categorially classified with other types, having qualities identical with those of men like-minded, in his own or in former times. Perhaps he aims (though unconsciously) at a self-portrait which should reveal the features of a type he has throughout life emulated. It may be only an ideal, but it is an ideal combination of qualities objectively viewed. We feel this, for instance, in Gibbon's *Memoirs* throughout, up to his final approval of the opinion of Fontenelle, "who fixes our moral happiness to the mature season, in which our passions are supposed to be calmed, our duties fulfilled, our ambitions satisfied, our fame and fortune established on a solid basis". What Bury terms "the immortal affectation of

---

[1] That which admits the close relation of psychology to philosophy, as, for instance, the work of Dr. William Brown and of Professor Aveling.

his style" reflects the mind of a man who aspired to go down to history as one who had lived in accordance with a certain style of life befitting the author of *The Decline and Fall of the Roman Empire*. In Newman's *Apologia* or J. S. Mill's *Autobiography*, on the other hand, we seem more intimately in touch with the experience of the real self. Possibly this is because these men, never satisfied that they have reached their ideal, always conscious of limits they strive afresh to transcend, are nearer to their own reality as subjects. A quality of the very life can thus enter into the autobiography, inasmuch as the individual writes it as still living the experience. It is not as with Gibbon a pageant of memory objectified. The past self is, as I hold, at times speaking. Similarly in such lives of action as those of Sir Ronald Ross or Sir Wilfred Grenfell the method is in certain respects almost the direct opposite of that of Gibbon. There is no suggestion that Ross is contemplating the events of his life as they might appear to posterity, the life of the discoverer of malaria, or Sir Wilfred Grenfell that of the never daunted missionary doctor of Labrador. Each stage of the life appears in its dynamic reality. We perceive the course of events with their original value, as in the workshop of the writer's mind. The individuality of each deed is almost realized as it was for the doer, a new experience not yet linked with others and classified. It is not as Gibbon's contemplation of the life of a man of letters, or Emma Goldman's presentation of the career of an anarchist, or that of M. Chaliapin, the life of an artist, and the inevitable clash with authority which would control for its own ends the creative impulse to which freedom is the breath of life. These writers portray themselves in part as personifying ideas, though it also happens that they produce the impression of intense individuality. These further references to the accounts by men of human lives, whether their own or those of others, remind us in the first place of the dynamic character of history, constantly evolving into fresh forms of which selves are the centre and are indeed the main source, though they may not will these forms. The beginnings of history, as Dilthey points out, are in the first expression in language of the brilliant impression made by the outstanding individual. "From the time in which, gathered round the fire, comrades in race and war relate the deeds of their heroes and the divine origin of their race, the keen interest of contemporaries has raised aloft certain facts, and preserved them out of the obscure flow of ordinary human life."[1] It is probably true that at this stage the individual is hardly yet disentangled as a subject-self, superior to events, continuously active and inactive. Only fragments of his being endure in memory and legend. We must therefore notice in the second place that the origination of the biography (and still more the autobiography) involves an unconscious metaphysic. That which was part of the process of events living in them, forgotten without them, has become a thing of another kind. The minds of those who contemplate the life as a succession of deeds engendered by the individual out of forces which begin to be separated and abstracted, strength, courage, love, hate, grope after the notion of the enduring, the continuing being, source of ever fresh and changing deeds. This which is only one aspect of the growth of recognition of individuals as selves brings out the fact that our cultural treatment of biography in relation to history involves a metaphysic of the self. At the primitive animistic stage anything may have an "anima".[2] It is at least something that can set itself over against us with definite attitude, good or ill. But the other self, the Thou, though the belief in its existence be intuitive,[3] is not clearly perceived as such, prior to the stage of thought at which the idea of a life as a whole, separable from events, is familiar, and the conditions for biography are thus present. In the modern age of innumerable biographies we often feel that the individual is only presented in certain aspects as he appears to observers

[1] *Gesammelte Schriften*, Band I, "Natur des Materials der Geisteswissenschaften."

[2] Not animus (which as by Lucretius) is used rather for the rational soul.

[3] See Chapter III.

possessed of a certain interest: "With all the biographies that
are now published, how little men know after all of the man
they are asked to love or hate!"[1] Such estimates of the limitation of the biographical view evidently imply the existence of
some real being whose nature cannot be exhausted by any
vision of friend or critic, or even by the subject's own perception of the meaning of his actions. No biography could be
written of the self as Hume discovers him, observing rather
the absence of such an entity from the bundle of perceptions,
feelings, etc., certainly no such autobiography as he himself
produced. In reference to Bryce's reflection that "Individuals
or even an assembly may be understood by dint of close and
long-continued observation, but to understand a whole nation
one must also have sympathy",[2] it may be pointed out that
the understanding of individuals, of which he speaks, can only
give the objective view as I have interpreted it. By the understanding of a whole nation he appears to signify an insight
into certain common qualities which are deeper than the
unique qualities of the individuals and shared by the observer.
The philosophy of the nation which this seems to imply
differs from that which I have outlined,[3] but might be brought
into harmony with it. The larger sympathy (in my view) can
only proceed from the finer personal form of understanding.
In Mr. J. M. Keynes' sketch of the characters and causes of
the Versailles Peace Treaty we may find, in spite of its comparatively slight character, materials for a study of the relation
of person and event which would throw some light on the
present problem of the conceivability of a new control of
that historic dualism in which lies the frustration of so many
forecasts.[4] His treatment might indeed be conceived as aimed
at revealing the intricacy of the problem whether the event

[1] Max Müller: *Auld Lang Syne.*
[2] *Studies in Modern Biography: Lord Beaconsfield.*
[3] In Chapter VI.
[4] See *Economic Consequences of the Peace Treaty, 1919.* Chapter on
the Conference. *Essays in Biography,* 1933. Fragment on Mr. Lloyd
George.

or the personal agent (if we abstract these two) is the central constituent of history. The accounts of the leading figures in the framing of the Treaty are hardly biographical. Paradoxically they almost take the form of studies of factors in the event personified. "A sense of impending catastrophe overhung the frivolous scene; the futility and smallness of man before the great events confronting him; the mingled significance and unreality of the decisions." The faces of the chief agents suggest to him "the tragi-comic masks of some strange drama or puppet-show". He thinks of the impression conveyed in Hardy's *Dynasts*, of "events marching on to their fated conclusion". The event, however, if we conceive it as central, does not march on without the agents, but with them as crucial aspects of it. A critic of Mr. Keynes' book on the Treaty objected that the author entirely failed to see Clemenceau in perspective. He sees only the cynical old man at the Conference. "He does not perceive in him the member of the National Assembly of 1870, the Mayor of Montmartre during the Commune, the destroyer of innumerable Cabinets, the courageous upholder of justice in the Dreyfus affair, the friend of England," etc.[1] Mr. Keynes' portrait is not, however, subject to this criticism if we take it primarily as the portrayal of an action in the drama of the event. Clemenceau is the spirit of this action, in a sense the soul of the event, though not completely so, since the significance of the event depends also on other men and on blind agencies. The rest of Clemenceau's life and activities are not a portion of this event, though in an attempt to define his total personality nothing available should be omitted. Similarly with the characterization of President Wilson. But here we may note especially the effect of a highly alien environment. In Bury's view, it may be observed, Thucydides the rationalist carried his methods of exclusion and omission too far. "In estimating the action of an individual in history his whole character must be taken into account." . . . In Thucydides' "impatience of biographical trivialities he went

[1] *Times* Review, January 5, 1920.

to the extreme of neglecting biography altogether", as in his silence concerning the personality of Pericles.[1] Mr. Keynes feels the making of the Treaty to require Hardy's interpretation of the Napoleonic catastrophe:

> *Spirit of the Pities:* "Why prompts the Will so senseless-shaped a doing?"
> *Spirit of the Years:* "I have told thee that it works unwittingly."[2]

In such an interpretation we seem to find a strange meeting-point of necessitarian science and fatalistic drama. Hardy's philosophy appears to include both points of view in the doctrine of the Immanent Will blindly working through necessitated agents. Science depersonalizes the human factor. Drama, of this type, animates or personifies the event, but though personified it is blind and senseless. The purely necessitarian view leaves wholly unexplained the meaning both in value and in disvalue. Once we include the significance which at each successive term of the process rises from it as it were in countless waves for every subject concerned in the experience, it is impossible to preserve the form of necessity, for meaning or value effects cannot be measured. But neither does personification of the event make the process intelligible. The imposition of a super-will which (senselessly) works through the human wills, driving them to actions and ends they did not purpose, poetically expresses an impression which demands another interpretation. In the event of the Versailles Treaty we ought to recognize as its core the work of personal agents, but there is a true sense in which it was not the freely willed outcome of selves in co-operation. As earlier pointed out, the factor we have characterized as alien and other in relation to any personal agency may intrude, so to speak, into a course of events strictly brought about through human activity. An unforeseeable effect of the clash of wills perhaps, a combination of intentions avowedly for a common end, but in fact for ends

---

[1] *Ancient Greek Historians*: *Thucydides.*
[2] *The Dynasts*, quoted by J. M. Keynes, op. cit.

differently conceived by each up to any degree of difference, may eventuate in happenings, as "unwitting", or anti-personal, as any catastrophe of nature. The coming together in a course of events of minds whose subjective points of view, visions of good, memories and experience are separated by deep spiritual gulfs, may produce impediments or obstacles to valuable common action, destructive of real collaboration, like a natural force clouding the mind through injury to the brain. When Mr. Keynes observes that Clemenceau alone of the chief agents could speak and understand both French and English, and that "it was of historical importance that Orlando and President Wilson had no direct means of communication", these facts belong to "contingency" in the sense given to this in Chapter V. The result is unpredictable, rather than necessarily determined. Forces, or more strictly visions or ideas in a multitude of individual minds, and desires to realize these visions in the construction of a very different type of treaty, certainly existed as the basis of a prediction of another outcome. The unpredictability was not due to the freedom of man so much as to a certain unlimited indefiniteness in the event which included factors many of them incalculable, the effect of whose conjunction was to produce something unlooked for—certainly in all its potencies unlooked for by the majority. If this interpretation suggests a kind of wild freedom in the events (or their historical significance), how is this freedom to be estimated? Is it capable of being so used by greater personalities as to increase the good rather than the evil tendencies of the process? This is an important aspect of our problem, but the question is perhaps unanswerable. If there is any road to a tentative answer, it seems that it could only be found by way of the more general argument which will be suggested in the next chapter. At this stage our brief empirical reference seems to point to the following results. The question of determinism becomes irrelevant. This may have been seen to be involved earlier, in the doctrine of the basis of history and in the conception of freedom. But unless we can show that the impossibility of proving historical determinism has more than a negative significance, it has not much value in relation to any speculation concerning the future. If the "gates of the future" are not closed, scientific necessity will not conflict with any achievement of value that human freedom can bring about. Mechanical necessity can be treated as irrelevant because of the contingency in events which results from the inconceivably complex relations of selves to the environment to which they give meaning. Or again, we are relieved from the incubus of necessity because, even though it may hold good in the sphere of natural processes abstracted from relation to man's mind, the self is potentially capable of increasing the value found in the process. This value entering into its course, as later found also by other selves, makes the result through their activities to be different. This potentiality is no doubt limited, but we cannot know its limits.

The other point of greatest importance which has been dwelt upon in this chapter, as bearing on the problem of the future, is the necessity of admitting the freedom of the person whose activity has evil results. We cannot then be assured that we have in personality a principle whose increasing efficacy would necessarily bring with it an increase in the value of human existence. For a pluralist philosophy this is the greatest enigma. Personality is the principle of value in our experience. The exercise of moral freedom means, as Professor Hartmann says, "standing upon the summit of humanity". The misuse of this power cannot be made intelligible. We can only point (as was hinted) to the possibility of an ultimate ground in the anomaly of that very nature of the self which gives the human creature his unique status. That there should be in the universe beings capable of limitless claims for knowledge and power, this is in the end the source of the chief problems of human history.

CHAPTER X

HISTORY AND THE FUTURE

B

"Everything may happen in the immensity of time."[1]
HERODOTUS, Book E 9

IT results from the previous considerations that experience cannot disprove the possibility of a change in the relation of our ideals of value to the actual course of history, such as is conceived in all theories which treat moral progress as characterizing history on the whole, but that it can do little to reveal principles which show this kind of change to be either inevitable or probable. We may first observe the impressions which arise from any point of view we may adopt, setting ourselves as far as possible in relation to one or more past civilizations of which we have some knowledge, of the failure of any realized good to maintain itself in permanent security. Proceeding to seek the ground of this in factors universal in history as the process of events to which human activity gives meaning, we find that on the one hand the personal principle itself gives rise to activities which are frequently destructive of any continuous progress. On the other, the presence of conditions irrelevant to value, and in combination with human striving frequently hostile to it, is ineradicable from the process of change. We may characterize this as an empirical generalization of the widest or highest order (in Mill's sense), in experience conceived as a field for the realization of value. An even greater wave to surmount within the spheres in which value or good has been in a high degree realized, as judged by the mind of some age or community, is the fact of the relativity of value to points of view which can rarely if ever be assumed to be universal.

[1] γένοιτο δ' ἄν πᾶν ἐν τῷ μακρῷ χρόνῳ.

We have then to seek a somewhat different line of approach to the problem, enquiring whether there are any considerations of a more general kind based on the nature of the principal factors which permit of a more positive view in regard to the history of man's attempts to achieve a greater measure of value. This history may appear to us to be already old and to furnish immensely varied illustrations of experiments, with a preponderance of failures. But as was argued in an earlier chapter, our knowledge extends but to a fragment of human history, in so far as we are able to conceive its limits, and the unknown, even of man's history, may be greater than we conceive. Whilst then we cannot turn to any *a priori* principles in the logical sense from which to deduce the conclusion that experience must be other than it seems even in our immediate perception of it, or in the conception of a totality of events, since the principles of value are only known in relation to experience, we are not precluded from an examination of those principles with a view to their relation to a wider—perhaps immeasurably wider—experience.

Some reference must first be made to the bearing of our view of the reality of time on the problem of knowledge of the form of the future, since this question was postponed in the chapter on the temporal process. The philosophers who have maintained the unreality of time do not appear to have given much attention to this aspect of the problem of knowledge. The distinctions of past, present, future have, of course, a very different significance from their standpoint. Yet they must have some significance, if only in relation to differences in the nature of our cognition in relation to these distinct provinces in the sphere of experience (or the phenomenal). This significance seems to be necessarily much enhanced where the principles of value, especially moral value, are under consideration. If, as in McTaggart's view, the perception of events as succeeding one another in a temporal series is total misperception, and as implied in this position the functions of memory and of anticipation equally false in the forms of their report upon experience, it is not clear why the contents of those reports should have respectively a wholly different status for empirical knowledge, if empirical knowledge has any relation to knowledge as it might be of the real. It must at least be regarded as a shadow or reflection of this, even though distorted. And we are at least (*ex hypothesi*) able to affirm from our standpoint as members of an apparent process of change that the real is non-temporal. It is to the contrast between the character and claims respectively of memory and anticipation themselves that our contrasting estimates of their credibility are primarily due. In the second place they are due to the strong empirical evidence that memory has access to sources more nearly related to the actual. But how much validity or applicability is retained by these distinctions, once all experience under the form of time has been degraded to misperception? On Bradley's view that our ideas of past and future are alike constructions on the basis of the present, it is difficult to allow much importance to the distinction, difficult to understand why the construction of the future should be inferior in credibility to that of the past.[1] McTaggart, who appears to be alone or most unambiguous amongst neo-Hegelian idealists in holding that definite relations between the misperceived temporal experience and reality can be affirmed, allows in the first place that there *is* a series, though it is misperceived as temporal. In the second place, he so conceives the relation between the phenomenal or temporal series, and that real series which is misperceived, as to conclude that the terms which appear future in the phenomenal order are nearer, in proportion to the degree of their futurity to the whole in the order of reality, and thus the futurity of the whole can be asserted.[2] This result

[1] In the chapter on "Memory and Inference" (*Essays*) he is not comparing memory and anticipation, but Memory, Inference and Imagination. "As against fancy, memory has necessity. Memory is a judgment and an assertion about its subject."

[2] *Nature of Existence*, Vol. II, Book VI, Chapter XLIX. It is not necessary to the present subject to give McTaggart's argument for this position.

is of great practical importance for McTaggart, though this corollary is not, of course, allowed to affect his argument. For in his view it is in favour of a more optimistic position in regard both to the nature of the whole as containing more good than evil, and to the course of our experience in finite time, than would otherwise be possible. "We shall in a future time reach an endless state which is infinitely more good than bad."[1] This part of the theory, however, throws no light on the question why, if the forms of experience, as future, present, past, are alike illusory (though as to the order or direction of the series there is a perception which can be termed correct), that part of the experience with which we appear to be in contact, through memory of "the past", should rank as knowledge or the basis of knowledge for our apprehension, whilst the part we conceive as future lacks this character. Yet unless we are to follow a philosophy for which all finite experience is wholly illusory—and the philosophies influenced by Hegel, in particular that of McTaggart, must dissent from this in their exaltation of certain human values—it is surely required of any metaphysic that it should afford some interpretation of the phenomenal experience.

Professor Broad gives consideration to the problem of the status of the future in reference to the question of the metaphysical contrast between future and past. Reference was earlier made to his view in regard to the past—that "once an event has happened, it exists eternally".[2] As regards the future, his theory holds "that the future is simply nothing at all".[3] My view of the nature of the self, that a continuous being in its own past is essential to it, would be, as earlier noticed, so far consistent with Professor Broad's theory. With reference to the future in his argument, it is to that unanalysable change which we call becoming that the fact of an increase in the sum-total of existence is due. McTaggart criticized Professor

[1] *Nature of Existence*, Vol. II, Book VII, Chapter LXVIII.
[2] C. D. Broad: *The Mind and its Place in Nature*, Chapter II.
[3] *Scientific Thought*, Part I, Chapter II.

Broad's view of the non-existence of the future on the ground that this "must be false if the past can intrinsically determine the future. If X intrinsically determines a subsequent Y, then (at any rate as soon as X is present or past, and therefore on Broad's view real) it will be true that as soon as there is an X there must be a subsequent Y. Then it is true that there is a subsequent Y. And if it is true that Y is not itself present or past, then it is true that there will be a future Y, and so something is true about the future".[1] This refutation does not appear to me valid. For granted that there is a temporal succession (as Professor Broad assumes), then the intrinsic determination of Y by X does not involve the existence of Y, as Y *together with* the existence of X. It is not then existent in the present, and the not yet existent does involve non-existence in Professor Broad's sense. McTaggart's criticism appears to be based on an illegitimate identification of causal with logical necessity. The event would not less possess these causal tendencies though its occurrence were to be the final event in the history of the world.

This debate raises the question of the relation of the scientific deterministic view of the process of change to the problem of our knowledge of the future. It was argued above that determinism in history cannot be proved, and this also results from the conception earlier outlined of the origin of the categorial principles of our intelligence and the real individuality of the process. From our point of view it cannot be argued that it is only because of the weakness of intellect and the inconceivably greater complexity of the data in the province of human history that uniformities and evidence of universal laws cannot be found to prevail here as we find them on the whole to prevail in the natural sciences. It is rather because individuality is here at its height, and also here more discoverable on account of our more intimate understanding of the process through human affinities. The desire to find order—that order which as "the principle of the same" is everywhere

---

[1] *The Nature of Existence*, Vol. II, Book V, Chapter XXXIII.

in Plato the good and beautiful principle, source of the harmony of the celestial movements, and the pure music of the soul—proceeds (in our view) from the fundamental life of personality freely seeking rhythm, coherence, regularity in every department of experience. The physical and physiological tendencies meet and harmonize with these principles, but could not be their source. This part of the view differs from that of Plato, seeing that the human soul has in his philosophy a much larger proportion of the element of the Other in its nature than has the soul of the world[1] in relation to that of the Same. From the interpretation I have advanced of the need to find order, all forms of order proceed from the fundamental need for value. The uniformity of nature is thus an ideal, and in every law of causation we can trace the footsteps of Plato's measure and symmetry in the cosmos. How then should it be a tyrannical mechanism suppressing the liberty of the individuals who move in accordance with it? How should it swallow up the freedom which gave it birth?

These considerations suggest that the problem of the conceivability of a stage of scientific advancement being reached at which knowledge (at least in a general sense) of future history will be within the grasp of the human mind, is wrongly stated and does not arise in this form. Even though nature proceeds according to expectation in the fulfilment of those regularities which prevail in regard to the properties in which members of a species are similar up to the limit of non-identity, we must leave open the question of the inner freedom of the individuals. But as has been more than once suggested, it is in our "insight" (though it is something less than this) into the *an-sich* nature of selves that we gain some notion of a possibility of knowledge of a higher type than that which is accessible to us in relation to the processes of all else that is other than self. The type of human history which is nearest to those processes of natural change is the history of races, tribes, hordes of men, amongst whom individuals seem hardly

[1] *Timaeus*, 41 D.

to have emerged at least as subjects. But it is more exact to say that we can have no knowledge of such subjects. When we turn to history under civilization, in so far as the events concern the mass of men, under such categories as the nation, the community, we are nearer to the scientific order with laws of causation, uniform sequences, than when we conceive the collection of individual histories as the centre of the process. But the type of generalization possible in relation to human communities, civilized and also primitive, is of an extremely empirical character and liable to falsification.

If then such similarities as there are do not lead to results which have great value for science or practice, if even a statistical determinism is not possible here, how far does this negative for knowledge help in the dilemma of the present chapter? We ask concerning the conceivability of knowledge of a different type such as would afford the most exquisite satisfaction possible in the fields of knowledge to perhaps the majority, knowledge of principles which promise an outcome of the travail of human history in a state in which the greatest values of existence would be much more fully realized. On the other hand, since (as has been maintained in this work) it is through the freedom of the personal principle that value enters into experience, any discovery of principles pointing to necessary development even in a desirable direction would appear to conflict with this outcome. Thus Herbert Spencer's doctrine of evolutionary development, inevitably terminating in the goal of an Absolute Ethics, even if on its own basis it were not self-contradictory, could not have satisfied the ideal which has been expressed again and again in individual lives, though they may constitute a small proportion in the long procession of history. In a striking passage Professor A. N. Whitehead speaks of the profound inconsistency running through a great deal of Western thought. It is, he says, as though men believed at once in two incompatible religions. "A scientific realism based on mechanism is conjoined with an unwavering belief in the world of man and of the higher animals, as being composed of self-determining organisms."[1] We might thus describe the attitudes towards past and future respectively, which in spite of all argument we find to be implied half unconsciously in our thoughts when we attempt to contemplate history as a vast process stretching behind us and before, with ourselves in the midst at the point of the present. In our own past we were ourselves part of the process. Our contemplation of it is probably attended by the feeling that it might have been different. There is perhaps remorse, there is regret, there is the interest of speculation as to other possibilities untried. Thus the self admits continuity with its own past, and as member of the human race it feels an obscure connection with a much longer past. But the irrevocable for action soon takes on the form of the inevitable or the necessitated for knowledge. In relation to the future, on the other hand, we are agents, and as Dr. Whitehead points out the world of men must in this relation appear to us as a world of self-determining organisms. Here then is the distinction of our attitude to the future, which seems to imply a metaphysical difference. The individual as self is conscious that it is his function to assist in however small a degree in the determination of that becoming which has not yet become. This is the causal predicament of practical man of which the theories of the timeless real suggest no interpretation. It is possible that the enigmatic character of the free will problem is due in part to the fact that freedom cannot be shown in the documents of historic knowledge. Our organs for the interpretation of these documents cannot include the instrument for the discovery of freedom. For this instrument can only be present experience, not yet recorded, and the relation to the future with which exact knowledge[2] appears to have no concern. The issue in respect to the possibility of the increase of human freedom, and of its control of the non-

---

[1] *Science and the Modern World*, Chapter V (1926).

[2] With reference of course to human events. I am not referring to such anticipation of future events as is possible through physical and astronomical science. This is highly abstract.

personal factors in history, as conceived in this chapter, lies
pre-eminently in the sphere of value. It may be said that we
have narrowed it down to this, or that it can be nothing else
from the standpoint of this work. This might be exemplified
in relation to any illustrations taken from unsettled questions
of present-day history: the future of democracy, the development of communism, the closer union of nations, the endurance
of European civilization, etc. In the last resort the existence
of all such problems is significant in relation to the increase
or diminution of the experience of value attendant on their
solution. From our point of view, indeed, they could not exist
except for the value found by selves in the events whose
general meaning is expressed in these categories. If it be
assumed that human nature has remained the same since
culture began, this sameness must consist in something that
persists through great divergences of political history, forms
of government and of economic life, religion, warfare, diplo-
macy, ecclesiastical and other organizations, types of state, life
with and without applied science in every stage of application.
The divergences and the similarities are alike unimportant so
long as the movements and activities of human beings are
regarded as we regard those of a species remote from ourselves, as not essentially in their ultimate nature differing (to
an observer of a higher species) from those of bees or ants.
It is only because human experience has value that similarities
and differences in its forms have any significance. It is in this
light that history has a meaning incommensurable with the
effects of human actions in changing the surface of the earth
or modifying the physical processes of which it forms a
material part, however tremendous these modifications may
sometimes appear to our intelligence. We are brought back
then to the point reached in the last chapter. At that point
it appeared that investigation of experience could not throw
light on the possibility of the principle of personality permanently acquiring a greater superiority to the conditions which
restrict freedom. A more general consideration of the problem,

in view of the narrow limitations of experience, seemed, however, not to be excluded, though it must be speculative. As noticed in the chapter on knowledge, Troeltsch does not admit the validity of the purely contemplative attitude to history. The point referred to above, that the attitude regarded as proper to knowledge renders almost or wholly impossible the perception of freedom in history, seems to support this view. We may ask whether the dynamic attitude enables a truer insight into the developing spirit of history, granting for the purpose of the present problem that such a conception as the "spirit of history" is justified. Troeltsch supposes a "material philosophy of history which is teleological—in the sense of the teleology of the will constructing its past into the future out of the present moment".[1] But he proceeds that if such a unity of the whole were given as objectively constructible, it could only be for divine knowledge. The reference to divine knowledge in this connection must be a reference to a power which is wholly unknowable to us, and therefore different in kind from any knowledge of which we have experience. This is involved in the view of the historical process which has been outlined, as depending in its very essence on the originative activity of selves. The question also arises whether it is conceivable that there should be such a union of the active principle of change and the contemplative attitude of knowledge in the subject as is postulated in the notion of a cognition which is dynamic in quality. But it might be maintained that the problem lies in fact rather in the division than in the union of these functions.

According to Höffding "the core of religion consists in the conviction that no value perishes out of the world".[2] If this conviction could be grounded on past history, then history would at least guarantee its own continuance as the succession of events in which value is constantly created and experienced in the lives of human beings. For Höffding the principle

---

[1] *Historismus*, Kap. II, 1.
[2] *Philosophy of Religion*, Chapter I.

appears to be *a priori* in the sense that we perceive in the nature of value that it is eternal. From the standpoint of this work, since one event would be barely distinguishable from another but for its meaning for man, apart from this fact history would seem to vanish as well as value, and the black monotony of dead worlds to be nothingness. To some the spectacle of history has seemed to postulate the permanence of principles which would justify the immeasurable travail and labour of those agents who have been the chief factors in its events. Without necessarily assuming with Lord Acton that it is the stage for the conflict of good and evil, they cannot as students and thinkers admit the moral chaos of a temporal universe in which all values would finally lose their significance. In spite of the fragmentariness of our knowledge, the relativity of values, the uncertainty of progress, the evidence of total disappearance of civilizations in the past, their faith is inextinguishable, that the world for humanity is a "vale of soul-making".[1]

The postulate which we have found to be necessary to the intelligibility of history is that freedom as we have defined it is the real principle of personality, and when we reflect on the nature of freedom, it is possible to argue that in a temporal universe this principle must, however slowly, increase in efficacy. This is one of those considerations for which we are seeking, based on the ultimate facts of experience. The principle cannot be demonstrated from experience, but in the length of time to which the human race may look forward within the present form of experience, there is scope for its realization. If the form of experience as succession in time be taken as a mere framework or receptacle for events, or the bare form which the mind brings to perception, no truth in regard to the ultimate can be discovered in it, as, for instance whether it is itself ultimate as form, or is a symbol of some principle more real in the nature of things. If time is an eternal

[1] Bosanquet: *The Value and Destiny of the Individual*, Section III, from a letter of Keats.

image moving according to number,[1] we know this not because we see it to be implied in the nature of time, but because we know that there is in the end only the eternal, whilst we are compelled by experience to conceive a descent from this into the temporal order. If on the other hand we understand the temporal succession to be the aspect or form of an experience from which it is inseparable, we may ask whether there is any quality in the content of that experience which can lay claim to reality under this form. We have seen that experience cannot show that progress as usually understood can be treated as a necessary character of history. If we enquire, after the manner of Kant, whether there is a relation either analytic or synthetic between the temporal form and progress, no such relation is demonstrable. Professor Driesch holds that we can point to continuous advance in the two great values of knowledge and charity.[2] It is doubtful whether increase of knowledge can be regarded as an intrinsic or more than instrumental value, except for the minds who seek and contemplate, as distinguished from those who receive the result as established fact. In regard to the increase of charity the difficulties in the way of treating this as continuous and universal are evident. If love has increased in its manifestations, in any one civilization, so also it might be plausibly contended has its contrary. There only remain as data on which any arguments for the endurance and even increase in the future, of the struggle for value and its expression in human history, the principle of the free self with its law of activity. We may then put the dilemma, following Bosanquet's principle in the treatment of a different problem,[3] Either this or nothing. Can we as thinking beings, as Bosanquet in effect asks when dealing with the "ontological argument in the Form of to-day", face the possibility that thought has no relation to existence? In like manner, in a very different connection,

---

[1] Plato: *Timaeus*, 37 D. [2] *Wirklichkeitslehre,,* IV C.
[3] See *Meeting of Extremes in Contemporary Philosophy*, Chapters III and IV. Referred to in the Introduction to the present work.

Heinrich Rickert asks whether we can suppose that the culture-world in general has no more significance than any other process. Are "the few known millennia of human development to appear as insignificant as the differences of stones in the road or ears in a cornfield"? Coming as it were to the rock-bottom of our being, can we renounce the belief that there is some significance in human history? If we cannot, he argues, we must assume that there is a unity and objectivity of value, that its validity can be established.[1] He adds that if we abandon this possibility, we must not assume that there remains the scientific system of nature as an intellectual possession free from any postulation of value, because the development of knowledge has depended continuously on the desire for the value of truth. The postulate that the creative principle in the self is real would have then to be accepted, or all belief in the meaning of life and culture be abandoned. The choice of the former alternative does not, however, necessarily imply belief that the potency of this activity must increase. I suggest, however, that such increase seems involved in the creative quality of the principle. As both a general or (in a secondary sense) an *a priori* view of the nature of the self and also a particular reference to history would suggest, the greatest difficulty in the way of achieving an advance of this kind lies in the fact of the relativity of value to which reference has more than once been made. The possibility of a real novelty in this respect, such as for instance it was hoped by not a few might result from the effect on men's minds of one of the greatest catastrophes of history after the European War, cannot be denied from the present standpoint. But since it seems impossible that value should be perceived in identical form even by two minds with close affinities and experience, an impoverishment of the separate energy of each constantly takes place in common action. This does not happen apparently or at once since the less personal forces of mass psychology seem for a time to enhance the effect. But this enhancement

[1] *Kulturwissenschaft und Naturwissenschaft*, concluding chapter.

does not frequently endure, and the true form of combined endeavour for closely similar ideals is rare, or at least for the most part brief. I speak of the more usual course of events, in which either love or moral genius does not make a new law.[1] Freedom then it seems must have wider scope, ethics must go further towards the mastery of history, if what may be called historic evil is not to continue to characterize the events, the evil which happens with blindness in the men who are agents, and goes further than their intent or responsibility, yet results mainly from human work in past and present.

In spite of the above grounds for doubt, it is then urged that, granted the reality of the temporal process, a creative principle must increase in power. This view may, at least, be reasonably argued, though, as has been pointed out, it is not demonstrable. From my standpoint creativity is logically prior to time, in the sense that the temporal form is the condition required by the principle of the "creative advance".[2] Since it is in the unique sources of personality that the novelty arises, it results that we cannot limit the possibilities of the future. The argument may be attacked at the root by denial of the proposition that personality is a principle such as has been assumed. Or the objection may be made that granting the indispensable part it has played in the history of past civilizations, or at least of that to which we belong, experience does not disclose that history must always be of the same character, and there are even indications in the present age that the control of events by humanity will take in time to come an essentially different form in which the individual is subordinate.

In reference to such an objection it must in the first place be pointed out that the view here advanced must obviously not be limited in its application to any one civilization or series of civilizations. Any such limitation would indeed be

[1] Cf. Chapter III.

[2] *Process and Reality*, III, 3, etc. Although this is Professor Whitehead's expression, and I agree with the position that there is a "creative advance into novelty", I do not think he would ascribe creativity to personality in the sense intended in my argument.

fatal. For the fact of the relativity of values to the culture and the age, the difficulties in the way of pointing to steady progress even within a single civilization, would abase the principle of creative personality itself to the status of relativity, and even to the contingency in which as we saw all history, with the exception of this principle, seems to be involved. The conclusion that the personal principle, though in an important sense the source of relativity must itself be set beyond relativity, is one to which the whole argument tends. Are we to conceive the different civilizations with their diverse manifestations of value, each seeming to its members to have the finality of rightness, as all alike experiments whose several types of good are incommensurable, so that the achievement of an absolutely higher or better can never be a fact of knowledge? Have any of the claimants of a supremacy *quod semper quod ubique* withstood the revolutions of time? From the standpoint of this book a higher form of human history is conceivable, and if experienced would be known to be higher with a new kind of certainty. It is not to be thought of as any achievement of Utopia, or even as Kant's Kingdom of Ends. The dualistic factors cannot be expunged from history, nor the potentialities of evil from personality. These admissions imply the absence of any possibility of dogmatism on this subject. The position which leaves an open way to the genius of the future is based on the view of the human force of personality with its primary potentialities, which has been set forth, and the ultimate basis of which is undemonstrable, being intuitive. Here, if anywhere, as has been argued, we seem to find a principle beyond relativity, but the conclusion in regard to its heightened strength in the future cannot rank as more than a probable speculation. The dilemma expressed in the form, *either this or nothing*, is, however, regarded as inescapable.

It is perhaps unnecessary to point out that this standpoint is unaffected by the ebb and flow of movements in our own civilization, towards and away from theoretic conviction and practical applications of the opinions that individual or personal force is either everything or nothing in historic and social achievements. If the influence of these movements were of essential importance to our view, it could not escape relativity, and the principle admitted by Troeltsch, that the ethos and culture of an age can only be measured by the standards they produce, must be applied. To take an example, the significance of the Bolshevist doctrine of the Collective Mind would have to be examined, and with it of certain widespread tendencies in modern life towards increasing uniformity of type in large societies, and the comparative rarity of original individuality. Also the contrast between the proportion of men of genius in the tiny city-states of Ancient Greece and in the huge communities of modern Europe and America would demand investigation. The general view of sociology and anthropology, that on the whole human advance has been characterized by increasing scope for independent individuality, is challenged in the most emphatic way by what appears to be the dominant philosophy of Bolshevism, and the tendencies of thousands of years of development denounced. We have the extraordinary phenomenon of a scientifically directed attempt to compel a community to the sameness of thought supposed to pervade the primitive tribe, the fear of novelty in ideas and initiative in action, private judgment in any sphere. According to the more philosophic accounts of this point of view, it is presumed that the true way of progress is by means of the movement of a collective or mass mind.[1] According to more recent expressions, the making of the collective man, the product of social groups and forces, proceeds by means of every possible external channel of influence on beliefs, not founded on thought, organization, propagandist education, the Press, radio, drama, cinema. The aim is the production of "standardized man".[2] Yet if the facts are closely examined, we find that in

[1] Cf. R. Fülop-Miller: *The Mind and Face of Bolshevism*, 1926, the most philosophical treatment of this subject I have seen.

[2] *Making the Collective Man in Soviet Russia*, article by William Henry Chamberlin.

a present-day community, not overshadowed by the numinous presence and sense of immemorial custom, this can only be brought about (in so far as it is a real achievement) by the efficacy of the original individual at some point in the process. Ultimately it is the leader, the man of ideas, consumed by the passion to impress these on the world, who is the source of this principle of standardization, and even in Russia there is unmistakable recognition of this in the adulation of the memory of at least one individual. As regards the powerful agencies of modern scientific genius in application, working as it might appear for the natural coming about of a monotonous uniformity of ideas, estimates of value, production of goods and pleasures, the radio, the cinema, the mechanical character of industry, the psychological effect of trust-controlled and commercialized journalism, etc., it is yet to be shown that the superficial impression of similarity in mental type corresponds to an increase in the fundamental similarity of the individuals whose lives are thus affected. Into this question, however, it is not necessary further to enter. The position in regard to the principle of personality may well be illustrated by impermanent social tendencies, or questioned from the standpoint of these, but its roots go deeper. The civilization to which we belong is perishable, the possibility cannot be excluded that it might vanish into an unknowability as complete as that of some ancient races of whom little more than their existence is known. This admission is compatible with the view that no form of civilization can exist even for a time without the continued realization at least in some members of the creative potentialities of selves. The following facts, then, have to be faced. Let it be granted that we have perceived the absolute nature of personality, and the necessity to it of historic experience. Throughout known history, on the other hand, we can trace no endurance in the forms of human social relationship such that it could be affirmed:—Here is realization of the absolute type of ethics. Nor again can a succession of events be observed during a sufficient period showing a continuous indubitable increase for mankind in the greatest experiences of value. The conclusion seems necessary that whether in the order of actuality conforming to our experience, or in other forms of existence, in the illimitable future (or even the unknown past) there must be other types of historic actuality, and some of them more adequate to the ideal of a spiritual world. The dualism inseparable from history which has been throughout recognized would not be eliminated, but, consistently with our view, its unfavourable effects might be incalculably diminished.

CHAPTER XI

THE CONCEPTION OF THE WHOLE AS PERSONAL

"To help a God in his struggle more or less doubtful and build, with resisting evil, is no inferior task. And if the issue were taken as uncertain, or if even the end were known to be God's indubitable defeat, and our inevitable disaster, our religion would have risen thereby, and would have attained the extreme of heroism."

F. H. BRADLEY: *Essays in Truth and Reality*, Chapter XV

IT is possible that some consideration of the philosophic doctrine which ascribes personality to the Universe as a whole may help in the further definition of personality as conceived in this work. The emphasis on personality does not seem to characterize the earlier monistic views of the nature of things, whether mystical or logical, but naturally arises in the course of attempts to reconcile the deeper modern interest in the significance of individual selfhood with the philosophic need for unity. An important line of thought leading to this result is indicated by Professor Clement Webb. Once the idea of the "Absolute" has formed itself definitely in our minds, he argues, this idea cannot maintain itself in separation from the idea of God. "No conception of God which takes Him for less than an Absolute Reality will satisfy the demands of the religious consciousness." In his view, moreover, the thought of the universe as a whole "primarily presents itself as a religious thought". The conception is thus regarded as the culmination of two movements of the mind, the one scientific and philosophical, the other religious, both essential forms of the search for reality. The one seeks to understand, to find the rationality of the world in a concept which will finally satisfy reason, therefore in unity. The other seeks an object the existence of which will assure the being who lives for values, for love, beauty, creative action, greater knowledge and power that his ideals and strivings are not wholly vain

They have a significance which is not swept away with all other things in the stream of change. The power manifested in nature and history is the source of value. It may be argued that these two paths must terminate in a single object if either end is to be attained. Otherwise there would remain outside the native and intrinsic determination of the mind to the discovery of a wholly intelligible universe, another distinct and equally irresistible impulse which threatens to be incompatible with the first. For if unchecked, unaffected by the intellectual demand for unity, may not the expectation which primarily proceeds from the emotional nature that value will be found at the heart of things terminate (unless merged in mysticism) in a dualistic rather than a monistic view of the sources of our total experience? Again, it may be maintained that once freedom of speculation is in some degree achieved by the human mind, the two tendencies or forms of "nisus" do proceed from the same root, namely, that need which Schopenhauer characterizes as the "metaphysical hunger of man". Since, however, men constantly labour in ignorance of the ultimate sources of their impulse, limited by the shortness of human life and the physical conditions of mental activity, they inevitably become in general confined to one or other of the great methods to which the impulse drives. And these tend to grow more divergent to the degree to which one or other is persistently followed. In many, though by no means in all cases, each pursuit claims to satisfy the whole need. The values of religious thought may be attracted to attend on logical and philosophical labours and the energies of scientific pursuit, from youthful passion to the waiting concentration of age on the last verge. Scientific truth may be sought with an ardour hardly less burning than that of the search for God. Or the struggle to discover and clearly conceive an object of the highest value may be carried on with a regard for exactitude of thought and repression of emotion no less austere than that which characterizes the toil of the mathematical physicist. Yet is it possible that the results of the two movements should be mutually consistent and the ultimate goals be identified? From the standpoint of religious thought it seems that the combination is possible only by means of the fundamental religious paradox. Our inability to conceive what nevertheless, if inescapable human needs are to be met, must somehow be assumed, permits or even necessitates the bringing together in the idea of God notions which reason cannot join. The difficulty appears in its most intractable aspect in this attempt to equate the notion of the whole with the idea of God. How in the first place can we have a personal relation to that "in which we live and move and have our being"?[1] This relation appears to have meaning only in a spiritual world which is not, at least at that stage of thought at which the relation arises, identified with all that is. The poet may develop a religion of beauty whose power is enhanced by the introduction of the personal principle. He must be able to commune with beauty as spirit with spirit, experiencing

> "A sense divine
> Of something far more deeply interfused
> Whose dwelling is the light of setting suns
> And the round ocean, and the living air,
> And the blue sky and in the mind of man."

But human history is far away, and Wordsworth can dissolve the thought of humanity into "still sad music". The grounds for holding that it is only through a religious paradox combining concepts which cannot be united whether from the point of view of logic or of philosophy of value, that the two relations to the universe as a whole and to a supreme Person can be assumed to be one, become clearer on consideration of the metaphysical aspects of Professor Webb's argument. Once the concept of the Absolute has been formed, he pleads, no idea of God which treats Him as less than this can be satisfactory to religion. He criticizes Bosanquet's theory of the Absolute as transcending personality, since in personality,

[1] See Clement Webb: *God and Personality*, Lecture V.

according to Bosanquet, there is something which falls short of that concrete universal which is also individual. He concedes, however, that personality would be ascribed to the Absolute in a very different sense from that in which it is attributed to human beings. He appears in fact to admit in some degree the logical difficulty of his position, without perceiving that the change in the meaning of personality when it is ascribed to the All is one which removes what is essential to "person". It is in the main on logical principles that Bosanquet conceives his whole argument in respect to the relation of human experience to the Absolute to rest.[1] The person can only correspond to a finite centre in the All. But as each part, fragment or atom of the Universe implies all the rest, and we are driven on in our attempt to understand, to perceive it in wider and wider relations—("self-development", as Bosanquet and Bradley term this process on the objective side[2])—so each individual strives to the whole in the endeavour to transcend its unreal abstraction. The view which seems to be treated as all but axiomatic by this school of thought, that the highest value cannot be ascribed to any being short of the whole, determines Bosanquet's religious attitude to the Absolute,[3] in which personality is transcended, and with it in the end the moral order as possessing incomplete reality, since it involves a world of persons claiming rights as individuals.

That it is logically inconsistent with the essential meaning of personality that the Universe as a whole should be personal, is cogently argued by McTaggart in his article on Personality.[4] Here he exposes the fallacy of the argument that, assuming a Being who has knowledge of the experience of all selves, these selves must form part of the All knower. In *Some Dogmas of Religion*[5] he observes with reference to the doctrine of an

---

[1] *Principle of Individuality and Value.*
[2] F. H. Bradley: *Principles of Logic*, Vol. II, Terminal Essays, I.
[3] Cf. *What Religion Is.*   [4] *Encyclopaedia of Religion and Ethics.*
[5] VI, 167.

Omnipotent Personality that human personality is never found
to exist without a recognition of the existence of something
not itself. The position that no self can be part of another self
is re-argued in *The Nature of Existence*.[1] The form in which
the problem is of most critical importance for the present
work is that which it has assumed in recent thought. The
ethical philosophy of Max Scheler provides an argument in
which the principle of personality as correlative to value is
used in support of the idea of the world of persons as unified
in the being of the divine Person. Only a brief reference can
be made to Scheler's subtle doctrine of the person.[2] This is
the concrete being the presence of which in its acts makes
them to be truly acts, or without which these are mere abstractions. A concrete act then can never be understood except in
its attachment to the nature of the individual person. Every
collection of acts remains a mere conjunction of abstract act
entities, if the person in whom it is a collection is not given
together with it. The person is not a thing or substance, but
an act-completing being. Correlation between every person,
and the world within which it experiences and acts, is an
essential principle.[3] So far I am in agreement with Scheler,
as also in the view that the person is never object, but always
subject. His distinction between the person and the ego (*das
ich*) is more difficult to follow. Presumably this I which is in
every sense an object, "the individual I, an object (*Gegenstand*)
of inner perception", is the I of empirical psychology. "If
we understand by psychology . . . a science of occurrences
accessible to observation, description and explanation, then
every genuine act, as well as the person, fully transcends
psychology". To the total sphere of acts Scheler gives the
name Spirit (*Geist*), thereby naming all that constitutes the
nature of act, intentionality and fullness of meaning. All spirit

[1] Vol. II, Book V, Chapter XXXVI, "Spirit", Chapter XLII,
"God".
[2] *Der Formalismus in der Ethik und die Materielle Wert-Ethik.*
[3] Ibid., II Teil, VI, A, 3 (c).

R

is personal from the necessity of its nature, and the notion of impersonal spirit self-contradictory. His view that in no sense does an I belong to the nature of spirit, and neither therefore the separation between "I" and the external world, may be accepted if he means the object-self conceived in distinction from the original subject. But when he proceeds from this to the position that since person is the necessary and only form of the existence of spirit, an absolute term, it is not like "I" inseparable from the reference to a thou and an external world, I am unable to follow him. It results for him that God can be Person but not an *I*, since the opposition I—Thou, I—the external world, has vanished. The argument for the supreme Person is led up to from the principle of the correlation between the person and his world. In the personal world every realm of objects we can distinguish is included, "objects of the inner world, the external, the corporeal, including the whole possible kingdom of life, and the realm of ideal objects and values. All these have only an abstract objectivity, except as worlds of a person".[1] Any concrete act I select from a person contains in it an original character peculiar to the world of this person alone. It results that the one single world supposed to exist for various individual persons is mere appearance (*Schein*). Thus absolute truth can only be personal. Must we then be limited to the multiplicity of the personal worlds, or is the idea of the macrocosm valid? If this is possible, all microcosms or individual personal worlds are parts of the macrocosm. But the personal corresponding member (*Gegenglied*) of the macrocosm would be the Idea of an infinite and perfect spiritual person, who must be concrete. "The idea of God is then given with the unity, identity and individuality of the world."[2] In spite of this argument Scheler holds that it is not philosophy which enables us to posit this idea of God. Only to a person in immediate communion with a Being corresponding to the

[1] *Der Formalismus in der Ethik und die Materielle Wert-Ethik.* II Tiel, VI, A, 3 (*c*).
[2] Ibid., II Teil, VI, A, 3 (*d*).

Idea can this revelation be given. He insists, however, that any attempts to replace the personal God, whether by a general world-reason, a transcendental rational ego, a moral world-order, an *ordo ordinans*, an infinite logical subject, an impersonal or so-called super-personal unconscious, etc., are assumptions philosophically unmeaning. Whoever posits concrete thought or will posits further the whole personality. With the latter principle I am in entire agreement, as also with the correlation of the world of every subject with his own personality. Scheler's philosophical argument, however, admittedly not by itself a demonstration, for the existence of the macrocosm in correlation with an infinite supreme person does not appear to avoid the inconsistencies earlier referred to in the notion of the Personal Whole. Or rather it has its own inconsistency analogous to though not identical with those. If every world is an abstraction apart from the person who knows and acts in it, then the Supreme Person can only be in correlation with the macrocosm of all worlds, *qua* immanent in all persons. Does not however this immanence involve a principle of unity in the individual persons which would nullify that essential peculiarity of the correlation on which he insists, constituting the individuality and incommunicability of the worlds of each? The difficulty is increased by the fact that Scheler accepts the relativity of the individual to his own age.[1] The practical character of men is, in his view, wholly relative to the ethos of their age, and cannot be measured by the ethos of another age and people. How is this to be made consistent with the communion of all with the Absolute Person? In these ways Scheler's philosophy well illustrates the accentuation of the difficulties of the concept of a Universal Person by the deepening in the modern view of personality. Amongst the chief of these is the metaphysical paradox of a Whole of Persons. This notion, hardly tolerable when the idea of person is vaguely determined as an object

[1] *Der Formalismus in der Ethik und die Materielle Wert-Ethik*, II Teil, V, 4.

amongst other objects, the object self member of a greater self, as the cell of an organism is member of the living body, becomes intolerable when the person is realized to be the subject which is always subject, source of all that is unique in a living experience and activity. If we examine the concept of a whole which is the unity of subjects we perceive that it lacks logical validity. It results from the transference of a category from the objective world of thought in which it has significance to the subjective, in which it loses meaning. Either the whole is not a true whole because its *ex hypothesi* members cannot form a unity, or the members lose their essence and are no longer selves. A greater subject cannot include in itself a lesser without destroying this. Up to this point the concept under consideration has been mainly, though not entirely, examined as a subject of knowledge. This however is an abstraction which we do not meet in experience, though it seems to be approached in a certain degree for a limited period in some human experiences. The legitimacy of postulating the being of this, and attempting to deduce what is or is not possible in regard to the problem of a universal mind, may be called in question. There remains for further examination in relation to this problem the nature of that something in the point of view of the individual subject which must necessarily (as I conceive) be left out if we assume the experience of the unique "I think" to be included in that of a supreme thinker. Let us grant for the purposes of the discussion that the All Thinker could gather together into a unity of consciousness all the wanderings of thought, errors, inferences and hypotheses, valid and invalid, all human visions and imaginations in their limitless degrees of obscurity, and mutually incompatible significance, even if we include only the controversies and discordances of a single generation.[1] Yet there remains a uniqueness in the thought of every subject which cannot be absorbed. The subject of knowledge, however imperfectly he knows, has in his subject nature the seed of a

[1] Cf. F. H. Bradley, *Logic*, Vol. II, Book III, Part II, Chapter IV, § 5.

creative mind. With recognition of this we must restore the principle which is essential to the person (as Scheler of course insists). It knows and acts in experience as having value. Let us admit the hypothesis of a world of such persons the unity of which is also personal. We may then ask whether in such a universe the personal members can be conceived as having different degrees and kinds of perfection and of imperfection? There are familiar arguments from Plato downwards in support of the view that the members or parts need not have the value-character of the whole to which they belong. Because the whole is beautiful or good, it does not necessarily follow that the members taken individually have the same beauty or goodness. Is this applicable to persons as members of a whole? It will be found that this kind of whole cannot be treated in the same way as other types. The analogy breaks down at a vital point. A whole of persons is not an organic whole. It does not form a unitary being. It may be a spiritual whole, i.e. a unity in the sense that all its differing members are striving in a single direction towards closely similar ends. But such a whole is not a real unity, since the members possess as persons severally incommunicable sources of activity. If waiving this formidable difficulty, we frame the idea of a perfect whole of persons who should always be in complete harmony in their strivings, we see that the essential condition of the validity of this concept is that all members should be perfect. A marred, distorted person could not appear in the whole which has absolute personal value, as an ugly feature in the whole which is beautiful, because the marred personality could not contribute to the personal value of his universe. This is the law of personality from which it cannot escape and preserve its own essential being. It must, so to speak, save its own soul. It cannot contribute to the production in the universe of a good which is not its own good, and be redeemed by the good in the whole. It appears from this consideration that the doctrine of the Personality of the whole, namely, that the Absolute Reality is a kind of being to which we can attribute the same type of being that we experience in the human person, is confuted by the occurrence of a single wrecked personality, a single individual which, possessing the type, shows it in a defaced form.[1] The Neo-Hegelians who recognize that, since they admit nothing in the end to be real, except the Absolute Whole, they must sacrifice the reality of the person, appear to be more consistent than those Personalists who ascribe personality to the All. Neither the part nor the whole is personal where all is One.

It is interesting here to note Kant's attitude to the Wolffian doctrine of God in connection with the difficulty of conceiving a divine unity of all things. As Dr. England observes, "Kant's language sometimes indicates that he is thinking of the transcendental ideal as an *ens realissimum* in the rationalistic sense of the term, i.e. as a being which embraces all reality. He falls short, however, of lapsing completely into Wolffian rationalism in his characterization of the Ideal, for in the first place he has argued that, since there is real opposition amongst realities, they cannot in their totality exist in God, as his predicates or determinations"[2] (Kant, A. 273, B. 329, etc.). The opposition of persons in respect to values would seem in a philosophy of personality to be parallel to Kant's real opposition amongst realities.

Before leaving this subject some reference ought perhaps to be made to the problem of the unity of value. From the standpoint of an objective theory of value this is of the highest importance. In the present view it is also of importance, but in a different sense. The unity of good is put in a strong light by Plato, and the derivation of the Forms of virtue and knowledge from that Idea, whilst beauty is on the whole treated as an aspect of Good, or even itself the supreme form.[3] From our standpoint the striving of the personal principle in the

[1] This argument was used in the writer's *Study in the Philosophy of Personality*, Chapter V.

[2] F. E. England: *Kant's Conception of God*, Book VI, *The Ideal of Pure Reason*.

[3] Cf. *Republic*, VI, 504; *Philebus*, 64; *Symposium*, XXIX, 210 E–212 A.

self, to transcend the limits within which it is entangled, so to speak, in dualism, gives rise to the pure experiences which we objectify in their main forms as the great values. Other forms there are which are less definable, or not defined, and there is no ground in the nature of value why a limit should be set to experiences of selves in this respect. An interesting example of modern objective theories of the unity of value is presented in Johannes Volkelt's *System der Ästhetik*.[1] Holding that aesthetics must ultimately rest upon metaphysics, he conceives the realization of value as the world-purpose. The nature of things is founded on absolute value. There is also an absolute ought, by which he means nothing else than the indwelling tendency of absolute value to self-realization. Thus absolute value must eternally enter into existence. Being is the self-realization of absolute value. "In absolute value I see the only possible world principle supplying content." Since in his view value can only be in relation to consciousness, the absolute value can only be as recognized and realized for an absolute consciousness, namely, the self-consciousness of absolute spirit. He also posits a striving in the absolute value or an active will-tendency. As against Hegel, the absolute value realizing itself can only be thought of in the form of striving. All being must be conceived as self-realization of the absolute striving. Thus voluntarism and intellectualism would be united in metaphysics. He regards it as only a small step from the recognition of the necessity of the absolute Value to the recognition of a plurality of "self values". So far as the human world is concerned, and "in accordance with the finite, temporal, individual nature of the human, the absolute manifests itself in a number of separate values (*Teilwerten*)". These partial appearances of absolute value are equally values, and, in themselves, values of unconditional validity. He aims at the conclusion that those values of which through intuitive certainty we are assured, as self- (or independent) values are in fact the partial appearances of the absolute value in our world. They can be seen to com-

[1] Vol. III, Abschnitt 2, Kap. IV, p. 5.

plete one another, and form an organic unity, such that what is essentially human is creatively realized through their co-operation. "If the theoretic demonstration leads to the result that those intuitively assured self-values—the true, the moral, the holy, the aesthetic—form themselves into an organic unity presenting complete humanity, one may be assured of this that the voice of Intuition is right, and these values are in truth the part-manifestations of the absolute value."[1] The fundamental difficulty of Volkelt's conception of the union in metaphysics of voluntarism and intellectualism is the irrationalism which seems involved in the notion that value is not on this assumption either eternally realized, or necessarily realized at any point of infinite time in a temporal process. It seems that the striving for the realization of value can only belong to the experience of finite beings, not to the nature of an absolute value, correlated to an absolute self-consciousness. In my view this absolute value is an object of contemplation for the minds of personal beings objectifying their highest experiences. Granted that the principal values take the forms in this experience which Volkelt indicates, there appears to be no ground in the nature of the striving self why there should not be other kinds, too rare perhaps, too unique, transitory, or elusive to be objectified. Whether all the values can be seen to be derived from love, as some philosophic aestheticians hold, is a problem which it is not necessary here to examine. Volkelt regards love as fundamental. Love would appear to be the primary value of the historic process in so far as we can conceive this as the experience of persons, abstracted from the dualism of history. It was earlier suggested that the fundamental value of concrete history as a whole must be sought in the relation of the eternal and the changing. Volkelt's doctrine of the absolute value, which is in the end identical with the absolute consciousness, is open to the difficulties to which we have referred in connection with the idea of the whole as absolute person.

[1] *System der Ästhetik*, Vol. III, Abschnitt 2, Kap IV, p. 5.

It must finally be pointed out that the idea of a supreme person *not* equivalent to the All appears to contain no self-contradiction, and that the postulation of such a person seems even to be required on the grounds of the logic of value. If personality is the source of value throughout our experience, and if the examination of the nature of the historic process is valid showing that its content must have the qualities of value in the relation to selves, and that its course is to a considerable degree determined as a result of their value judgments, it follows that the realization of the principle of personality in a person whose nature is superior to changes and loss in value is a necessary principle of order in our idea of history. To this position the view is also necessary that whilst evil is at least in some degree inescapable in human experience, good has a real priority such that the adjuration "Evil be thou my good!" has significance, whilst the reverse, Good be thou my evil! would be devoid of meaning. It appears then that the priority of good must be exemplified in the perfect goodness of the highest person. Whether such a being has existed within historic experience, as known, is a problem for empirical investigation. I omit the possibility of a special intuition of the religious consciousness, since I am unable to speak of this from personal experience. I know, however, that a conviction may arise having the quality of certainty from the historic records of the life of the founder of Christianity. It is then the belief of the present writer that in these records a very high probability that there has been a morally perfect person in history is given. Now though such a person is conceived as superior to the principle that personality is the source of evil as well as good, no historic individual can escape historic dualism. Thus the extraordinary manifestations of contingency in the circumstances and events of the life of Jesus would be intelligible, the problem of His entry into the course of history at a particular moment, after countless millions had lived without knowledge of this event, the seeming moral injustice of the ignorance of untold multitudes in all ages in respect to it, the appalling mystery of the large place occupied by evil developments in the history of so-called Christian communities, and not least the organizations purporting to be based on His teaching.[1] His existence in human history could not but be in accordance with all historic conditions. But there is no logical contradiction and a clear moral necessity in the concept of His perfection, seeing that without the occurrence in history of one such personality we lack assurance of the principle that "value shall not perish out of the world". And as has been argued, without this principle history passes to meaninglessness and therefore to nothingness.

[1] Cf. Chapter VI.

CHAPTER XII

CONCLUSION

IN conclusion a few aspects of the position maintained in these pages may be restated. The work does not aspire to the character of a philosophy of history, as generally understood. For it does not put forward an interpretation of history as a whole, whether based on an *a priori* view of the meaning of the universe, from which, granted that there is a temporal process, its nature must follow, or on an empirical view of the actual course of history. That a view of the nature of things which is *a priori* in a logical sense cannot show the necessity of the temporal process, even as an illusory experience, and neither therefore the necessity of history, seems evident when we survey the history of *a priori* systems. From our examination of historic knowledge it resulted that in respect to its proportion to the unknown our knowledge is wholly inadequate to the establishment of any universal principles based on experience in a purely empirical sense. It may, however, be argued that the *a priori* of historic knowledge should be sought, not in the order of logical principles, since with the assumption that there is historic knowledge we are admitting a type of a-logical knowledge, but in the independent nature of the principles essential to history. If this be granted, we may turn to the nature of the self, as disclosed in self-knowledge, and knowledge of other selves—admitting the limitations of knowledge in both these forms—and seek here for the principles which must condition our interpretation of history. Here we meet with an ultimate of experience unanalysable into any simpler elements, namely, self-consciousness, of which we find the essence to be that it is subject, and only in a secondary sense capable of presentation as object. On this account it is never completely knowable. In regard to this ultimate fact I hold that subject or "spirit" is necessarily individual. Its individuality seems involved in the nature of a subject. That there exist other subjects with which it is in relation appears also to be involved in the nature of experience for any subject, even the purely contemplative experience. For all such experience implies self-transcendence, and self-transcendence begins in the apprehension of other selves. Without this the individual could not be aware that his knowledge involved any relation except to the parts and elements of his own being. Should it be objected that knowledge of this type is conceivable, and is such as would characterize the experience of a universal consciousness, or the Absolute whole, I should reply as follows. In such a conception the attempt is made to combine the metaphysical doctrine of the Absolute with the conception of knowledge we derive from experience as individual subjects. And that no clear idea of knowledge can result from this combination seems evident. This appears to be admitted in the most powerful presentation in British philosophy of the doctrine of the Absolute as all experience, that of F. H. Bradley. For reality is beyond truth.[1] Selves then are individual and unique as subjects. That their nature involves experience in a historic process results from considerations which are based both on analysis of the conditions of history, individual and general or categorial, and on a metaphysical view of the person, i.e. the self *qua* possessing qualities that point to a super-empirical origin. From analysis of the self it is seen that it is in great degree constituted by its memories, having its nature in the past as well as the present. Considerations which, though not demonstratively conclusive, possess great force lead to the view that a world of selves enjoying an experience which can be regarded as common in important respects affecting the life of all is impossible without a past for all selves. Past, present, future belong to the very being of the self, even though the past into which the future (through present) is ceaselessly moving has alone existential being in its content, the future being a form with imagined content.

[1] Cf. *Appearance and Reality*, Chapters XXVI and XXVII.

The imagination of this content is indispensable to the activity of the self. History then seems implicit in the being of a society of selves. Its being is found to depend on the meaning given by selves to events, though in the events of history there are all but universally present factors alien or irrelevant to the values of personality, or the creative activities of selves. To these blind factors (as I have termed them), together with the principle of the relativity of value to the individual subject, and therefore in a secondary sense to the age, the race, etc., is due the irrationalism of history as history, i.e. its failure to exhibit clearly the type of temporal process proper to the experience of persons. It is not inferred that in this type, if realized, experience would be completely valuable, since history in every form testifies to the fact that evil as well as good may arise out of the principle of personality itself. But it is held that the conflict would be clear and unobscured by the irruption of factors whose effect on the process is constantly unpredictable, and often unfavourable to good. These factors arise at times from the physical and psychical nature of men in interrelation, but nevertheless have a blind or impersonal quality.

The metaphysical principle of the theory of the person is rooted in truths which appear to be implied in all our experience. It is not based on the Cartesian argument because this involves a view of the self as substance which points to a static form of the concept, not true to its nature as active subject. Also we cannot penetrate to reality by self-observation. How is the process to be secure from illusion? The only secure basis for the belief that we have found reality is the discovery that we have come upon something, doubt of the existence of which would involve that nothing else is real. This is obviously closely similar to Descartes' argument. But even here it seems that the latter does not prove enough. I cannot doubt that I am doubting. Does this however prove that I have more than a quasi or transient existence? That there is some ultimate reality is indeed involved in the very admission of illusion.[1] And this must be sought in that without which it is inconceivable that man should grasp an experience as his own with clear consciousness. This is the quality of value for self, which is attendant on all such experience. On examination of this we find that it is brought by the self and in this sense is *a priori* (as Scheler insists). Now a being having a naturalistic origin such as we attribute to things inanimate and animate, when contemplating them in abstraction from their relation to the subject in its concrete nature, could not bring value to experience. We conclude therefore that the personal principle in the self is trans-empirical. This argument distinguishes the view both from the rationalistic metaphysic of Descartes and the metaphysical ethics of Kant. For the "noumenal" element in experience, to adopt Kant's too committal term, is in this view not the purely rational but that spiritual or value-conferring element which is potential in all human individuals, but does not show its activity until certain external conditions of free activity are present, together with a certain degree of development of the rational capacity.

History is necessary to the value experience of selves, or to their experience as giving scope for the striving to self-transcendence in which the values definitely arise. This striving seems inherent in the nature of personality. It is not necessary to have resort to the biographies of unusual men and women to be convinced of this. Daily experience of widespread activities, under conditions individual and interpersonal which appeal strongly to the higher emotions, make it unmistakably evident as a principle of human nature. It is then according to this argument empirically discovered, and this seems to support the argument from the original fact of value-experience. For the striving to self-transcendence is primarily a striving to a world of complete value, with exclusion of the alien factors of experience, and those impulses in the self native to it, though in a secondary sense in which disvalue

---

[1] "In theory you cannot indulge with consistency in an absolute doubt." F. H. Bradley: *Appearance and Reality*, Chapter XXVI.

originates. Though secondary, it was argued that these impulses result from a distorted striving after self-transcendence. It has been noticed[1] that the existence of the self with its claims is from one point of view an anomaly and a paradox, and here may be traced a possible clue to the significance of evil. But no claim can be made that light is thus thrown on the solution of the most insoluble problem. Any serious consideration of it must, however, give equal rights to all the facts. If evil has to be denied in the interests of the idea of a perfect whole, this perfection must be beyond good as well as evil, as Spinoza, when most consistent, recognized.

The history of mankind, as of communities, races, peoples, nations, is conceived as a secondary form of history, inasmuch as it deals with categories rather than with unique individuals, and cannot present the subject in all its individuality. The truth it possesses is in one sense less, in another more than that of the sciences. More because it approaches nearer to the portrayal of the nature of the individuals (though these must be presented as objects), since their primary experience is in the historic process. Less because its generalizations belong to the order of those empirical generalizations which can only have a low degree of generality, and from the standpoint of scientific knowledge it is least a science where it is nearest to its own ideal. The peculiar sources of disorder, in the course of history from its own standpoint as depicting the human process, chance, contingency, the casual, the other or blind factors, do not, in the sense they have for history, enter into the sciences. But their very presence, indication of a more exacting standard, is sign that the historian has to go deeper, further into the roots of his agencies than the student of other subjects of knowledge. Historic knowledge then is least in the kingdom of the sciences, but greatest in its orientation towards original being.

This book sprang as one of its chief sources from an intense impression of the paradox of our contrasting attitudes in

[1] Chapter IX.

historical and in ethical interest and judgments and a desire
to find the interpretation of this. Hegel's well-known doctrine
of the world-historic individual, or hero, whom the Litany
of private virtues does not concern, suggests, I think, a distortion of the problem, for it appears to signify (in accordance
with Hegel's own view) that events of great value to mankind
at large have been brought about by men who need not follow
the moral ideal in the sphere of personal relations which is
peculiarly its own. From my point of view it is recognized that
history, with its content as primarily major events rather than
the lives of persons, has a value which is not identical with the
moral. There may be a greatness in historic events which is
not due only to their moral quality. They may exhibit in a
high light the fundamental historic value, the opposition of
the eternal and the transient which is wider than ethical
tragedy. But the human agent as such cannot be an organ
of a world-historic movement superior to ethics. It is impossible
to deny, within the limits of our knowledge, that relatively to
some phases of history movements contributory to human
welfare may have been brought about in which the human
agents were not morally motived beings. It is even probable.
But such human agents must then be regarded as, as it were,
events, to whom the qualities of moral value are not attributed,
or as comparable to natural forces. As regards the effect on
ethics of a study in which the subject is approached from the
standpoint of history in all its concreteness, this is in the first
place to make the moral student and seeker realize that he is
in need of principles which will show the possibility of ethical
progress in the historical world. He cannot be satisfied with
the system of duties within the society and the age to which
he belongs, the table of the virtues, the moral ideal for the
individual moving within the well-known community. From
this comparatively sheltered world he must go out into the
historic worlds of the ages, recognizing no generally agreed
system of the best life for men and communities in their
interrelations. He must face the facts of relativity in all values,

and of the changing visions and standpoints of succeeding generations. The struggle to find some principle in human nature under the moral law to which the course of history also bears testimony, as possessing both value and power, results, as the argument seemed to show, in bringing to the foreground the principle of freedom. On the one hand this is of the very essence of personality. On the other, in spite of the slow growth in history of man's power to realize in society the highest ideals prevailing at any time amongst any people, the existence of cultures and civilizations, however restricted, in itself bears witness to his creative energy constantly taking new forms. In freedom then, and therefore in human personality, we find a principle which does not succumb to relativity. It is indeed vindicated by that condition of relativity which signifies the ever renewed effort of men in each new age to see truth, beauty and good for themselves. But if so, in the sphere of human relations certain universal laws do tend to be reaffirmed, once personality is freed from conditions which suppress and distort it, including the emotion of fear in the face of an ignorance too great for the undeveloped mind to bear. This may be called unnatural ignorance for the self-conscious being. Such a universal law is that which results from affirmation of the reality of other selves in all its implications. It was argued therefore that the historical approach leads both to a more ample conception of freedom as exemplified in all types of human creativity, in the different forms of genius in a wide sense, and in practical life, and to the personalistic view in ethics. The values arise in the experience of individual life. This is always unique, but certain great and closely similar experiences of men in all times have been objectified as ruling principles and forms, to which independent spiritual being is attributed in the Platonic and other types of idealism.

Moral philosophy has tended to ignore the factors alien to the activity of the free personality (however this is understood), which a historical view cannot overlook. As a result of the influence either of metaphysical theory or of a scientific

s

psychology, it inclines to concentrate attention on the problem of freedom in a narrow form as one of the relation of will in abstraction from the total personality to motives viewed as causal in the scientific sense. The individual may conceive his activity under these formulae. He then appears to objectify himself and create a system under which the true self is submerged. In this system his essential freedom cannot be exercised. As the philosophical psychologist points out, a false personality may be imposed.[1] In the process to which I am referring, however, it is rather a secondary self than a false personality which takes the place of the true self. The idea that he necessarily acts in a psychic system of causal conditions and conative outcome makes of the individual an object rather than a subject-self. Unconsciously he may cease to draw upon his own resources in the free energy of the subject.

The greatest difficulty in the attainment of historic freedom, as distinct from the ethical freedom which has its root in personality alone, lies in the nature of human constructions of the instruments and forces of history. Here we have to consider all that fabric of life and circumstance, in which together with personality many would find the very spirit of history. It belongs to civilization, and has appeared in some famous attempts at the interpretation of history as "objective mind". Institutions, organizations, established forms of life in communities, witness on the one hand to the creative activity of men in co-operation, on the other hand they are liable to become unfavourable to freedom, a new type of restraint, reproducing, though in more rational form, the oppression of the factors of nature at the earliest stage of primitive culture, and of blindly accepted custom at a slightly more advanced stage. This comes about on account of the changing spirit of men in the historic process to which it is due that the institution loses its original meaning and exercises a force no longer through the vitalizing meaning given to it

[1] Cf. William Brown: *Mind and Personality*, Chapter XV.

by its members, but in a mechanical way, as something alien to them, empty of any value they can understand. Corresponding to the importance and indeed necessity of institutions and organizations for the life of civilization is their place in historic knowledge, as the categories with which this is in great part concerned. The instability which attends on men's valuation of their institutions is more obvious to reflection at the present time than when nineteenth-century idealists treated the existence and development of institutions as affording material for knowledge of the direction of human progress, though we may not know the goal. According to the thesis of this book, as will be obvious, it is the value of the individual which must never be lost sight of in the endeavour to find some intelligible principles in history. Hence the rejection of any philosophy of history which is deaf to the voices of the individuals of the past in their countless millions, in its exclusive attention to a far off goal in which all will be well with history. The idea of this vast being, spirit, or process which on the basis of all the travail of men and women in ages known and unknown attains the ideal for humanity, neither satisfies the metaphysical concept of a perfect whole, for its value cannot include the value of all subjects, nor receives any moral historic justification. It is a quasi-logical notion which can have no place in a view which posits the reality of the temporal process and the creative spring of history in the personal principle.

INDEX

NAMES

SUBJECT INDEX